MW00627557

Dedication To Duty

Written by
Harvey Dahline

Edited by
Doris Dahline
Steve Koskovich
Britta Arendt

Consultant
Ron Stoesz, brother

This book is dedicated to
Doris Dahline

MY SAVING GRACE

I will speak few words today
As Doris, my saving grace, my friend, my lover,
my wife, has gone from me as promised to be with the
Lord her God.
I, who thought I was so strong have been brought to my
knees. My grief unbearable.
I met this young woman and was married over 60 years.
She brought into my heart a fullness I never had.
Five beautiful children with many grandchildren.
Her main thought in life was she would bring them all
to the Lord before leaving us.
My house is now empty but alive with memories.
I knew as I sat down to write this, that I could not cap-
ture in a few words the virtues of this woman of God.
My Saving Grace,
Amen

CHAPTERS

CHAPTERS

CHAPTERS

PREFACE

A book written simply because a friend, Joe Piskel, took the time off work one afternoon to come to my house saying, "Harvey, I know some of your stories, there are so many of them. It's been 17 years since you have been retired, if you don't start writing them they are going to be lost forever to your family and Grand Rapids."

So, I got my yellow pad out and started to write a few stories. It is not something I could ever have envisioned.

As I wrote on the pad, they were a mess! Then reading them to my wife, as she typed them on the computer, she would hand me a copy. As I read them they would come alive.

These stories would cover all facets of police work from a call that a child had fallen into a creek on Hwy. 38 to a shooting taking place at the high school as well as the senseless murder of a fellow law enforcement officer.

Doris, my wife of 60 years, kept encouraging me, lending moral support. Sometimes helping me remember as she had lived through these stories with me.

Soon, I had written well over 150 short stories covering my personal life, childhood, Army service in Korea and 40 years on the Grand Rapids Police Department.

During these years, I wore many hats: Patrolman, investigator, sergeant, assistant chief and eight years as chief. Never looking for the power of the position but the challenges to be met. I worked with men and women, I could never have asked for better coworkers than the ones I had.

These stories have now become a book for my family and friends.

Along the way to challenge myself, I have also written a book of fictional short stories always striving to bring a different slant to a story, "A Justifiable Ending?"

1
FAMILY - CHILDHOOD MEMORIES

Harvey & Harry Dahline

Some of my first memories: The warm cozy room, the glass of winter etched in frosty glaze, snow angels, blowing on glass and now you can see through it. Only your mind can see and put them there. The wind whipping across the snowy fields making wondrous huge snow drifts, the whistling through the eaves and sometimes through the cracks between the logs of that ancient cabin mortared with cement that sometimes fell out. The spring with the eaves dripping in the, oh, so warm sun, and sitting outside against the logs in the sun's rays. The call of the crows who were the first to announce that spring was here. The heat of summer and the flies that were always there, little sticky fly catchers hanging from the ceiling, everyone getting a towel and flipping them as we were walking across to an open door to drive the flies out. My twin Harry and I walking through the fields hearing the cries of the Whippoorwills, a sound never to be forgotten.

These are, as I remember them, the happier moments of my earliest years. We were not poor---as to say "poor" means you have something but not much. We had nothing of value. What a great way to start out.

Harry and I had a younger brother, Ron, who stuck to us like glue. Also a sister, Marge, who tried to take care of us although she was only three years older. I also had a brother, Don, who was six years older, but I didn't see much of him. Judie was around seven years younger than me so I didn't have much memory of her either. Kathy was just a baby when she was adopted out.

In around 1936 we moved from the log cabin in the woods which was a mile from downtown Remer to a tar paper shack some four or five blocks from downtown. While at the shack we could see the old steam engine go by on the tracks a block away and hear the whistle and the clang of its bell. Often we would put pennies or nails on the track to get them flattened out.

I must speak of my mother who was a beautiful woman with her own problems. She was loved by all of us. How do you speak of her when you are so young and seeing her through a kid's eyes? Ron was always very special to her, but after he was adopted out the two of them never got to see each other again; she passed away at 59 years of age. We do know that there were more than three fathers to her children and that she drank and was gone a lot. She also had some health problems. I think the Cass County welfare was trying to monitor us.

George and Minnie Maness (Harvey's grandparents) stand in front of their home in Remer where the Dahline children were born. Julia May Smith is in the center.

Dahline children

Something that will never leave my mind. Sometimes I have judged my mother quite harshly but she was a strong woman in many ways. Around 1939 something was going on across the field. The Peabody house was on fire. My mother and some other women headed in that direction. About an hour later I saw my mother coming back holding her arms out in front of her. She was in a great deal of pain with burns on her arms and some flesh sticking to them. When she had approached the burning house, there were a number of people standing around. She could hear the screams of the children from inside and she went into the inferno and carried two little boys out. They were still alive and taken to the hospital where they died later on that day. Some of the story told later was that the boys were asking for ice cream. Many years later we were in Remer for a family reunion and I was able to locate the graves of the children in the graveyard on the outskirts of town. Judge not lest you be judged.

As I said before, Marge tried to take care of us. One time my mother had been gone for a couple days and Marge killed some six-weeks-old chicks and made some soup. More than once we sneaked into our neighbor's basement and took some jars of canned goods. Many years later when I was a police officer I ran into the son of the people who owned the house. I got to talking to him in a filling station and he told me that his parents knew who had been in the basement, but we never did any damage, just getting something to eat, so they had let it slide. Marge, Harry, Ron and I had gotten a reprieve.

Other things happened while we were by ourselves. One time we were blowing up tin cans with fire crackers. There was a wash tub sitting there with the bottom blown out with some very jagged edges. Harry was backing up and fell on the tub leaving a deep gash on his rear---it was closed with tape. We all lived in spite of everything.

We had an old grandmother who was very small, less than five feet tall. She was first married to a man named Schmidt in Hinckley. It seems they had three children. When the children were very young, he had gone to the gold fields in North Dakota to make some money. As the story was told, he had written that he had made his fortune and was on his way home. He never returned. During that time the 1894 Hinckley Fire burned out of control and killed many people, but she and her children escaped on a train and spent some time in a hospital, but due to her mental health was never reunited with her children. She eventually married my grandfather George Maness; they settled around the Remer area and had six children. He was a horse trader and died from a heart attack when his house burned down in 1938. My Grandmother lived with my mother for many years until her death in 1951. In our younger years she tried her best to help raise us.

We had been roaming around Remer but this was not to last. Marge, Harry, Ron, Judie and I found ourselves in a Walker court room. Soon Harry, Ron and myself were on a farm in Hackensack where we spent the winter. Not much happened there except that on a warm winter morning we decided to go home so we ran away. It didn't take the farmer very long to track us down through the snow about a mile. He had cut a long willow switch along the way. I was singled out as the ring leader so he switched me all the way back to the farm with me hollering like I was being killed. I think he knew as well as me that I never felt a thing because I had a fur lined leather coat. The farmer's wife could make the best chicken and dumplings which I was not to see for a couple Sundays. We slept up in the attic curled next to the chimney to help stay warm. We would wake up to the smell of bacon along with eggs and pancakes being cooked for breakfast. Then it was off to the school bus.

That spring we were returned home but not to Remer. My mother had rented a two story house in Grand Rapids just north of Blandin Beach close to a mink ranch and across the road from the Newman sawmill. One day we were looking out our upstairs bedroom window when a truck pulled into the yard with a live horse lying in the bed. They tied a rope to the tree, put it around the neck of the horse and drove away. The horse flopped to the ground. They killed and butchered it in the yard; it was food for the mink.

We had to walk to the downtown Middle School. One day some boys held me while another boy beat me up. Then the other boy took off on foot. The boys let him get a block away then they let me go. That boy could sure run but I caught him by Blandin Beach and got in a few hits, then felt sorry for him. We were friends after that.

We were not home long and then ended up in the Holy Angel's Academy, a Catholic home in Belle Prairie just outside of Little Falls. Ron was still with us but after a short time left to go to California to live with an uncle and aunt. After a few months someone told me that he was coming back and we waited for a Greyhound bus to drop him off. We had really missed him.

We slept in a boys' dormitory in really small beds that looked like hospital beds which were maybe only around 20 inches wide and not much more than five feet long. We visited there some years later as adults and couldn't believe how small they were. The nuns were very nice overall, but they would make you hold your hands out and slap them with a ruler if you misbehaved.

Something I will always remember is waking up in the middle of a cold night to someone shaking me awake. It was Ron. "Harvey, Harvey," he said, "I'm so cold," his teeth chattering. He had wet his bed quite thoroughly. Since my bed wouldn't hold two, I tucked him into my bed then went to his bed for a very uncomfortable night. As young as he was, Ron never forgot that night and neither did I.

After some time at the Holy Angel's Academy, we were taken to the Gene Martin Brown Home, an orphanage that was a big red brick building on Como Ave. in St. Paul close to Como Zoo.

We were only there for a short time when we decided to run away. To prepare we went to the laundry room and got some bed sheets to keep us warm as they were light to carry. On the way out, Ron had to go to the bathroom and we somehow lost him. This was in the fall and quite cold at night. We ended up in Como Park for a couple days before getting caught by Mr. Dahl, the man running the orphanage. We could not have been happier. Those sheets just could not keep you warm at night and who wants crab apples for every meal. Upon returning, we found that Ron was being treated like a hero for not running away, We had to sleep in the fourth story attic for a week and all we could have was all the bread and cold milk we wanted. How I suffered; there is nothing I liked more than good bread and cold milk.

When it snowed that winter I would take a shovel and go to the neighbors and shovel their walks, sometimes making $5 in an evening.

The next summer Ron was adopted out and taken from us. Harry and I being older and twins were left together. For many years we had no idea where he was, but he was always in my mind and heart. At this time we didn't know where any of our sisters were either.

Harry and I were then placed with Emil Johnson's resort since we were getting older and they needed work done. The resort was located on Coon Lake a short distance from Wyoming, Minnesota. They had an ice house filled with ice and sawdust. We would chunk off 25 lbs of ice for customers as most people had iceboxes then, not refrigerators.

One winter they were hauling 300 pound cakes of ice off the lake on a sleigh pulled by a tractor. I had a small six foot sleigh with runners hooked onto and being pulled behind the big sleigh. The small sleigh had three inch metal poles sticking up on each corner.

I was lying on the sleigh being pulled when we hit a rough area; I bounced up and came down on a metal pole, getting the pole caught in my crotch. We were going maybe 10 mph. It was maybe a hundred yards before I got free. I didn't know what to do so I went home, but some of the Taylor boys knew what had happened so, Joe, their father came over for a look. He went home and had his wife make a sling to go around my body with a pouch in it. I used this with Vaseline in it for a couple weeks. I never rode that sled again and got a pretty good scar.

It may seem like we were good kids all the time but we had our fun. There was a farmer up the road who had a big farm that raised corn, watermelon and pigs. No one knew where the watermelon patch was but it didn't take much to figure out that it was in the middle of the cornfield. But that fun didn't last long. He came by and told us to stay out of the patch because we were damaging the vines. He said he would drop some off at our place on his way to market each week. They never did taste as good though after that. Some times when we were supposed to be in Sunday school we would be getting bullheads and northerns out of the game warden's fish trap in the creek.

Ron, Harvey, Harry, and
Judy Dahline

One winter the ice froze as clear as glass. Someone would pull us with an old car on the end of a hundred foot rope. We were on skates; they would go fast then turn in a circle. You would be whipped so hard at the end of the rope you couldn't hold on and would slide across the ice perhaps a quarter of a mile. In the spring-time the ice would be melting on the lake getting 50 feet from shore. We would run off the end of the dock onto the rubber ice. You could feel it giving way until you got out to thicker ice--- a few times we fell in. Sometimes looking down through the ice you could see piles of frogs in two foot circles on the bottom.

I remember my mother coming to visit us there one time. We were happy to see her. But I also remember we were to wait for her by the road one other afternoon. We waited most of the day but she never showed up.

We were at Johnson's place perhaps a couple years until one Sunday I came home from church and found Mr. Johnson dead of a heart attack in the yard.

Our next home was to be at Cliff Farber's farm five or six miles from Staples across the Crow Wing River Bridge and a mile down the road. We had 12 milking cows, a couple horses, chicken and pigs. There was lots of work. I worked outside and Harry was to work in the house. When we first got there, we were told we could have all the milk we could drink. Their minds changed quite quick-ly. I learned how to harness a team of horses and how to use a side rake and mower, plus I plowed with one horse and a plow that you'd walk behind. The work was hard but I loved it. We often went fish-ing in the Crow Wing River.

The school was about a mile away and I would run both ways. I loved to run in the woods too. Some times I would come to a barb-wire fence and just leap right over it, clearing it most of the time. One time I hit some wet grass and got a cut on my leg around five inches long. Tape held it together pretty good.

We had a windmill that pumped water into the watering trough for the animals. It stood about 40 feet high and I would climb it with a pocket full of seeds from a maple tree that spin like a pro-peller and watch them fly down. One time I was up on top of the windmill on a platform dropping them when I started to lose my

Staples Junior High School									
Staples, Minnesota						Home Room 22			
Name Dahline, Harvey									
Year 19 48 19 49 Principal *Alice Hutchens* (signature)					Grade 8				

PERIODS	1	2	3	4	5	6	Final Exam	Final Mark	TEACHER
Days Absent	0	0	6	0	3	0			
Times Tardy	0	0	1	0	0	0			
English VII	D	F	F	F	F	D		F	*Shirtle*
Mathematics II	D	F	D	D	D	C		D	B. Spahn
Social Science 9	D	D	D	D	a	a	a		Kummert
Ind. or Home Ec.	D	C	D			D	P		Edwards
General Science			C	C	C	C	C		Dittberner
Art									
Music	D		D	F	D	D	F	E	Maass
Physical Ed.	C	B	C	C	B	B		B	Rengel

A—Superior; B—Above Average; C—Average; D—Below Average; F—Failure.

TO THE PARENTS:
In addition to the achievement record above, a section on the other side of this card is devoted to certain habits and attitudes. Should you at any time observe anything unsatisfactory in any part of the report, please consult with the teacher at once. Parents are always welcome to visit the school.
P. M. ATWOOD, Superintendent.

EXAMINED BY
First Period *C. C. Farber*
Second Period *C. C. Farber*
Third Period *C. C. Farber*
Fourth Period *C. C. Farber*
Fifth Period *C. C. Farber*

Citizenship

This report calls attention to certain habits and attitudes. All affect the pupil's progress.

The pupil needs to improve in the items checked ✔. If no items are checked, traits appear satisfactory.

Periods	1	2	3	4	5	6
1. Sits, stands, and walks correctly	✔	✔	✔	✔	✔	
2. Is regular in attendance						
3. Uses time to good advantage	✔	✔	✔	✔	✔	
4. Keeps books and property in good condition		✔	✔	✔	✔	
5. Follows directions	✔	✔		✔	✔	
6. Starts and completes work on time	✔	✔	✔	✔	✔	
7. Is neat in written work	✔	✔	✔	✔	✔	
8. Makes use of ability			✔	✔	✔	
9. Is self-reliant	✔	✔		✔	✔	
10. Works well with group	✔				✔	
11. Is courteous			✔	✔	✔	
12. Keeps appointments	✔	✔	✔	✔	✔	
13. Is truthful				✔		
14. Takes criticism		✔		✔	✔	
15. Obeys quickly and cheerfully		✔		✔		
16. Is a good winner and a good loser				✔		

balance. I reached for something and put my fingers through the cogs of the windmill. They must have been old, loose and worn as my fingers went through the cogs and all that happened is that I have some scars.

We had been going to a little white one room school where some of the kids picked on us for a while but soon learned better. Next we went to school in Staples. While I was playing tag football one noon, the coach noticed me and that night had me out for spring practice. After practice I would run home the six miles to do chores. That summer I got a job for the Great Northern Railroad working on a track gang mostly throwing a 10 pound maul all day pounding railroad spikes in. I had to up my age a little on my application. After a while on that gang I was getting in quite good shape. At the end of summer I had to quit to start school. My paycheck didn't come in for a couple days, so I had to wait around, and having no money I went without food too. During the time I was working they had provided meals for us.

Our bedroom was on the second floor and sometimes rather than going out to the cold outhouse we would "go" through the screen down into the snow. The screen started getting pretty rusty, and Mr. Farber also saw the yellow snow and gave us a firm talking to and that it wouldn't be tolerated.

In 1949 when school was out my brother Don showed up and said, "Get your things; I'm taking you home." He was old enough now that he could sign for us. We moved in with my mother and grandmother. They had an apartment on 2nd St. N.W. which is now a parking lot for the paper mill. Mother was working in the Pokegama Hotel doing their laundry. Sometimes the heat would get up to 125 degrees. I started working for the Gambles Skogmo just next door.

That fall I went out for football although some guys said it was no use because the coaches had their favorites. They were teaching how to tackle which was to pick 'em up and drive them into the ground. Three days after starting Coach Nobel Hall came up to me and said I'd made the team but would have to back off a little because too many boys were getting hurt. We had some good teams and I still have connections with friends like Duane Helmer, Pete Peterson and Bill Hachey from that team.

Along the way I had again upped my age and joined the National Guard as I needed the money along with what I was making at the store. Then the Korean War started and the National Guard was activated and so I became a member of the Army. I was still going to school so could have gotten out of it, but I had signed the papers so did what I thought was right. We were sent to Camp Rucker, Alabama for training. While there I played regimental football. After my training was completed I was sent to Korea. I was home on furlough before being deployed and one day was walking past some school buses in the driveway of the Senior High. A very shy young girl named Doris was on one of those buses and saw me. It was hard for her to do but she went to her brother, Cecil, and asked who I was. He replied that I was that dumb Dahline who didn't care if he was going to Korea or not. She did not think she would ever see him again.

Not a long time after that I was on a troop ship bound for Korea. I ended up as a sergeant in a Machine Gun Platoon and had some troubles for a short time as some of the men were quite a bit older

and lower in rank. Some from WWII, but we worked it out.

Being on the front lines gave me pictures in my mind that will always be there. I was 17 and 18 years old at the time and saw some amazing things. How quad fifties, (machine guns) mounted on a half-track (truck) putting out 2,400 rounds a minute with every 5th one being a green tracer, could light up a whole valley. The smoke and fire from napalm bombs exploding near you. The sight of little parachutes shot up into the sky with flares on to light up the whole area at night so that you could see your enemies. Watching the accuracy of planes dropping bombs on targets in front of you. The planning and coordination to see troops taking a hill while you are firing a machine gun over them. There were two hills that were the center of our attention for some time. They were the highest hills in the area and were called Baldy and Breadloaf. We would fight and take them in the morning and were off the hill at night. The enemy would take them back at night and we would have to take them back again the next day. They were used for forward observation posts in no man's land. Sometimes it was raining so hard you couldn't see the hill or where your own ground troops were so you had to cease fire. I earned the Combat Infantry Badge, Korean Service Medal w/1 Bronze Service Star and United Nations Service Medal. I am very proud of them.

After being discharged in 1952 I went back to high school in Grand Rapids and played football. I tried out for the basketball team but had too much football in me. John Curran, the wrestling coach saw me and asked me to go out for the wrestling team along with Harry. We did quite well since it was the first year for wrestling. The coach appointed me as a co-captain of the team, and I was very fortunate to become one of the two region champs. 1952 was the beginning of the wrestling program which is still my favorite high school sport.

During this time a classmate informed me that there was a friend of hers who was interested in me. After reminding me of this a few times she asked if I would come over after the regional wrestling tournaments and she and Doris would make a meal for her own boyfriend and me. I said yes but I didn't have any money or a car. Needless to say, I didn't show up.

While in the service I had been sending my paycheck home each month, but on arriving back home I found my family had spent it all. Shortly after the wrestling season I quit school and got a job in the Oliver Iron Mining Co. as I found that the family had been charging on my name at the Johnson Food Store, including cigarettes and beer, and that I owed several hundred dollars.

After work one night I went to the roller rink. Guess who was there. She was quite unsteady on her skates and required a lot of attention. We seemed to hit it off very well, and since I had a borrowed car, I asked her brother if I could take her home and he consented. I'm not sure this was such a good idea on their part as I was very rough in speech and manner. Soon Doris took me home to meet her mother and father who seemed to be great. Later her mother took her aside and said that I made the hair stand up on the back of her neck with my rough language.

Along the way I told her about my family and that I didn't know where any of the younger ones were. She was always supportive about locating them.

We got married the next summer. We had a small wedding which included my mother and her boyfriend, Louie, getting married at the same time. At Doris's suggestion we contacted the welfare in Walker to see if they would give us some information about where Ron was. They said they couldn't. I think they actually felt kind of sorry for us and gave us a clue that he was around 250 miles away. We had heard that he may be with a farming family around the Mankato area. For a honeymoon we headed for Mankato State University. We looked for hours through yearbooks for someone named Ron. We had no idea what his last name was. We did not know how close we had come.

Out of the blue we heard that the welfare had contacted my mom and that Judie wanted to come home and see the family. We also learned that she was not legally adopted but was still a foster child. Later on when she was old enough she chose to be adopted. We had heard that Kathy was adopted out to a family in Walker, so during the time Judie was home we went over to the school and asked if we could meet her. They told us they couldn't do that but the principal took us to the classroom she was in and we could see her through the window in the door. Within a couple years she came back on her own to meet us.

After I tried various jobs, Doris saw an ad placed in the local paper by the police commission about an opening for a policeman. I said I didn't think I could make it because of my lack of education. She encouraged me to try it saying she thought I could. I took the test and got hired on the GR Police Department. I had only been on the force for a few short months when my sister-in-law, Betty, told us she got a call from a young man questioning all about me but who gave no hint who he was. We were living in a small apartment downtown, and I came home for dinner one day and there was a very handsome young man standing there in our living room-bedroom combination. Doris asked me if I knew who he was and I just stood there. There was something about him and then Doris said, "This is your brother Ron." I could not believe what I was seeing after all those years. Looking and wondering. I threw my arms around him and I have to admit I cried and cried. My brother had come home. There was an empty spot that was now full. It had been 13 years. I went and talked to the chief and told him the story and he gave me the rest of the day off, and we water skied with my brother-in-law's boat the rest of the afternoon. Now the whole family was accounted for.

Later Doris told me the story of his appearance. She had heard a knock at the door. When she answered it, a young man was standing there. He asked if Harvey was home and she said he would be home shortly. He turned to walk away and she said, "You are Ron, aren't you?" He replied, "What did you say?" and she repeated it. He got a smile on his face and came back and waited. He later said if she wouldn't have recognized him he wouldn't have come back. What happens to kids when they are taken away? In our talks he said he always remembered a cold night in a wet bed. My reward was priceless. He had felt abandoned and but for that memory he may never have come back.

It's been 50-some years since our reunion and over the years we have shared a lot. One thing he had told me was how frightened he was as his adoptive parents were driving him home. W.W. II was still going on. He was in the back seat and they were speaking in German and he thought they were spies. Ron grew up on a farm in the Darfur/Butterfield area, and I was very surprised to learn that the two "spies" had also taken in as a foster child and later adopted Judie, my little sister.

All seven of us have met and have kept the communication open with each other. We respect what each other has accomplished in spite of the sad beginning. Adversity can make you strong.

We found my real father through much hard work by Doris. He lived in the Hinckley area and worked as an engineer for MNDOT until his death in 1958. Much to our surprise he also may have ridden the same train out of the Hinckley fire as my Grandmother Minnie Schmidt Maness. My father's name was Earl Basil Currie. I never met him but found his side of the family, and they accepted us very well and we have maintained a relationship with them.

We also met the people who adopted Ron and Judie. They also accepted us and one day Ron's adopted father, Mr. Stoesz said, "I should have adopted the whole bunch of you." That was nice of him to say but that would not have worked. Ron has his story and I have mine.

I would not change what I went through for anything; the wonderful time in that frosty old cabin, running through the woods, appreciating our little grandmother. The remembered times with Little Ron and Harry; The wet bed, working on the railroad throwing a 10 pound hammer and feeling my strength grow; being so proud of a mother with so many weaknesses who risked her life going into a fire while everybody else stood and watched the flames while the kids were screaming, she getting burned as she brought them out; the hard work on the farm, playing football on some great teams and joining the Army and finding out what great teamwork was; going to Korea,   feeling as though you have done a small part for this country; having to quit school, a grown-up thing to do; having a brother, Don, and sister, Marge, who both tried so hard; meeting Doris who was to be my saving grace and having four young sons and a beautiful daughter. These things I went through all helped me grow a confidence within myself that was to help carry me through the next phase of my life. Over 40 years on the police department.

Success is not always reaching the top but trying your best.

~

2
COLD CARBURETOR - WARM BEER

On a very cold morning I was driving behind Anderson Glass Co. which is in the west end of Grand Rapids. This was before the dirt was brought in to fill a ravine which was eight to ten feet deep and 120 feet wide stretching from Anderson Glass to Rapids Flour and Feed next to the railroad tracks.

At this time there were a lot of junk cars in the ravine but also some good ones. Coming upon a black older car with a very warm radiator even though it was 20 below parked up by the side next to the tracks. Getting out of my car, I walked down a small incline and headed through the alley going west. In a short time I saw two young men working in the dark under the hood of a car. When I got within 40 feet or so of the car, the person closest to me looked up and saw me in uniform. He just kept watching and never said a word. I then walked up to the car, leaned on the radiator and watched the other young man trying to remove the carburetor. He was having some trouble doing so. With head down he asked for a screw driver, so I handed him one. Shortly, he picked up the carburetor and started to lift it out. I then told him that maybe he should put it back. He was a little startled.

Upon search of their car I found a warm six pack of beer in the trunk. When asked about the beer, one boy said his father had left it in the trunk three weeks ago. It had been well below zero for the last week.

Juveniles remanded to the courts.

~

3
HIDDEN MAN

The first few months on the police department were quite interesting. I was hired and put right on the street without any schooling or formal training.

One of the things we had to do was open and close the VFW Park gate with locks every morning and night. Go to the alley switch box by Miltich Jewelry; turn on the alley and street lights in town. Then walk the downtown to check all of the businesses. If we found any unlocked doors, we would have to call the owners to come and lock them up.

It was a warm beautiful night in the early morning hours when I was checking doors on the Marlon block and thinking there was no one around. Then I got to the Janicke Bakery. They had and still do have a small three-sided entry around a three feet by three feet area where you step up on a single step to enter the main door. I reached in with my right hand to grab the latch. Just then I saw a person to my right. I jumped back and went into a crouch, ready, for---I don't know what---action. I stared at my opponent and he stared back. I had not known Janicke Bakery had a 30-inch wide by 60-inch tall mirror on the right hand side of the entry.

To this day 57 years later my wife and I laugh over this. She always thought I couldn't be startled like that.

To have fun in your life you have to be able to laugh at yourself.

~

4
LONG COAT - HOT SUMMER DAY

The National Tea food store summoned me to their location on a hot summer day. The manager said that after much observation, he was sure an older man wearing an ankle length coat was shoplifting by putting canned goods in the lining of his coat.

I stopped the man after he left the store. The coat was full of canned goods that he hadn't paid for. After retrieving the stolen items, I didn't see a car for this person in the lot. I then asked him where his car was as he must have one since he said that he had just came over from the Range. He pointed to an old truck parked way over in the back of the lot. I thought it strange that he would park 300 feet from the entry to the store. I went to the truck and couldn't believe what I saw. The passenger side of the cab was completely filled from the window to the floor to the center of the floor board with loose canned goods. Probably at least three bushels full.

I then took him to the police department. He told me he was broke, no money or income. Also, that he had cancer and was going to the doctor. I then asked him were he had gotten all the other canned goods, which by this time were being boxed up and brought to the police station. He told me he had been stopping at different stores as he drove across the Range.

Some of what he was telling me did not ring true. Going out to the truck I did a more thorough search, finding a three pound coffee can with dirty oily rags in it. Under the rags was $700 in bills. Going into the station I made some calls to his home town police department.

It turned out he was a very well man with sticky fingers. But, I did treat him well. I set him up with a court date that relieved him of a good portion of his $700.

~

5
THE DANCING THIEVES

In the 1960's the Grand Rapids City Hall offices were all on the ground floor. The top floor had two bathrooms and a large gym area with a stage around four feet off the floor at one end of the gym. On both sides of the stage were small rooms with curtains coming out seven or eight feet on the front of the stage. In the back of the stage were a lot of canvas props eight feet high and wide leaning against the wall.

At this time we used to have teen age dances with live bands every Friday night.

We were starting to have reports that money was being pilfered each week from girls' purses left on stage behind the curtains.

One night I got on the stage early before anyone else got there, made my way behind the props, cut a small hole in the canvas on one of the props so I could see the area of the stored purses.

As the night wore on nothing of interest seemed to be happening. The Buddy Lawrence band was playing and around 150 kids filled the dance floor. Some of them were dancing while others just stood around, talked and watched. Around 9:30 to 10:30 two boys got up on the stage and started to dance and were actually very good. At first they danced just in the middle of the stage. Then as time went on they started running and sliding doing different movements. After a time many kids who were watching got tired and left. It got so their sliding and gyrating got them into the area of the purses. They would go through the purses very quickly, take some cash, leave some, put the purse back and come out dancing.

This was all going very well for them until they were getting ready to go. The two of them were standing in the middle of the stage. All at once it was a trio with me standing between them.

Juvenile court and restitution were waiting

~

6
SCHOOL YARD - BITING DOG

The police station was in the front of City Hall when I first got on the police department in 1955. You could look out the west window and see Central School across the street.

School had just been in session for a short time when a lady came running into the police station saying that a big dog had bitten several kids in the school yard. I ran onto the north side of the school and someone met me and pointed me to the west side. As I came around the corner, I was met face to face by a large Weimaraner dog. He came after me and I for him. He got my left wrist in his mouth, but I got my right hand into his choker collar. As we wrestled I managed to do a full twist of the collar and he went unconscious. When he came to he went after me again, but I had full control and twisted him unconscious again. When he woke up again, he loved me.

I then walked him over to city hall where the chief took over talking to the business owner and doing the paper work. I then went to the hospital for a couple stitches and a tetanus shot.

I still love dogs, just not that big.

~

7
BLINDING SUN - FAST STOP

Many years ago there was a very nice woman driving her brand new Oldsmobile through the parking lot of a store which is now KMart. She was having trouble seeing because of the evening sun. She was probably doing around 20 to 25 mph when suddenly she hit a light pole on a yellow concrete base, totaling her brand new car and seriously injuring herself.

In great pain she was taken by ambulance to the hospital with possible broken ribs and other injuries. Her husband was notified and shortly afterward showed up at the emergency room. I could not believe what I was hearing when I walked in. The husband was a prominent business man and was giving his wife hell over the damage to his new car in spite of the fact that she was obviously in great pain. I listened to him for a short time then stepped in. I asked him not too nicely what kind of a man he was by tearing into her while she was in so much pain. I added that he only had one wife but he could buy a hundred cars like that with his money. He seemed to grasp what I was saying and turned around and left.

She did manage to thank me later for coming to the accident scene and as she put it "rescuing her" at the emergency room.

~

8
THE TRANSOM BURGLAR

My partner, Clarence, and I were in the N.E. part of town just having picked up a drunk driver, and Clarence was in the process of driving the guy to the downtown lockup when I got a call that a burglary was taking place. It was at Gabby Clusiau's which was located at the back of the Coast to Coast store and across the street from the Old Mill Pond, which was a bar. Stopping at the Old Mill Pond, I was told that they had watched a man climb up the door of Gabby's and go through the transom. The transom is a window above the door that can be opened at the bottom. After looking through the windows I couldn't see anyone in the front part of the store. Not wanting to do damage to the door, I also climbed up the door and dropped through the transom to the floor. As I hit the floor, a man appeared from behind the counter and started for the back door. It was very dark, and I couldn't tell if he was armed. I told him to stop but he didn't. I then fired a shot into the door next to him. At that time we were only 8-10 feet apart. He turned to face me and I ordered him to turn around, face the wall, put his hands against the wall and spread his legs. All standard police procedures. He would not and told me so with some profanity.

It is preached that you should not get close to a suspect. In the movies the suspect does what he is told. But now in a dark room what do you do? Do you shoot? You don't have much time to think about it. I stepped forward quickly and nailed him. He went down. Finally he got up, turned to the wall, spread his feet and put his hands on the wall, all the time telling me that the next time he would have a gun and would kill me.

The suspect, Bill, was in his thirties, and this was not the first time he was charged with burglary. He had been picked up some years earlier for breaking into the Oldsmobile garage, taking a car from the showroom window, loading a safe into the back of the car and taking it out to the Big Woods. He then brought the car back and rode his bike home. He was caught because it had been raining, and another policeman, Arnie Witherill, tracked the bike tracks through the mud.

Some time later I took some flack for the incident at Gabby's place, some critics saying I could have injured or killed the poor boy.

I noted most of these critics were arm-chair quarterbacks, sitting safely in their chairs.

~

9
THE MAN THAT HANDCUFFED HIMSELF

A man was reported to be "holed up" in his house after shooting up the inside. Arriving at the house, I got the name of the person and learned that the incident may have started as a domestic issue. The address was located in the N.E. part of town, and since we didn't have a phone system as we do today, I went to the sheriff's office and made a call to Tim's house.

Tim answered the phone, and knowing him somewhat, I told him who I was and then asked him what in the world was going on. We had a lengthy conversation, and he admitted he was having some "women problems." At what I thought was the proper time, I asked him if he needed some cigarettes. He said he did, badly. I told him he would have to put the shotgun on the sink so I would be able to see it through the front window. If he did that I would bring him some cigarettes, and we would sit down and talk and he could have a smoke.

Before approaching the house, I had a talk with the other officers, and since we didn't have portable radios, I would signal them some way with a flashlight when it was time to come in. As I approached the house and looked in the window, I could see the gun on the sink and Tim standing away from it. After entering the house, I handed the cigarettes to him. Seeing a refrigerator in the corner, I asked him if he had any pop in there. At this time I concluded he had been drinking. As he was bending over to get the pop from the refrigerator, I used the flashlight to signal the other officers to come in, which they did with a flourish.

At this time I let Tim sit at the table as I had made him a promise to have his cigarette. The other guys looked at me as though I had lost my mind. Perhaps I had. I had a can of Coke with him.

After his smoke we stood up, and I explained to him we were going in the squad car down town. One of our rules in a case like this is that a person put in the squad car has to be handcuffed. He jumped into a corner saying that no one was going to handcuff him. At this I told him no one was going to, tossed him the cuffs, and told him to put them on himself. And he did.

We later counted the numerous gunshot holes throughout the upstairs and down. Tim continued to have problems through the years but nothing like this incident.

~

~

10
GRAVE YARD RUNNER

We were pulling a car over in the bowling alley front parking lot and could see there were at least three boys in it. As it was coming to a stop, a passenger door came open and a young boy around 15 years old jumped out, ran across the road at a very good clip and disappeared into the Itasca County Cemetery.

We found beer in the car with the driver and two more boys, none of who would tell us who the runner was. The squad left with the other boys.

Not wanting the boy in the cemetery to become lost or neglected, I turned out the lights on the boy's car and slumping down drove real slow through the cemetery just bumping the horn a little bit. After driving through most of the cemetery and getting to the far end, I saw a darting figure. He ran up and opened the passenger door and jumped in at which time we said, "Hello!"

~

11
LITTLE LONELY OLD MAN

The little old man standing off by himself in the pool hall appeared very quiet and lonely. Old as he was, there appeared to be something about him. I could feel it, courage and respect. I walked over and talked to him.

Over the next few weeks I got to know him and gave him several rides home as he no longer drove. I also took him some strawberry jam and checked on his well being. Over time he began to confide in me. He had just lost the love of his life of 70-some years. He was very lonely. He had a beautiful daughter but without his wife his life was empty.

The friendship grew and one day he asked me to come into his house as I was dropping him off. He wanted to show me something and talk to me.

When we got in the house, he said he wanted to give me a prized possession, adding I could turn it down if I wanted but that he had talked it over with his family and they said it was OK.

I had known that he was perhaps the best pool player in the area, having won several championships here and in other states. He took me upstairs and showed me a beautiful unique clock, pool balls with numbers on them for the time and pool sticks for the hands with green fabric as the background. He had won the clock some time back. I accepted the clock with hesitation, but I felt he wanted me to have it for some special reason.

I left my friend that day and never talked to him again. For he knew.

That night he went to be with his love.

The stones like sentinels rise
through the morning mist
There is pink in the east
and dew on the fresh mound
of earth
70 years they had been together
Now he is at peace
My friend.

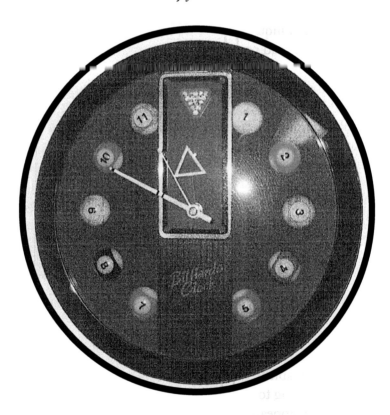

~

12
CARS BROKEN INTO - 8 TRACKS STOLEN

In the summer of 1970-1972 we had a rash of thefts from cars. Probably around seventy 8 Tracks and hundreds of cassettes. It seemed as though there was nothing we could do to get a line on who was doing this. Watching cars, doing stake-outs, talking to people. Nothing seemed to work.

One day I started going to places where they repaired cars, and to TV shops, anywhere someone would want to go to get an 8 Track harness to hook up to a car. Whoever was stealing them took the 8 Tracks but left the harnesses.

A couple days after being to Yelle's TV, he called me to say that two boys had been inquiring about 8 Track harnesses. His shop was located across the road north of Central School so it could be seen from the police department. I was standing looking out the window toward the school while I was on the phone with Dale. He said if you look out the window now you will see a car stopped at the stop sign by the village hall with two boys in it. I saw them and ran out to my squad car. I was able to get behind them. They were heading north on Pokegama Ave. going past the high school. Making a stop of the car by Ice Lake and walking up to the car, I could see through the side window several 8 Tracks and many cassettes all on the back seat and floor.

After checking their driver's licenses and other ID's, I asked who owned the players and cassettes. They were both very nervous and without any good answers to my questions. It was not long before they admitted they were all stolen from Grand Rapids and throughout the county. They lead me to a stash out in the woods of two big garbage bags full of more. At least 70 to 80 cases of car prowls were solved which had taken place over the last couple years.

We were never able to trace a lot of the owners. When asked what they were going to do with all their loot, they had no idea.

Both juveniles appeared in court.

~

13
WHY DID THE LIGHTS GO OUT?

While out patroling at around 10 P.M. on a very cold night with my partner Al Brooks, we received a call from a very good friend asking us to come to his house right away.

Upon our arrival my friend invited us inside to show us what he had found on his table when he arrived home a short time before. It was from his brother who I knew lived near by in a trailer house. The note stated he was going to commit suicide at 12 o'clock this night. His brother had mental problems and had threatened it in the past. We went right to his home.

Upon arriving I instructed Brooks to stay in the patrol car for now, as I had built up a trusting relationship with my friend's brother that made me feel I could approach him in a nonthreatening manner.

The night was dark and below zero. There was a small light outside on the side of the trailer which was about 60 feet long by 12 feet wide. Facing the side of the trailer was the entry door and the living room. It had about a three foot wide hallway on the far side with a bath and a bedroom on the side. At the end of the hallway was the master bedroom.

Reaching up to the side door and rapping, I heard Jerry asking who was there. I said, "Harvey Dahline. You know who I am. I've helped you out in the past. Times when you fell off your bike and gave you rides home." He asked me what he could do for me, and I told him I had read the note that he had written to his brother. If he would let me in, having helped him in the past, I was sure we could work this out. He replied that he knew I was a championship wrestler and that I would trick him.

We talked back and forth for the next half hour. My problem was that I was not dressed to stand outside without a heavy coat on. I was starting to freeze and shake. I told him that I didn't think it was right for him to let me freeze outside as I could not leave him under these conditions. Then an idea came to me: I asked him if he would unlock the door and then go back to the bedroom and that I would wait a few minutes before I came in. Thinking for a couple minutes, he said, "Ok, but you have to wait a few minutes before coming in." Hearing the door unlock and seeing the back bedroom light go on, I entered the very warm and well lit living room. It was quite a pleasure after standing in the cold so long.

I was carrying our old walkie talkie radio and thought I should let Al Brooks know what was going on. I lifted the radio to talk and when I hit the transmit button, all the lights went out in my end of the trailer. I told my partner what was taking place, and looking down the hall, I could see light from under the bedroom door. Hollering to Jerry, I asked him if he could hit the breaker switch in the box back there as the lights had gone out in my end. I saw his shadow cross the light under the door and about three seconds later the lights came on. Time went on with some small talk and again I lifted the radio to talk to Brooks outside. I hit the switch and the lights went out again. Now, I don't know how or why the lights went out nor have I ever heard of anything like this since. But, I have learned that if the Lord puts something in your hands use it.

Another thought came to mind. I called Jerry and asked if he would turn the breaker switch on again, watching as he crossed the light under the door again. The light came on again. Time was moving on toward 12 o'clock. I took my shoes, jacket and gun belt off so I could move faster without making lots of noise. Jerry was now saying, "It's about time." Hitting the switch on my radio again, the lights went out. First yelling for Jerry to turn them on and then watching the light under the door and the shadow moving across, I dashed down the hall at full speed and crashed through the door. There he was, astonished, mouth wide open, his right hand in the breaker box and left hand on the front sight of a .30/06 rifle with the butt trailing on the carpet.

A few quick steps and it was all over. I guess Jerry was right not to trust me.

Many years have gone by now. But we took all of Jerry's guns and he seems to be doing quite well.

Why did the lights go out that night for us? It does make you wonder.

~

14
THE SHOPLIFTING FAMILY

Called to Goldfine's in the late hours of the morning many years ago, I met the manager at the door. He said there was some shoplifting going on but that I would have to see it to believe it.

We found a good vantage point to watch from. What I saw was two of the most beautiful Indian girls in their twenties you are ever going to see. They were taking their time putting selected clothing for women and children in their carts. Along with the women were boys and girls 7-10 years old. As soon as the carts were loaded up, a couple of the children would push the carts nonchalantly past the cashier out the door to the back parking lot, and unload the cart into a car that was parked there. They would take the cart around the building and come in through a different door.

This went on for some time. After approaching the two women and getting the children together, the clothing was taken from the car and arrests were made for shoplifting. The women appeared in court, paying a fine of up to $300 which was a lot in those days.

They were both very intelligent with good personalities. I understood one had gone to Yale and the other to Harvard. I've also heard they have gone on to do great things for their communities, helping others and so forth.

We got to be friends. For a few years they would stop at the police department and say "Hi" when they were going through town. I wished them well.

It is not up to me to judge but to serve and protect.

~

15
THE SLIPPERY FLOOR

In the mid-fifties we on the police department sold tickets to a Policeman's Ball for $1.00 each. The money was to help out on uniforms and some police equipment.

This particular dance was being held at the Forest Lake Lodge on the shore of Forest Lake in the west end of town.

My wife and I were very young at the time, but most policemen on our department were at least in their forties and fifties. As neither one of us drank and most of the others were very good at it, we were somewhat chided and looked down on. As my wife had her pop and I had a glass of milk of all things at the table, it was very obvious we were out of place.

As the evening went on, one lady, who was getting well on in years and who appeared to already have had more than her share of the strong stuff, came to our booth and while holding on to the side started to heckle and give me a bad time. Asking, "What's the matter; can't you handle a man's drink? Do you need your mother? Go take your bottle and get in your crib," as quite a few bystanders were watching. This went on for some time with a few more digs and she was becoming more unsteady on her feet. Suddenly her bladder let loose. Apparently she had more than her share of liquid as the floor got very slippery. She went down and try as she might she could not get up.

Her husband finally appeared and after some difficulty on the wet floor got her to her feet and with great pride walked her through the onlookers then out the door to take her home.

Being a gentleman somehow I was able to restrain all signs of a smile.

~

16
JUSTICE SERVED??

Sears contacted our office one morning saying that an expensive, brand name tractor had been delivered to their back door that morning. It was in a crate with all the paperwork in it and was valued at $3,000.00. It was now missing.

With this information I contacted the company that had delivered it, and they verified it had been delivered. I decided before too much time had elapsed that I would contact the newspaper. They put an article in the paper describing the machine and its value, also asking for anyone who might have any knowledge to contact the Police Dept.

A day or two later I received a call from a woman saying her husband had such a tractor. She said that he had found it discarded behind Sears next to the dumpster. We all know the garbage men will empty the dumpster but they aren't going to pick up a new tractor in a crate.

He was arrested and appeared in court. He testified that he had been picking up discarded objects behind Sears for years. Hearing this testimony, the judge found him not guilty, but at least he ruled that the man would have to return the tractor to Sears.

Justice served??

~

17
THE BLOW TORCHING CAR

One day as I was in the police office, I heard a horrible screeching of tires and the revving of a car engine. I ran to the window and saw something that most people won't see in a life time. An older car was going by very fast leaving a 25 to 30 foot blow-torching fire trail behind and heading for the fire dept around the corner.

Someone had called ahead to the fire department so they were ready to put the fire out and the car was saved. Good job by the fire department as usual.

Someone had been installing a trailer hitch using a welding torch at Neuman's sawmills and had cut into a gas tank.

~

18
PLANE OVERTURNED ON LILY LAKE

About 2:20 on a Friday afternoon we received a call stating a float plane had overturned on Lily Lake which is right next to the airport in the S.E. part of town. The report stated it was in the middle of the lake.

We saw a boat and motor about a block from the lake. We stopped and asked the owner if we could use it. He said we could but there wasn't much gas in it. We arrived at the scene and could see a man standing on the overturned plane around 200 yards out. Launching the boat went fine, but the owner had been right because around 100 yards out we ran out of gas.

One other boat had been launched, a one-man shell. It was able to pick up the pilot. While we rowed our borrowed boat back to shore, Warren Anderson went by us with one paddle and the pilot.

So much for a heroic rescue, but we did have a good laugh. We had tried.

~

19
INTENTIONAL COLLISION

On June 19th at 2:00 A.M. we received information that a bloody man had been trying to get into the police station. Upon arrival at the station we found two cars in the street that had hit head-on.

The driver of one car, M. Douglas, was still behind the wheel of his car which had come around the corner, hitting the second car across the center line. M. Douglas was taken to the hospital with injuries. The owner of car two, Dan, also injured had left the scene of the accident, breaking through a glass door at the sheriff's office and seeking medical help as well as protection from M. Douglas.

These two men earlier had some type of altercation. M. Douglas had started to chase Dan around town on several streets trying to ram him. Dan had circled around, heading to the police station where he had stopped for help he was met head on.

We met Dan at the sheriff's office, got his story and took him for medical treatment. The doctor said that without immediate treatment it was possible Dan would have bled to death.

M. Douglas was charged with criminal vehicular operation which is a felony. He appeared before Judge Spellacy and pled guilty. He was fined $750.00 and received a three year suspended sentence.

~

20
THE RUSTY SCREW

In the early sixties, R. Borg had a restaurant called the Mileage Cafe located on Highways 169 and 2 on the east side of Grand Rapids.

Early one Monday morning we received a phone call reporting a break-in and the week's receipts missing. Several hundred dollars.

After arriving at the cafe, I checked out all the doors and windows but couldn't find any signs of forced entry or attempts to enter. Further examination showed you could slip a knife behind the door trim to the office and spring the lock, gaining entry. I did this with Borg and John, the cafe manager, present. I asked who had access to the key for the office door. The reply was just the two of them. John told me how and when he had hidden the bag with the weekly receipts. No one seemed to have anything of value to add at this time.

For a couple weeks the case seemed to be at a standstill. Then on a Monday morning another report was received from Borg. That entry had again been made, but this time several thousand dollars were missing. Arriving at the café, I found that both Borg and John were present. John again took me through his routine of where he put the money. He was very helpful with me every step of the way. He told me that he thought whoever had done this burglary had done the same thing as the last time, entering the offices by slipping the knife under the door trim and tripping the door latch.

John did not know that after the last time I had come back and with no one present nailed the trim with some finishing nails. It was now impossible to do it the same way. Now we had a problem with just Borg and John having keys to the door. I showed John how the trim had been nailed and stated it must be someone with a key.

But John came up with a very quick answer to his dilemma. He said, "Come with me, I bet I know how he got in." I followed him out to the alley behind the office and there was the answer! Right under a small window opening that had an air conditioner in it was a large green metal dumpster. We got up on the dumpster; John lifted the air conditioner out of the opening and set it on the flat roof just above the window. We both agreed there was plenty of room for a man to slide through and get back out. He then slid the air conditioner back in place. Things seemed to be falling into place; John had been super helpful and I thanked him for that. He replied that if there was anything he could do at any time that I should just say the word. I said there was one thing he could, in fact, do. If I could I was going to line up all the employees to take a lie detector test, and I asked if he would take it too. He replied that he would.

It so happened that we had a lie detector operator giving some tests at the sheriff's office at this time. So I said, "Let's go and get this over with as fast as we can." He looked a little taken back but had already agreed to take the test at any time.

John took the test but failed. The operator said there was no doubt in his mind that John was the culprit.

Talking to John at the office, I told him the "good news." At first he denied that he had taken the money, pointing out that we had agreed on how the person had entered above the dumpster. I replied that not only had he not passed the test but also that I had concluded before the test that he was lying. I then told him about the screw. I had noted a rusted, damp two inch screw in the middle of a board under the air conditioner. There was no way one could have slid in over the window sill and back out without moving the screw out of its own rusty thread prints.

After a little more discussion he finally admitted he had entered with the key and taken the money. I added that Borg had been a good boss to him and deserved to get his money back. The money was soon recovered. He then gave me a written statement to the facts of the case. He was charged and pled guilty.

The strange twist to this was that he was soon out of prison and had been such a good worker that Borg took him back, and he had no further problems.

Perhaps it pays to give some a second chance. (Sometimes)

~

21
PROFESSIONAL COURTESY

In all law enforcement we try to extend what I would call professional courtesy to each other in the law enforcement field. I would do the same for the everyday citizen, such as using common sense in enforcement of speeding, over the center line, time of day or night or danger to the public, for example. Giving warnings instead of a ticket when appropriate.

In the early morning hours I approached the corner of 4th St. and 1st. Ave. N.E. which is the corner of the Itasca County Courthouse and is where the law enforcement center is located. I observed a plain car turn onto 4th St. E. in quite a hurry, not even slowing for the red light, then proceeding east at 60 to 70 mph, and blowing through the red light at the Mileage Cafe corner. Other than the two of us there wasn't anyone else on the road.
He then proceeded to pick up even more speed.

At this time I turned on my red lights and siren and got the car to pull over to the side of the road close to a mile out of town. Approaching the car, I could see the driver had a St. Louis County deputy uniform on. When I asked what his hurry was, he responded that he had just completed some work in the Itasca County jail and was in a hurry to get home.

I told him that I respected the work he was doing but his driving was way out of line and that I was giving him a verbal warning not to drive like that again in Grand Rapids.

Would you believe---the very next morning in the same area and at the same time this same car went through the same red light. He turned east toward the Mileage Cafe and at speeds in the 70's went through the next red light. The same deputy as the night before was pulled over and issued a ticket. He was not happy but neither was I to be put in this position with a fellow law enforcement officer.

He made the call, I answered.

~

22
THE CADILLAC WON

It was 2 A.M. and I was coming into town on the east end and approaching the stop lights at the Highways169 and 2 intersections. The lights had just turned red. Two cars were stopped at the light. In the lane to my right was a green Buick convertible with four or five teens in it. Sitting just in front of my squad car was a new, big black Cadillac. Neither one of them seemed aware that there was a squad car sitting right behind them as they were revving their engines.

They both revved their engines a couple more times, then the convertible jumped about six inches and stayed there. Meanwhile the Caddy took off through the red light, smoking his tires for 50 feet and accelerating up to 45 or 50 mph.

A couple blocks down the road he saw the red light from my car and pulled over. He was issued a ticket. Receiving the ticket he said, "What about that convertible back there?" I looked back and replied, "It's still sitting there."

The Cadillac had won.

~

23
WHO ATE THE BACON

Around 1990 a man came into the police department to report that someone had entered his home during the night and had taken two pounds of bacon from the fridge. As this was a very serious charge, I took it upon myself to start a thorough investigation.

Talking to the man, he said he knew of no one other than his wife who had knowledge that the bacon was there. I then knew I was going to have to extend my investigation further. I knew the wife quite well from years of contact with both parties. She was known to evade the facts but with a little patience and understanding would tell the truth.

I did talk to the wife alone and she admitted she had gotten hungry during the night and getting up quietly went downstairs and ate the bacon. Asking her how the husband had not smelled the bacon cooking, she said she had eaten it raw so he wouldn't smell it.

We did not tell the husband. She went away with a smile on her face. The case is still marked unsolved.

~

24
ON THIN ICE

What's a mother to do? She had always tried her best with Conner. He had always been dear to her heart. She had other children, had been married more than once. The fathers had always treated the children well but for some reason, Conner could not stay out of trouble. It seemed through his teens, it was just one thing after another. If it wasn't for tampering with cars, drinking and drugs, it was burglaries. Now he was wanted again.

She had told him many times that she loved him very much but would not put up with what he was doing and would not protect him if the police came looking for him.

Conner was out on the prowl on a cold night on the 23rd of November, 1988. Starting over on 2nd Street N.E. in Grand Rapids he chose a few cars to go through, not finding much of value in any of them. Tonight as he walked through the fresh snow on foot he knew if he was careful he wouldn't get caught. One thing he was good at with his long legs, he could outrun most people.

Close to 6th Street, walking up the alley, he came to a garage. Entering, he went through the car taking a few tools. He was on his way. The snow coming down pretty good, that would cover his tracks. Soon he was forcing his way into a locked garage. Nothing in the car, he wasn't doing well. Maybe the next alley up he would do better.

He was now getting close to 9th Street, still in the alley; coming to the garage door, it was locked. Looking through the window he could just make out some tools and a car. He put his shoulder into the door; it made a loud noise and gave way. He stood there a little while expecting to see the lights come on in the house. Waiting, nothing. A little more time and he stepped into the garage trying not to make any noise. He opened the car door, the light went on. He quickly shut the door.

Now he was stepping out of the garage door with a battery charger and some tools. There was a man almost on him saying, "What do you think you are doing?

Dropping everything, he was gone up the alley running north. Looking, the man was a hundred feet back. The trouble was, due to the snow he was having trouble with his footing. Cutting between some houses then back up the alley, he could not seem to lose his purser who all he had to do was follow his tracks. Conner had been running for some time and was getting tired. He had to do something. Looking, he could see Ice Lake a short distance north. It looked to be frozen over. The guy was getting closer. Soon he was crossing the road hitting the ice on the lake at full speed. Looking back, the man stopped on the side of the road. Conner thought he was going to make it. Then he was clawing at the ice trying not to go under.

The man was just standing there and he was freezing. Looking up the hill he could see the flashing red lights. The man's wife must have called the police.

As Conner was struggling to get back on the ice with the police on shore waiting for him, he must have thought, "Here I am on ice and they are going to put me in the cooler."

It took some kicking and clawing. Crawling on his stomach, Conner finally reached shore where the police helped him into their warm car.

Soon they were backtracking Conner's footprints to each of the garages and cars he had gone through. Then, he was booked into the Itasca County jail on charges of burglary, tampering with a motor vehicle and damage to property.

On March 1, 1989, Conner was sentenced on two felony convictions. He was to serve 22 months in Stillwater and to make restitution.

Even though he is in the cooler now, I'm sure it's warmer than where he had been.

~

25
THE MAN WITHOUT A HEART

I just walked out of my office door and there he was. A small man with pain all over his face. Tears were starting to come, and he appeared to be on the verge of collapsing.

Looking at him, I said, "How can I help you?" He stood there saying nothing, then sobbing, he said, "All I want is my house, all I want is my house."

Taking him into my office, I sat him down in a chair and told him to just sit there a few minutes and relax. What he told me, I could hardly believe. How could anyone with any decency in their heart attempt to do to this old man and his wife what a local realtor had already done? It's hard to believe this story, but it happened right here in Grand Rapids.

Here is his story as he told it to me: Mr. McGee and his wife wanted to sell their house and move into an apartment as they were getting old. A reality owner, Dan, offered to sell their house for them at what he said would be a small fee to help them out. He would come over often and sit with them and just chat over coffee. Over time they were starting to think of him almost as a son. Time went on and the place was not selling; he was getting more forceful in suggesting what was best for them such as adding their furniture into the sale of the house. It wasn't long before everything in the house was included. Next it was McGee's old pickup truck, which was the old guy's only means of transportation. By this time Dan had gained full control.

This morning he said he had great news for them as he had been unable to sell the house. He was going to do them a favor and buy it himself. They could move into an apartment. He had all the paper work with him and soon had the signatures on all the legal documents. He then informed them that he now owned the house, all the furnishings and the pickup truck. McGee asked about his money for the house, and Dan said that starting the next month he would be getting monthly payments over the next 15 to 20 years until the house was paid for. The old man realized he would never see his money because he was already in his eighties. He asked about the down payment as that was to be his so he and his wife could get an apartment. Dan informed him that as he had sold the house he was entitled to a commission and that the commission was for the same amount as the down payment so they were even.

Dan informed them they had a day to move out of the house and to leave the truck. The old man was broke.

He had come to the right place. My first thought was that I had two vulnerable adults on my hands. I didn't know how but I was not going to back off on this one. I took him home and told him not to move or let Dan in. If he had a problem he was to call me.

I then called Dan, asking him to come to my office and see me. We had a very nice talk. Dan was very righteous over how he had done everything by the book with the McGee's. He even had witness signatures on the proper places on the legal papers, although it turned out that they had never been to the McGee's. He told me he had taken all the legal papers to the courthouse and properly filed them. I told him that I could see he was a very intelligent man by the way he had crossed his T's and dotted his I's. That a blind man could see he had picked his victims well, two vulnerable adults in their eighties with no one to step up for them. That I was going to do my best "to help his realty company out."

1. I was going to call the newspaper explaining to them what he was doing to two vulnerable adults; you could bet when I got through they would have printed the story. 2. I was going to call the State Realty Board. 3. I was going to the County Attorney on a vulnerable adult charge. 4. Also, I would be contacting my friend, Pat Medure, the Itasca County Sheriff to do an investigation into his background and to talk to anyone doing business with him.

Pat Medure and I did start doing an investigation on him which was quite extensive. In less than a week Dan came to my office informing me that he had been to the court house. The house, the contents and truck were back in the name of the McGee's. He now hoped it would be the end of this. I applauded him for his thoughtfulness and kindness. I don't think we parted as friends.

It is my understanding that he left the area for some time.

Some names have been changed on the advice of counsel.

~

26
'TIL DEATH DO US PART

George Porter was a very good friend of mine for a long time. A retired highway patrolman and a happily married man of more than 50 years. It was a surprise to receive a call to go to his house in the N.W. part of town close to 2 A.M. Upon arriving, I was met at the door by his wife who thought George was having a heart attack. As I entered the bedroom, it was obvious to me that he was gone. A few minutes later the ambulance arrived and they went in to take care of him.

I was talking to his wife in the living room for five to ten minutes when she said, "My God, Harvey, what am I going to do?" Then she slumped toward me. I caught her and helped her over to the couch. I ran into the bedroom and told the medics, "You had better leave George as he's gone and his wife just collapsed." They did go to her but she had slipped away. It was a trying but amazing moment.

Til death do us part---Death could not part them.

~

27
SOMETIMES I AM ANN LANDERS

Some years ago, probably close to twenty, since I have been retired sixteen years now, I was driving around Ice Lake when I recognized an 82 year-old young lady walking by herself. I recognized her because she and her husband had owned a local business for many years.

Having worked for them a couple times, I had formed a good relationship with them. As I pulled up next to her she waved saying, "Oh, Harvey, it's so good to see you again" as she was coming to the window of my squad car. We must have talked a good half hour. I knew her husband had passed away two or three years ago, so you can guess that I was sure to ask, "How are you doing, are you getting along well?" Her reply surprised me. "Harvey, I am so lonesome. I need somebody or someone to share my life with. I love my kids but they don't come around and once you are single even at this age you don't seem to fit in, couples or otherwise."

I asked her about some men friends, if there were any possibilities there. She replied that she did know an older gentleman that was well off and several times had asked her to travel with him but her kids were strictly against it. "So, Harvey, what do you think?" I thought for a while then said, "You are a lovely woman with lots of life in you, go for it. Kick up your heels and go for it. Make these last years fun." "What about my kids?" I responded, "They'll get over it."

In the fall of the next year I ran into her again and of course, asked, "How are you doing now?" A big smile, "Harvey, I am having the time of my life! I have a couple men friends, am doing some traveling and have someone to share my life with. I'm having a ball and I want to thank you, I just needed a push!" I asked, "What about the kids?" Her answer, "They haven't said a word."

I haven't seen my friend since but I know she went with a song in her heart.

~

28
FLASHLIGHT IN THE SNOW

On a very snowy day we were called to a burglary that had occurred at Walters Electric, a business located on 4th St. N.E. just past Ray's Sport Shop.

A window had been broken on the back side of the building to gain entry. Missing were several hundred dollars worth of stereo equipment.

The snow in the area was fresh and about two feet deep, and it was very easy to see the tracks from the road to the window. The window was about six feet from the ground. Leaning out and looking down from the window, I could see a flashlight still lit shining up from one of the foot prints. Going out the side door and wading through the snow, I retrieved it. It was a black two-cell, and on the side was a strip of sticky tape with a man's name on it. "Ted" and a phone number which was not local. I spent most of the afternoon trying to find a Ted but wasn't having any luck. The phone number was no longer in service.

I finally got some information that led me to a house on 10th Ave. N.E. The house was located some five blocks from Walters Electric. Approaching the house, I could hear very loud music. Knocking on the door didn't get any response, probably because of the loud music, so I started banging harder until someone finally opened up. I got the feeling he was expecting friends at his door, not a police officer. A young man of around 16 years of age was across the living room. Between us I could clearly see that all of the stolen stereo equipment was being put to good use.

When you're caught, why not "fess up" which is what they did. The flashlight belonged to his father who just happened to be out of town for several days with his mother. Having just moved to town, they were given a scenic tour of our courthouse.

I hope this taught them to always return their father's tools (and flashlight) when they use them.

~

29
MY SISTER-IN-LAW'S HUSBAND

A police officer is sometimes put into sticky situations. For example, however reluctantly, he may have to arrest a relative. Sometimes it made it a little more comfortable to have a fellow officer step in and take over.

I received a call in the late 1970's on a late summer night. The call was on my police radio from the Asst. Chief stating there was a black truck driving up Powers Hill and at the wheel was his sister-in-law's husband. The driver was all over the road and obviously drunk. I was to stop the truck and take appropriate action. At the time I was a block away and soon was behind him. Observing him for a bit, it was quite apparent he was indeed impaired. I turned the flashers on, and the truck pulled to the side of the road.

The driver did turn out to be the Asst. Chief's sister-in-law's husband and he was very irate. At first he would not open the door of the van truck which had a lower glass panel. Telling him my foot was about to come through the glass, he opened the door and threatened me bodily harm. As he put it, he was a Marine. He was still talking this way as he was safely tucked away for the night.

Brothers do what they have to do.

~

After 31 years on the Grand Rapids Police Department, Harvey Dahline was named chief in 1987. Dahline succeeded Harold Snyder at the post. Dahline's appointment was approved by unanimous vote of the city council. He would retire in 1995.

30
HOW TO BREAK UP A MOB

Before the High School was where it is now, it was located on Poke-gama Ave. N. starting at 9th St. and extending almost to Ice Lake.

Senior Night celebrations started somewhere in the 70's. The kids had a pep fest, football game, a bonfire, street dance and other fun things. However, as the years went by, this night seemed to be getting more and more out of control.

Bands of kids were starting to raid gardens, taking tomatoes and various produce and throwing them at cars. Added to that were drinking and fights.

This Senior Night they were taking gourds out of gardens and putting rocks in them which resulted in broken windshields. The police were out in force but we couldn't be everywhere and the kids were.

I picked up one boy that could hardly stand, taking him to the police station then putting him in a back room. I called his father who was a business man and very well off. I asked him to come pick up his son with the explanation that he had been drinking. It didn't take the father long to come storming into the station. Without asking where his son was, he tore right into me. He very angrily stated that his son did not drink. That he had beer in his refrigerator at home all the time and his son had permission to take some but the boy would not touch it. He kept up this torrent of words for some time, saying he believed in his son and that he would back him up.

Listening to the father I, too, was becoming a believer in the boy. I told the father that he was right that all parents should believe in their children and protect them but that they should not be stupid about it. This may not have been the best choice of words to use at this time. Jack became even more irate and demanded to see his son. I was happy to oblige, taking him back to a small room where there was a large wooden bench. There, leaning to his side almost lying down was his son (with a thick glob of snot hanging almost down to the bench). Without further words the father finally got his son's arm around his neck; he left half carrying and half dragging him out the door. I don't think Jack said, "Good night."

Then it was back to the streets. Where the library used to be across from the Fire Hall there was a large group of students yelling and being unruly. As I crossed the street, it must have been the pitcher from a baseball team who threw a strike from 30 feet, slamming a green tomato into my right ear. I kept on walking; ignoring the tomato, but it did help me make a decision. Looking around I spotted the biggest, oldest boy there. I do not normally talk to anyone the way I talked to this lad. Walking right up to him I said, "I know who you are. You are chicken shit and got no guts and if you don't get your ass for home right now, you are going to jail and there's nothing you can do about it." I had torn him down right in front of all his friends. Things had gotten too far out of hand; I sent him home.

Next step was to look for the biggest boy left, heading straight for him and doing the same thing. Finishing, I turned and there appeared to be no one else left that wanted to chat. They were all melting away.

The first big boy turned out to be a good man.

I don't remember exactly when the tomato fell off.

~

31
LUCKY TO BE ALIVE

Flames could be seen from blocks away as I responded to a report of an accident on Pokegama Ave and 6th St. N. at 1:15 A.M. 3-10-79. A blue van had struck a car that was parked on the right side of the road facing north, pushing it into a car in front of it. The first car struck ended up 50 to 75 feet to the north. The blue van had spun around and was now facing south, the way it had come, with the front left next to the curb and the rear out 8 to 10 feet from the curb. The third car struck was sitting right front wheel to the curb, with the rear out 8 to 10 feet. Both the car and the van were at angles from the curb. The car was shooting flames from its ruptured gas tank 10 to 14 feet into the broken back window of the blue van.

Upon arriving, I went first to the van. Seeing no one in it, thinking the driver had gotten out, I then went to the car. It was not possible for anyone to be alive in those flames so I returned to the van. Looking more closely, I was able to see a man wedged between the driver's seat and the engine cowling. The van was built with the engine between the two front seats. His feet were also twisted into the brake and clutch pedals. I tried to break a window as the doors were locked, but I wasn't having much luck.

Officers Barry Larson and Kirk Skelly had by now arrived and were assisting. I finally got the little window to break and reached in, opening the passenger side door and then the sliding side door. We finally got in and pulled hard on the person, trying to dislodge him without any regard to injury. Larson and Skelly were pulling hard on his arms. He finally came loose; Larson and Skelly tore out the door with him. Just as we were clearing the door, the inside of the van went "poof" and was totally engulfed in flames. They had him by the arms and did not stop running until they were 25 to 30 feet from the van.

The fire engines arrived and soon had everything under control. Bill, the driver of the van, was transported to the hospital where he

~

was treated, tested and arrested for DWI. After recovering he appeared in court, pleading guilty.

I don't know if he ever knew how close he came to burning up. I know he never called to say thank you. But I do know our officers ran their own risk that night and saved a life. This was the type of law enforcement I worked with for over 40 years.

~

32
DON'T HIT A DRUNK

In the early 70's I picked up a fellow I knew very well for drunk driving, James was quite vocal on his dislike for me but overall things were going well.

We were now in the jail booking area. James was sitting on a bench, and I was standing by the end of the counter with my left side to the bench. All at once I must have seen a fast movement, and I drew my left arm up to protect my face. James' right fist hit my wrist, breaking my watch and coming across and striking me in my right eye. I reacted with a right cross. James went back and down and may have lost a tooth. I don't hit drunks, I don't believe in it. Generally they can be handled in different ways. It was simply a fast reaction on my part to protect myself. Given time to think, I would not have hit a drunk and he definitely was. He was treated and put away for the night.

You would hope this would be the end of it. It was not. The next day our family was out at the in-laws at Pokegama Lake. We were in the yard when a car came barreling down the hill. I looked and knew who it was right away. It was Bill, James's brother. I had known Bill boxed in the Navy, now weighed 170 pounds and was in good shape. Me, 180 pounds and in pretty good shape. He came charging out of the car saying he wanted me for beating up his brother who was drunk last night. I walked up to meet him and said, "You are right, Bill, I should not have hit your brother, but give me a minute to explain something first, then you can swing if you want to." I then told him how I was doing paper work and did not see the blow coming and had just reacted. Then I showed Bill my busted watch and the bruise on my right eye and face where James' blow had landed. I added, "I don't believe in hitting drunks and he was." He looked at me for a minute and then said, "I believe you," and we parted as friends as we always had been.

Later I thanked God I hadn't hit James harder when I heard he

~

had gotten into a fight at the Fireside Inn bar and was knocked off a barstool and broke his neck.

I don't believe to his last days he got off the drink.

~

33
THE "BRAVE MAN"

I received a call to go to a domestic about 3 A.M. just up the hill from Blandin Paper Company offices, where there is a small white house on the side of the hill. Being met at the door by a crying woman saying that James had been beating her wasn't a surprise since I had known the family for years and since this was not the first time. She obviously was in great distress. It was obvious that she had just gotten out of the hospital because of the tubes coming out of her back on both sides just above the kidney area and running down to small packs. The floor had 12 inch white tile squares over cement and almost every tile had some blood on it.

James was in the living room and was highly agitated. He had been drinking and was spoiling for a fight. After talking to the woman and learning of how he had been hitting her and pushing her around, I told James he would be going with me. I realized I might have some trouble as he and his brothers were well known for their fights around town when they had been drinking. James was especially brave after having just beaten up his wife. He approached me, bringing his fist into a fighting stance, which I appreciated as the fist gives you something to grab onto. I grabbed a fist, spinning him around so I was behind him. I'm not a coward; I just don't like to be hit. Grabbing his left wrist from behind, I lifted him in the air in a wrestling move, and he went over backward to the concrete floor not too gently. He grunted and said, "You don't have to be that way about it." I put the handcuffs on him. Now he refused to walk out to my car in the alley, so I picked him up like a log on my right hip with my arm around him and carried him out to the car. Arriving at the car we had more problems as he would not bend over to get in the back seat. Leaving the door to the car open, picking him up like a log again, getting back about 10 feet, and running him head first, I slid him nicely across the back seat. He held his legs out so the door would not close. I told him it was

~

his choice but the car door was going to be slammed shut on the count of three. It was and he made the right choice.

As James was standing in the booking area at the jail, he was telling what he would do to me when the cuffs were removed. I said, "James, just remember one thing." He said, "What's that?" "Just remember who put them on you."

Shortly after that James was a divorced man. After a few years his ex met and married a wonderful man who treated her right.

James did quit drinking and was a different person but lived a lonely life by himself until his passing.

~

34
POCKET PICKED

On Jan.1st, in the early 1960's I was on Pokegama Ave by the bridge a couple minutes into the New Year.

We had 8-10 inches of new snow and the snowmobilers were out all over town. Seeing a snowmobile going up the sidewalk on Power's Hill over 40 mph and not stopping or slowing for any reason, I followed him up the hill. The driver turned to go left across Pokegama Ave. by the Country Kitchen. He was still on the sidewalk but looking south because traffic was so heavy he could not cross. For some reason he had not looked back or to his left and hadn't seen the squad car pull up and park close to him with its red lights on or me getting out of the car and walking directly in front of the snowmobile. About 10 feet away he saw me and hit the throttle hard, hitting me with the snowmobile. I grabbed him as I went over the top of the windshield, and we landed in the traffic lanes wrestling. He looked to be around 18 years old and maybe 180 pounds and in good shape. Fearing he might get away from me, I picked his pocket of his billfold and identification.

All of this time cars were driving around us as we wrestled in the deep snow. No one stopped to help or see what was going on. After a few minutes I was able to get full control and snapped the handcuffs into place. He turned out to be a juvenile. He spent the night in the Itasca County jail, charged with aggravated assault, a felony, with other charges pending.

Other than being out of breath and a little sore it was a fun way to bring in the New Year.

And, oh yes, he did get his billfold back.

~

35
DID NOT PEE MY PANTS

Some things you do not expect when you answer a "domestic."

I arrived at the home of a well known family and was met by the lady of the house who was very easy to recognize because of her "boxer nose," having been put to the floor many times in the past by her not-too-gentle husband. It seemed they both had a little problem with their drinking and would have some real drag-out fights. Looking at her, it was quite obvious she had lost again.

Arnie, it seems, had been to war, earning not only a Combat Infantryman's Badge but some other medals. Having done so well in the service, he had brought the war home.

Deciding enough was enough; I arrested him and was trying to get him into the police car when the little woman decided this was not to be, jumping on my back. After some maneuvering, I decided she was going with us to the jail as well. She was now in front of me with her back to the open squad door. Having some problems pushing her into the open door, I put my knee into her crotch at which time she let loose with quite a large volume of urine. Needless to say the front of my pants was soaked.

After bedding down both of my opponents for the night, I went home. After explaining to my wife that I had not done this to myself, she did get me a clean pair of pants. But to this day, I think she still gets a little mad at the other woman who was a shirttail relative.

~

36
LOBSTER FOR EVERYONE

Driving south on Pokegama Ave. by the Country Kitchen there was a fairly new car in front of me with four young men in it.

Something all officers learn to watch for is the reaction of drivers and passengers when they first see a police car. Do they turn around real fast? Do the other passengers seem to react in some way? Such as, does the right or left shoulder rise as they are trying to put something in their pockets? Do they appear to be trying to bend over to put something under the seat?

This car was going over the speed limit. When one of the young fellows looking back saw the police car behind them, there was a flurry of movement in the car. The right front passenger leaned way over. Both back seat boys looked back then turned and were bending over as though they were putting something under the front seat.

Pulling the car over in front of where K-Mart was, I walked up to the car and asked the driver for his driver's license. The young man looked very nervous. Looking down at the driver, I could see what appeared to be, of all things, frozen lobster with white frozen crystals on the wrapping just behind his feet. I asked him if I might examine the package. He handed it to me, and on examining it I saw a tag with the National Tea food store name on it.

Thinking that it did not seem right for expensive lobster to be treated in such a way, I asked the driver where he had gotten it from, and he responded that he had bought it from the National Tea just a short time ago. Looking over I could see one more package sticking out from under the right passenger seat. I asked the driver for a receipt as they had just paid for it, but for some reason he was not able to find one.

I then made some calls to the National Tea to see if they had made a sale of lobster this afternoon. After some time they got back to me stating that none had been sold that day.

I then had all of the young men exit the car and sit on the grass boulevard while a further search of the car was done. Turns out, each of the boys was going to have lobster this night as more was found pushed under the seat from the back, plus some other items.

While the boys were sitting in the grass, they were not being ignored. Seeing a couple of the boys moving around I walked over to them, I had them stand up, revealing some film containers in the grass that turned out to have drugs in them.

The boys were taken to the sheriff's office and we learned where they were staying. They had rented a cabin on Splithand Lake south of town for their weekend getaway. They had been in town getting their supper. With the information we now had, search warrants were issued. Other stolen items were found including some expensive jewelry.

They were all over 18 and appeared in court on various charges. The boys were up for a holiday from the Cities and must have enjoyed our hospitality of room and board. But, I don't believe any seafood was served in the county jail.

~

37
THE PROLIFIC BURGLAR - THOMAS FRANKLIN CLEMES

This is the story of Thomas Franklin Clemas, a prolific burglar we had in our area over a span of 15 years.

Some times an officer will go to the scene of a B&E, break-in or burglary, whatever you may want to call it, and think this is too sophisticated or different than any one I have seen before. So they are going to think of someone out of this area, perhaps from the Cities. You have to be careful with this kind of thinking or you may not do a good job investigating because you're thinking you won't get them anyway.

We had several burglaries over the years we thought were different. Some with a different mode of operation such as using lock pullers on doors, drilling a hole in a roof then using a keyhole saw to cut a 25 inch square hole in the roof, then dropping through or putting a bar across and dropping down with ropes.

Some of them would case a drug store in the day time looking at where the drugs were and on what shelf. Also, where the waste basket was. They would come back in the night using a lock puller on the little round locks on aluminum doors, opening the door, and sliding the metal round cylinder back into the door. Now you can't tell there had been a break-in. Then they would run to the back of the store, dump the wastepaper basket, then walk along the shelves where the drugs were, push them into the basket and be out of there in under two minutes.

This is a list of the M.O. of lock pullers or roof entries over the 15 year period I could recall:

1. Nip and Sip---enter window above the marquee---safe---also left a sign of a fish in the alley dirt which the Walleye Gang left as their sign they had been there.
2. Country Kitchen---roof entry.
3. Reeds---pulled lock---1980---drugs.
4. Reeds---through roof---Nov 4, 1981---drugs.
5. GR High School---1978.

6. Globe Drug---lock pulled---drugs.
7. Globe Drug, second time---lock pulled---drugs.
8. Miner's Grocery, west end---roof, back entry---safe.

On Nov. 4, 1981, the police department received a call from Reed Drug saying someone had come through the roof some time during the night and took drugs. Responding to the call we found an opening had been made in the roof by drilling a hole using a keyhole saw, then cutting a square hole through the roof big enough for a man to get through.

It appeared to me something had gone wrong. There was a false ceiling about four feet down, and it looked like someone had fallen through. Also, a bowling ball bag was still up on the false ceiling. I was able to retrieve the bag from its perch, placing it in my car for further inspection. Further investigation showed the hole in the roof was just above a platform to the downstairs. Looking in the basement I found a broken wrist band and watch which I hoped would be the magic clue. Reportedly there were a large number of drugs missing, some having just arrived the day before. They were to get us a list of the missing drugs.

Going back to the police department and setting the bag on the table, I discovered a number of tools in it. One was a five pound metal maul with the long handle cut off to about 15 inches. The rest were a variety of pry bars, screw drivers and so forth. I examined them for signs of identification with no luck. Sitting back and for some time just thinking, I recalled that detectives always find something in the movies! I decided to turn the bag inside out. The bag had a zipper top with a wood floor. Poking under the edge of the wood with a screw driver, some coins fell out. Then to my surprise, I discovered what appeared to be a tooth with some pink plastic stuck to it. This was in the days before DNA or computers, so I decided to take it to Dr. Charles Sherman of Grand Rapids to verify my thoughts. He said it was an upper, right, front tooth that had been in a false plate.

What was my next step? My mind kept working and came up with one thing I could do. I sat down and made up a brochure with all the information on it, when and how the entry was made, roof entry including drilling, keyhole saw, dropping through the roof with rope, and the use of lock pullers on cylinder locks. After I had the brochure done, I sent it to different police departments throughout the state. One of the departments responded a short time later. Det Swanson from the Minneapolis Police Narcotics Division said he had a lot of information on a gang called the Walleye Gang being led by a Thomas Franklin Clemas, age 39, and an accomplice.

Swanson said the gang had been operating for years with most of the gang spending some time in prison including Clemas, who had served some 17 years.

Somehow I was able to find out that Clemas had spent the night of the break-in at a McGregor motel. Swanson and I thought we had enough evidence to get a search warrant for Clemas's place. Shortly thereafter I went to the narcotics offices in the Twin Cities. We had a good exchange of information. He said he had a search warrant made up and he could serve it this day; however, if we did, it would screw up a deal that was going down the next day. We had some discussion and it was decided that my warrant could wait until Swanson thought the time was right.

I then went over to the Hennepin County Jail to talk to a prisoner because I thought I had someone in jail that didn't belong there. But that is another story.

Two weeks later I was contacted by Det Swanson. He had very good news. They had served the search warrant on Clemas. Among the things collected was an upper plate for false teeth with the upper, right tooth missing. They had found the plate at the head of his bed. When asked who those teeth belonged to, Clemas said they were his. They were confiscated as evidence. Det Swanson also said that they had a room full of confiscated goods and that I could come down and take whatever would help my case. A couple days later, I did go down taking the tooth with me. They showed me into a large room full of items from Clemas. With the hordes of items in that room, the only item I took was a four inch high white box with some numbers on it. After getting the upper plate from Det Swanson, I bid him good bye and thanked him for all they had done for my case.

Next I proceeded to the Minnesota Bureau of Criminal Apprehension in the Cities and gave the upper plate and tooth to Don Melander of the Bureau. After laboratory analysis, which took a couple weeks, they concluded the two were a positive match.

Going back to Grand Rapids, I thought what next? The next day, I thought, why not? I took the little white box to Reed Drug and showed the box to the pharmacist in charge. He looked at the numbers on the box and had a positive match. The box was in a specific Lot of drugs they had received the night before the burglary. Thomas Franklin Clemas was picked up and charged with burglary. Pleading guilty before Judge John Spellacy, he was sentenced to four years in Stillwater Prison.

I talked to Clemas at the jail before he left for the Stillwater prison. Even though I had just completed the investigation on him through his guilty plea, I tried to treat him with respect and told him I would return his watch and upper plate to him. I noted at this time that the years had not been kind to Thomas. At 40 years he looked like an old man. I asked him if he would talk to me about some past crimes he had committed in this area, noting that the statutes on the crimes had already run out and that I was not trying to charge him on anything else but trying to clear my books. Some of these burglaries went back more than 10 years. At this time he just said he did not talk to cops so why should he trust me? I responded that I thought he could help me out as I thought he had done the Nip & Sip some years ago and had done a professional job. He repeated that he did not know why he should talk to me, but he did. I asked him some very frank questions about being good at the burglary trade.

Q. What is the best time to do a burglary?

A. Before 12 p.m. You can be walking down an alley with tools in a bowling bag, but a police officer will not stop you.

Q. How and where should you make entry?

A. Always above eight feet. No officer looks up over eight feet for a break-in. That is why we go through the roof.

Q. Do you carry a gun?

A. Yes, I have already served 17 years in prison. What do I have to lose? And yes, I would even use it on you.

Q. Why did you choose Grand Rapids?

A. It is close to where we operate from.

Q. I have heard that you belong to a gang called the Walleye Gang. Did you burglarize the Nip & Sip bar years ago and if so, how did you do it?

A. Yes, that was a window above the front marquee.

Q. That is how entry was made? Now, next question, did you do something else in the alley before leaving?

A. Yes, I drew a sign in the dirt of a fish, a walleye. But I must add that the last couple years I was starting to get leery of coming to Grand Rapids for some reason. I started to think we were going to get caught here. That feeling was starting to get stronger.

Q. What other places have you hit in Grand Rapids over the years?

A. Globe Drug, a couple times; Reed Drug, a couple times; Country Kitchen, a roof job; Miner's Grocery, west end, roof job; and the school some years ago.

Q. Are you going to do any more jobs when you get out this time?

A. I don't know. This is something I've done all my life.

Q. How did your tooth happen to be in the bowling bag?

A. I had two sets of choppers made in Leavenworth prison, carrying them back to Minnesota in the bowling bag. I could never find the tooth. I didn't think about looking under the wood floor.

We parted then with me saying I would try to get his teeth back to him some day.

The next time I heard of Clemas, I was reading the Duluth paper and there his name was, Thomas Franklin Clemas. It could be no other. He had been picked up by the Duluth Police Dept. It so happened that I was going to Duluth on business the next day. So why not as they say, "Kill two birds with one stone"? Going to the property room, I signed out his upper plate and his watch.

The next day entering the detectives' division and talking to the detective in charge, I told him that I had not seen Clemas for a couple years and that I had his teeth and watch for him and would like to talk to him. He told me that Clemas was a hardened criminal and would not talk to any police officer so don't waste your time. He said they had questions they wanted answered and he would not speak to them. I asked the detective to make a list, so he made me a list of 10 questions.

Clemas did not appear to have changed much. We did say a cordial "hello" and some pleasantries. I then gave him his upper plate and watch. He said he was surprised but he did need them badly. I then explained to him that the detective had said he would not talk to anyone and I told him I would see what I could do. He looked at each question and then told me what to answer each one. I wrote down the answers. We said goodbye and I hoped he would stay out of trouble. But, I don't think this leopard will change his spots.

Meeting the detective, I gave him his answered list of questions. He shook his head and smiled.

I have heard that finding the tooth, then finding the upper plate with the search warrant was a one in a million chance. But what are the odds finding the little white box in that big room and bringing it back here to really seal his fate---another million to one?

Grand Rapids Herald Review
March 1, 1982
Volume 87-#17

Harvey Dahline

~

This is a copy of a handwritten letter I received from Thomas Franklin Clemas while in the Stillwater Prison:

Mr. Dahlene
Dear sir;
May 2, 1953
- the last time I talked to you, you told me after a few months I could maybe get my Dental plate back. the one used as evidence in the Reids Drugstore Burg. Its been almost a year now and I will be getting out in another 9 mos. If you could send it to me here, I can get it repaired here before I get out.

Getting along fine and getting short. maybe I'll see you again someday. If I do get up there, I'll try to stay out of the drug stores ☺

Thank you,
Thomas Clemas 103952
P.O. Box 55
Stillwater, Mn
55082

~

38
INNOCENT (OUT OF PRISON)

In the winter of 1980 we started to get calls of someone window peeking in the S.E. part of town in the River Road area.

Then early one morning around 3 A.M., as I remember, we received a call from the Pine Ridge apartments. A young, single lady contacted our department saying she had been asleep and woke up to a man with a knife in her bed. He had put a pillow case over her head and raped her. She lived on the ground floor level and the man left through the window on the east side of the building. Further investigation showed the screen to her window had been cut around the outside edge and the window just slid open since it wasn't locked. There weren't any noticeable footprints since there wasn't any snow. She did not recognize the man.

Another night close to midnight I was on the Pokegama Bridge when I received a report that a woman in River South apartments had just had a man come in the front door of her apartment and threaten her with a knife. He suddenly left. She described him as not a very large man and thought she would recognize him if she saw him. I found a small footprint in the snow but lost the trail in the road. I talked to Wally Herschbach who was an investigator for the county. We decided to make up several photo line-up cards with possible suspects in the area who would match the description we had.

We took the cards to several witnesses. Some of them picked out Ted and were very sure that this was the person they had seen. With that and other information we were able to get a warrant for his arrest. He had moved out of state. He was soon picked up and placed in jail in Jacksonville, Fl. Wally Herschbach and I made the trip to bring him back to Grand Rapids by airplane.

I had known Ted for a number of years and knew that he had a drinking problem and drug use. In June of 1981 Ted was found not guilty of a similar charge in district court which was 1st degree criminal sexual conduct.

When Ted went to court this time, he pled guilty to the 4th

degree criminal sexual conduct and a simple burglary on July 8th in a plea agreement. If he had not taken the plea agreement he could have been sentenced to many more years. He was sentenced to 18 months.

When entering the plea agreement, he also had to explain his crimes. On the crime that took place at River South, he told how he had gone in through a window and approached the woman with a knife. I thought at the time he was just mixed up from his memory loss from alcohol and drugs. Later I got to thinking the woman had just come through the door and he said he had come through a window. If the door was open, why didn't he use the door? Later something else had started to bother me because the shoeprint outside in the snow had been smaller than Ted's shoes.

This is how the case set, with me wondering.

On October 1, 1981, as I was sitting at my desk I received a call from a Bloomington, MN police officer telling me they had arrested William Merritt, age 37, for a series of rapes and other crimes across Minnesota including Duluth. He then asked me if I had any open cases of rape or other sexual crimes. I told him that I didn't, but I did ask him why he had called me and how was Merritt committing these crimes. He told me that Merritt was living in Duluth but was working in Cohasset helping to build the large stacks for the Clay Boswell plant. That Merritt's M.O. was to cut a screen and enter through a window using the knife as a threat. Also at this time I was thinking of him getting off his afternoon shifts and going through Grand Rapids to Duluth. This would correspond to some of the times we had reports of window peepers and prowlers in the River Road area. Also when I had been on the bridge when receiving the call to the River Road South apartment, I hadn't seen any cars as he would be using the River Road to go to Duluth. Cutting screens, rapes, using a knife, working in Cohasset, going through Grand Rapids, the time element, Ted's shoe size, Ted saying he went through a window not the open door 6 ft away. Why would you plead guilty to a crime you didn't commit? Because it looked like there was a strong case against you and a plea agreement would give you 18 months rather than many years in prison.

There were just too many coincidences here. At this time I asked the officer if he would ask Merritt if he would talk to me if I could get down there. He said that he would. The consensus around here was that Ted had pleaded guilty and had it coming---let sleeping dogs lie.

While lying in bed one night my wife asked me why I was awake and what was I thinking. I told her about Ted and what was going on and what did she think I should do? She said, "You do what you think is right." Well, I think the Good Lord was shining on Ted this time as it turned out I had to go to the Minneapolis Police Dept on the Thomas Franklin Clemes case (Reed Drug burglary). I went to Minneapolis and talked to their department and then made arrangements to talk to Merritt in the jail.

When Merritt was brought in, I was amazed at the resemblance that he had to Ted. I explained to him why I was there: that the Police Department in Minneapolis had a lot of charges against him that were very solid, that he did not need any more charges, that I had just sent a man to prison for something I no longer believed he did and that man should not be in jail.

I then told him in front of witnesses that I would give him immunity from prosecution for any sex crimes he may have committed in Grand Rapids, but he would have to tell me and convince me how each crime was committed and the location with no prompting from me. He then went on to tell me that he went through the door of the River South and told me what was said to the woman. On leaving in the snow he had gotten into his car and went down the River Road to Duluth. He explained how he had cut the screen on the Pine Ridge apartments, putting the pillow case over the lady's head and threatening her with a knife. Some of the things that he told me were facts in these cases that only I knew.

I was convinced that Ted was innocent. Now what would you do? I came home and talked it over with my wife then went directly to see Judge John Spellacy, telling him the story in its entirety. When I was through, he sat there for a while thinking, then said, "Harvey, you really believe Ted is innocent?" I said, "Yes". He then said that there was nothing he could do as he was not the presiding judge. Bemidji Judge Saetre had handled this case and promised he would be contacting him. In a short time a hearing was held in

Bemidji before Judge Saetre. After the hearing he ordered the immediate vacation of Ted Flannigan's conviction and his immediate release.

He told those present in the courtroom that in his 30 years in law and 14 years as a trial judge he had never had this type of a thing happen before.

Ted and I talked a few times after his release. He thanked me for the extra work I had done to get an innocent man out of prison. Ted lived a quiet life after that until his death a few years ago. We remained friends.

This is a copy of a letter I received from Ted's lawyer:

December 17, 1981

Mr. Harvey Dahline
Assistant Chief of Police
Grand Rapids Police Department
Grand Rapids, Minnesota 55744

Dear Harvey:

Thank you for your invitation to join you and John Dimitch for lunch following the hearing regarding Ted Flannigan in Bemidji. I am sorry that I was unable to join you, but I had a number of other things on my mind which I had to attend to.

It would have been very easy for you to ignore the possibility that William Merritt was guilty of the offenses with which Ted had been charged and to not follow up and do the investigation that you did. You are to be commended for your honesty and courage in following up on this matter.

I have explained my feelings regarding your efforts to Ted. I believe that Ted understands that you bore him no malice when you actively sought convictions on the charges last summer. I believe Ted understands that you were doing your job as it should have been done based upon the evidence then available and that no one person nor the system was truly responsible for what happened. I also believe that Ted knows that you applied the same zeal and effort in obtaining Ted's release as you originally did on the investigation.

I know the whole incident was beneficial to me. It was nice to see in operation a premise which I had begun to lose faith in: That is, that law enforcement officers can work with equal eagerness and effort to free a person wrongfully convicted as they can to convict a person who should be convicted. In addition, it reaffirmed my belief that eyewitness testimony is too subjective and is inherently unreliable because of this subjectiveness.

PAUL F. SCHWEIGER
700 LONSDALE BUILDING
DULUTH, MINNESOTA 55802

Mr. Harvey Dahline
Page 2
December 17, 1981

I recall that during the Abis trial, your daughter came to watch part of the trial and your testimony. Let her know for me that she can be very proud of her father.

Sincerely,

Paul F. Schweiger

~

39
THE SILVER SPUR "HITCHHIKER"

I received a call from the sheriff's dispatcher asking our assistance on a possible break-in attempt being made at the Silver Spur bar just out of town on Hwy. 2 South. Two men were trying to gain entry through the north door.

I responded that I was close by and would cover the bar on Hwy 2. This would cut the highway off, and other cars coming in from the east could close the field off behind the bar. At this time the bar was set off by itself. Coming from Grand Rapids there was a dirt road that would V off to the left about a hundred feet from the bar. Between the road and the bar was a field with high grass and brush in it. The other patrol cars were coming in from the east on the far side of the field.

Driving past the bar at normal speed like I did not see them, I saw two men appearing like they were trying to get in but not paying attention to the squad car going by. I made a U turn off the highway into the second driveway. As I pulled up the men saw me, with the smaller guy running into the field. The other guy ran out to Hwy. 2, stopped and stuck his thumb out like he was hitchhiking. The only thing wrong was that he was facing the ditch, not the highway. I secured him in the back of the squad car.

The other police and sheriff's cars were on the other side of the field. I radioed the other cars that I had one man in my car and the other one was in the field. Stopping by the edge of the field, I hollered to the officers, "I'll drive through the field to flush the second guy out and you guys shoot!" This might not have been very nice but it had the desired effect and the guy jumped up in the middle of the field yelling, "Here I am, here I am, don't shoot!"

It turned out they were two regulars who had seen the inside of our jail before.

The hitchhiker got a ride right away.

~

40
SOME PEOPLE ARE GRATEFUL

Late one night while approaching the stop and go lights at the intersection of Hwys, 169 and 2, the Itasca Dry Goods corner, I saw a white '65 Chevrolet a block away that went speeding through the red light going east. Stepping on the gas, I was sure I would catch him, but he must have seen me and had cut his lights. He headed north on 3rd Ave. E. As I came to 3rd Ave., I could see brake lights as the car made a right onto 8th St. E. heading in the direction of Murphy School. As I made a right turn onto 8th, no car was in sight, but there wasn't any dust after a couple blocks. Being a police officer there are many things you pick up on; one is that almost always there is a lot of dust in the air in the direction of a speeding vehicle.

As I traveled up Murphy Hill a few blocks, the dust was gone. Then down the alley to my right I saw the blink of a brake light a couple hundred feet away. I parked the squad car blocking the alley and walked to the driver's side. I shined my light into the vehicle and saw that there were also passengers. I then asked for the driver's license.

The young man remarked that he would have gotten away if he had kept going. I then told him to turn his lights on. Forty feet in front of him was a big rock and a drop off of 25 to 30 feet. He was on the upper side of the Murphy sledding hill. If he had kept going he might have been easier to find or what was left of him.

But I heard no complaint about the ticket.

~

41
BRAVERY ON HIS KNEES

Feb. 9th, 1962

On a Friday night in 1962, Officers Dale Fox, Arlis Hopkins and I were called to an accident at 169 N.E. and Hwy. 2 which is the Mileage corner.

A grain truck had struck the back of a car stopped for a red light and had pushed it fully through the intersection. Merle Schmidt and Jennith Schrunk were both badly injured and taken by ambulance to the hospital.

Joe Johnson the truck driver was not injured but was drunk; he was arrested and jailed.

While we were doing our investigation of the accident scene, an older dark car drove by a couple of times.

Some time later Fox, Hopkins and I were in the police station doing paper work on the accident. The phone started ringing. Picking it up I found I was talking to the clerk of the Riverside Motel, R.J. Barse, saying he had just been robbed at gunpoint by two men. I asked for a description of the get-away car and which way it had gone. It was a dark, old car going north was all we knew.

I gave the phone to Dale Fox telling him to try getting more information and saying to Arlis Hopkins, "Robbery. Let's go." We ran out to the car and Arlis headed south from the police department. He said, "Which way?" as we were coming to 4th Street. I said, "Let's try 4th St. W." As we made the right turn onto 4th St. W. by the Central School, there was an older dark car making a left turn onto 4th St. heading west in front of us. We fell in behind, pulling it over between 9th and 10th Ave. W. Arlis stayed back behind the open driver's door with his gun out to cover me. Approaching the car from the right rear blind side, I ordered the passenger out. Securing the passenger, we then had the driver step out. After securing the driver and passenger in the back seat of the police car, we found that neither one of them had any weapons on them. However, when the car was searched, we found two knives, a .38 and a

.32 pistol. The men were taken to the Itasca County jail where they were questioned. They admitted they had robbed the hotel saying that it looked like a good idea at the time and telling us they had seen the accident on the east end and thought that the police would be busy for some time. It would be a good time to knock over some business.

Wayne Muldenhauer age 24 was the one that went into the motel. Robert McKerby drove the car. Both of the men had criminal records.

We then went to the Downtowner Hotel to see the clerk, R.J. Barse. R.J. was a man in his eighties, small but with the heart of a lion and very pleased that his "visitors" had been apprehended so quickly. He said the phone was right in front of him as he was on his knees and that he was dialing the police before the man was out the door.

We then went back over what had taken place. Barse was behind the counter looking up he saw a man come in brandishing a gun and demanding Barse open the safe. Barse replied he was the night clerk and did not have the combination. When he was told to open the cash register, he said that the man with the key would be in at 7 A.M. Last, he was told to empty his pockets---less than $3.00. He was then ordered to lie on the floor. Barse said he had arthritis pretty bad and the floor was cold, so would it be alright if he just got on his knees. The man then said "Hell", turned and started for the door with Barse's $3.00. Barse was dialing the police before the robber got out of the door.

The men did plead guilty to the charges and got jail time. Now I don't know if R.J. Barse ever got his $3.00 back. But I do know the last time I saw him, he had a big grin on his face.

Monday Feb 12, 1962

Herald Review Volume 60 #141

~

42
A GREAT COMPLIMENT

When I started on the police force in 1955 we had six men, one police car and no radios. Often we only had one man on at a time. To get our calls we had to watch for a light to light up on top of a tall pole that was next to the police office. Then you would have to find a phone to check back in with a telephone operator.

Most law enforcement officers were 40 years old or more. The town was pretty much wide open with very loose enforcement of the law. It was nothing to see a couple of drag races down 4th Street in a night. The Marlon block was another "playground" for the young drivers. It was a very wide street and the kids had hot cars and would do "donuts" in the middle of the block. "Donuts" were spinning your rubber or wheels while going in tight circles. The fifties up through the seventies were the years when kids had really hot, fast cars. We officers had the Ford Interceptors. Something had to be done so "fishing" was really good down in the Marlon block. It was nothing to catch four "donuts" and a couple cases of beer in one night. In those days if you were of age you could have open containers in your car. In other words, you could drink and drive. Another example was catching and ticketing four sets of dragsters going down 4th street. One night I saw a pair racing and I got one but the other got away. Some years later that driver and I were talking; he said he spent half the night in Baker's gravel pit changing the lights on his car. Ticketing them slowed things down but a high-speed race was something you came to expect.

Over all most of the kids were pretty good. Talking to some seemed to help, warning of a license being taken away or maybe even taking them home to Mom and Dad. It paid to give breaks in some cases.

We did have a gang called the Beagle Boys in their upper teens that operated out of a white house back in the woods across the road from the Sawmill Inn. To get into the gang as the story goes, you had to "make out," drink so much beer and try to outrun a police car. What else I don't know.

I do know that over the years I chased and caught most everyone in this group, some more than once. Sometimes they got a warning, sometimes a ticket. Some of the gang didn't have cars and I might find myself driving one of them home on a cold winter night. But, I still considered them my friends. I never did look down on the motley crew that they were because if you saw where I came from, a log cabin in Remer, foster homes, orphanages and a "vocabulary" second to none, you would understand.

Fred belonged to the gang. I knew him well having chased him at least four times at a hundred mph or more. One of the pursuits was to Marcell on a very narrow highway with hairpin curves. The only reason he stopped that night was because the kids in the car were so scared they got on him.

I did get a surprise around 10 years ago. I got a call from Fred my old friend of 50 years ago. I asked him what was up. He said that one of their gang was very ill and probably wouldn't make it, so they were having a going-away party for him with the old gang, and they would like for me to come and be the guest of honor. I did not make the party because we were going to be out of state and I was sorry about that, but I considered this an honor and possibly one of the greatest compliments I have received. I think I knew what Fred was saying. These were their memories, their fast cars, and their youth. Maybe a little nostalgia.

Fred is gone now; some of my memories go with him.

~

43
MY HEART CHANGED -
TWO BOYS IN THE LAKE

Sitting down to write about an incident that happened some 60 years ago and not knowing how to approach it is not easy. Are you going to hurt someone after all this time? Do you really remember somewhat accurately?

I'll try to tell what happened to me and the boys. Sometimes you feel you have seen it all. Nothing can change you and you're happy with that.

I spent the first part of my life with three brothers and three sisters in a broken home without a father and with a sick mother that could not take care of us. With a lot of drinking involved, the welfare stepped in and the next ten years were spent in foster homes and orphanages. A brother and two sisters were eventually adopted out.

I came home in 1949 with nothing and soon joined the National Guard at 16. Within a year or so, I was in the Korean War as a sergeant in a machine gun platoon. The army loves young soldiers. You think you can't be killed. But during this time, you are all alone, you grow tough, you grow strong, and you have full control.

By then I had a wife, four sons and a little daughter. I sometimes wondered if I had those deep feelings others talk about.

I received a call in my car that there were some very frantic parents waiting for me on the west end of Forest Lake at the Stoltz place. The parents of two little cousins had been waiting for them to come home for supper.

I arrived at the home and was shown the clothes on the edge of the water. Looking out in the water, I saw a small raft. You think you know what happened. You're a strong swimmer. Should you go for it? But in your heart you already know it is too late. You do the smart thing by calling the Itasca County sheriff's office for help.

In a short time two boats are in the water. Each boat is pulling a 10 foot metal pipe with three-inch treble hooks about a foot apart being pulled by a long rope. In the boat with me are two other men.

We are going slowly to do a pattern search between the raft and the shore. The water is warm and up to 12 feet deep. We hear the other boat which is near the raft say they may have something. Almost right away we say we do too. We start to pull on the rope very slowly and something light starts to appear. It's a young boy around 7-8 years old. I look down and he looks like one of my sons coming up slowly out of the deep.

Something happens inside of me, it is such a deep, full emotion for the boy. It is so deep and full, like nothing I have ever experienced before.

We soon had the boys on shore. I know I will never forget what I felt that day or how I felt for the boys and their parents.

When I arrived home later that day and saw my family, I knew through the tragedy that had occurred that I had been given a gift.

~

44
HOW TO CATCH A DANGEROUS CAR THIEF

In the early eighties we were having some problems over the period of a couple weeks. Someone would steal a car, drive it a short distance and then dump it at different locations. Officers were finding the cars and returning them to the owners.

Coming to work one afternoon I saw on the books that a white Chevrolet had been stolen but not recovered. Remembering that all of the others had been dumped at different locations around town, I cut the town up into grids: N.E., N.W., S.E. and S.W. Then I would run the avenues and streets back and forth. Surprisingly, I found the car in about 20 minutes.

Going through the alley behind the home for the nuns, I found the car was parked just off the side of the alley. This would be three to four blocks north from the old library. I could hardly get inside the car since the seat was pushed up as far as it could go. The mirror was tipped down as far as it would go. The keys were in the ignition.

I wanted to catch him. I thought that if I couldn't go to him, with a little bit of luck maybe he would come to me. Opening up the hood, I reached in and took out the rotator from the distributer cap. I replaced the cap and left the keys in the ignition.

It was close to getting dark, so I went down by the library alley and parked a good three blocks away in some bushes. Looking down the street, I could see the stolen car with its rear toward me. I had not been there five minutes when a young boy who was known to have stolen a couple cars himself came up to me and asks, "What are you doing?" Taking a good look at his size, I guessed he was probably around 5ft. 8in. and 140 pounds. Thinking of the seat and mirror in the stolen car, I made a decision and told him what I was doing and suggested that maybe he would like to help me catch rather than being caught. He thought it sounded like fun.

I told him to jump in the other side where we sat and talked for some 20 minutes. Then a person crossed the alley by the car that was under observation. I waited a minute and the person opened the door and got in. Because of the angle of the stolen car, he would not see me coming up the alley in the police car. I told the boy with me what the plan was. I was to get out and take the driver's side; he was to go to the passenger side. We neared the car and stopped around 50 feet away and I told the boy to make sure he didn't slam the door. As we approached the car, we could hear it turning over but for some reason it wouldn't start.

Walking up to the car, I could hardly see him in there. He seemed a little startled when the door opened, all four ft. five in. of him and 80 pounds soaking wet. I felt quite secure having my back-up with me. The little guy must have been all of 9-10 years old. I thanked my other friend saying we would have to do this again some time.

Then I took my other new friend home to mother, father and the paddle.

~

45
SHOTGUN SHOOTER (ASSAULTED)

Around 1985 I was just getting up and ready for the day when I received a call from the police dispatcher. I had only been Chief of Police for a short time but due to the nature of the call would have been called anyway.

Our guys were out looking for a man in the northeast part of town walking around with a shotgun and who had shot at a boat and some garage windows. There had been several shots fired but no one seemed to know exactly where he was.

Dressing quickly and going outside, I was struck by how cold it was. It had to be 20 below zero. Every once in a while I could hear a shotgun go off in the distant northeast part of town. Getting into my unmarked car and hurrying to that area, I could hear shots ring out but the person was moving quite fast. Hopkins, Serfling and Johnson were doing what they could to locate the man. Meanwhile one of the officers told me that there had been a loud party at a house on 5th St. N.E. last night so I drove there, taking a chance that there could be a connection. Also I figured he would be heading back to the house shortly because it was so cold that a person with bare hands on a shotgun could not stay out much longer.

I parked close to the house and pounded on the door. A young man answered the door and I asked him outright if he knew anything about someone with a shotgun. He replied, yes, a young man had left the house with a shotgun about an hour ago. The kid had been drinking and acting funny. As we were talking we could hear the shotgun noise which appeared to be coming closer. Meanwhile I had been in contact with the other officers in the cars. They were trying to stay behind the shooting while working toward the house where we thought he was heading.

Seeing a running figure on the sidewalk about a block away, I told my men to keep coming. Standing across the living room from the front door, I waited, trying to judge the time the door would open. Just as the door opened he was about to step inside, but having started from the far side of the living room I tackled him, driving him out over the steps around eight feet to the cement sidewalk and landing straddling him. Having lost my radio I started to drag him to it, but by this time the boys were all there.

We took Brad to the lockup and he appeared to be coming around. He had been read his rights and did not want to say anything. Then realizing I was in charge, Brad said he wanted to file a complaint against those other officers for using too much force against him. I told Brad as a citizen he did have a right to file a complaint and that I would take a taped statement from him.

He told me how he had gone around shooting and was headed to the house when he was attacked from behind and knocked to the sidewalk by the officers. That was the sum of his complaint.

I don't think Brad ever really knew what hit him.

~

46
BURNING CELL (SORE NOSE)

Itasca County Jail sits over the top of the sheriff's office. It is made up of steel doors, bullet proof windows, cement block walls and some narrow hallways with cell doors down the left side from the entrance.

Some things you can plan for but there is always the unexpected.

There was a prisoner in the middle cell and as I recall he stood around 6 feet 2-3 inches and weighed 220-230 lbs. So what? Well, the man had mental health issues and was considered physically dangerous.

On this particular afternoon he set his bedding on fire. The room was heavy with smoke. The jailers had to get him out of there. They opened his cell door and he bolted out and down to the far end of the hall to a locked door and stood with his back to it. He waited. Along with other officers I was alerted that help was needed. Entering the hall we could see he was a tough physical specimen and ready to fight. Walking down the hallway toward him nothing was said. As I got close, suddenly raising my hands and saying, "Hi", he reacted. His arms came up high and I did a "duck under" which is a wrestling move; I went under his arm and slid around to his back, then jumped up and put my left arm around his neck. My right hand came over his head and I buried two of my fingers about an inch or so up his nostrils and yanked hard up and back. He stiffened out like a board. As this was happening the other officers had rushed in and pinned his legs. Now what? There was a cell close by that was all metal with a cement bunk. We carried him into the cell with me still holding his head. My fingers pulling back in his nostrils, I sat on the bunk with his head in my lap. The other officers cleared the cell. Then when I let go and got up, the man exploded, jumping up and kicking out with several powerful kicks. I did notice, however, he did this while staying back several feet. The nose did look a little tender.

This was not the last I heard of the gentleman.

~

47
WATERMELON HEAD

Generally you try to treat people that have been drinking with respect and most of the time that works out really well. But other times they force you to take other measures. That is what happened with my partner Clarence this night.

We were called to the VFW Club as there had been a fight going on. There were two large men that had more than their share and simply were not going to leave peacefully. The bartender wanted them out. We finally arrested them for disorderly conduct.

Getting them out of the door to the side of the patrol car was somewhat of a pushing match. The right rear door was open and the men had been told to get in. One was standing five or six feet from the car with his back to the door. It looked like more trouble. Clarence was standing on the far side with the man between us. I nodded to Clarence. We both grabbed an arm, throwing the man off balance toward the car. All of him started to go into the car except his head which struck the car just across his ear.

It sounded like you hit a watermelon---thud. The man screamed and got into the car.

The second man wasn't dumb. He walked over and got in never saying a word.

~

48
SHOTGUN (DARK NIGHT)

Sometimes you are out there thinking it's a quiet night, nothing is going to happen tonight, but that's when you get your little surprises.

This night was one of them. The sheriff's office called and said they didn't have an officer in the Singing Pines area out of town where a domestic was taking place. Could I handle it? It was west on Norway St. in the 2000 block. The time was 2:30 to 3:00 so all the bars were closed and most people would be at home.

Driving up Norway St., I could see lights on in a house. Thinking this was the house; I parked my car on the street and walked around the front onto the driveway. At this time it was very dark as there weren't any street lights. Then a little light by the door came on. A woman came out onto the steps yelling, "He's got a shotgun." Looking up the driveway, I saw a shadow against a light colored garage. I could just make out a man 30-40 feet away standing there aiming a shotgun at me. I just kept on walking. Getting close, I knocked the shotgun into the air, stepped in and took it. The man lunged for me, threw his arms around me and started to cry.

He had been at the Silver Spur and had a fight and went home. He then got in a fight with his wife. Thinking the guys from the Silver Spur were coming after him, he had gone out with the shotgun.

The shotgun was loaded. Why didn't he shoot? He seemed to have had plenty to drink. Perhaps he could see that it was a police car on the road? I never did get an answer to that.

I took him inside to his wife who put him to bed. Sure seems like there are a lot of shotguns around lately.

~

49
HIT-AND-RUN STOLEN CAR

On a hot muggy night in 1957 a call came in that two or three brand new 1957 Chevrolet cars parked by Corcoran's on 2nd St. had been struck, with a lot of damage done to the rear ends. The cars had recently been delivered to Swanson's Chevrolet across the street. While investigating the hit-and-run I was summoned to the police station. Arriving at the station I was told by Harry, a man I knew well, that his car had been running in front of a cafe but was now missing. He added that whoever took the car wouldn't get very far as the gas tank was empty.

I got all the information on the car and the names of the young men now present, one of them being a close relative. I thought I knew what had happened. We had a hit-and-run, plus a car stolen that had been left running without much gas in the tank. We started a grid search on the Southeast part of town and within about 20 minutes the car was found on the River Road about a half mile out of town. It was well off the road, but would you believe that although it was supposedly out of gas, the motor was still running.

Well, some of the people can be fooled some of the time, and some can be fooled all of the time, but this was not to be one of those times. Going to my close relative, I explained very carefully how possibly five people could conceivably end up in court or just one.

I then went to Harry, the owner and driver. He was very understanding of my point of view. He did not want his car to be confiscated until we could sort this out. He decided that perhaps he had gotten a little close to the parked cars and did not want his close friends involved any further. He elected to go by himself.

And yes, the car did make it back to town on the "empty" tank.

~

50
THE MISSING MAN

In the early 1980's the police department was contacted by a very concerned lady whose son was missing. She had not been able to contact him the last couple days.

The young man in his twenties had been in the service and possibly had come home with some mental problems. There may have been some disagreements with his father before he had left his parents' home in the Cross Lake area to return to Grand Rapids where he lived by Ice Lake.

The mother had driven up from her home and gone to his house. There weren't any signs that he had been there recently. She drove around looking for his car and finally located it at the Sawmill Inn in the lower parking lot. A search of his car produced the keys, his billfold with credit cards, a few dollar bills and a receipt from Cole's Hardware dated two days before. The receipts showed he had purchased a four-inch pipe with a metal U clamp. The items left on the seat gave the investigators the feeling this young man would not be coming back.

We searched his car as well as his house for a note or anything that could help us. Local hotels and motels were all checked and a follow-up done to see if there had been any use of credit cards. All areas close by were searched including sewer and drainage pipes. There was a path west of the Sawmill Inn and the area around it was searched. The foliage was very heavy on the trees at this time of summer, and we searched up in them as much as we could see. After the initial searches, Russ Johannsen, the sheriff, and I went back a couple times with his wolf dog. The mother was also checking relatives and not having any luck.

Time went on, as I recall maybe two or three years, and nothing. The mother kept on checking and even driving up once in a while.

Then one day I received a call from the dispatcher with some information. A group of young boys were playing out in the woods by the Sawmill and had discovered something. Two of the boys were my nephew's sons, James and Tony Dahline.

They took me back into the trail that we had previously searched when the young man had disappeared. We went up a trail a couple hundred feet under some oak trees that had shed their leaves since it was fall. Then going down a slope perhaps 20 feet off the trail, James showed me what he had found. He had picked it up earlier thinking it was an animal jaw. Looking at it more closely he could see it had dental fillings. Dropping it where he found it, he and his friends ran to the Sawmill to call the police.

We saw the jawbone and it did have fillings in some teeth but some teeth were missing. Moving some leaves, we found a couple more teeth. The area was covered with many new fallen leaves plus a lot of decayed vegetation. As we were looking we could make out a khaki green Army jacket. In the jacket was what was left of him after all that time. Mostly bones. At this time I knew we had found our young man from the years past.

Stepping back onto the path and looking up, many questions were answered in that one look. I could hardly believe what I was seeing. Hanging out from one of the upper limbs of the oak tree was a rope with a four-inch metal pipe and the U clamp. The rope came down through the pipe and circled back up and was clamped to the side of the four-inch pipe making a perfect noose. The noose itself was at least 30 feet from the ground. We must have been under that body many times. Looking up through the trees, we would not have seen the body due to all the leaves unless we were very lucky. Also, we had not been looking up that high.

It didn't take much to figure out what happened. The weight of the body had pulled it loose after some time. The body landed on the side of a slope, sliding down the hill a short distance. The head had gone farther. The leaves from the trees eventually covered the body. There was some plastic in the noose leading me to believe he had put a plastic bag over his head.

He was identified through his dental work. It was ruled a suicide. The mother was notified.

Bless her heart, her long wait was over.

~

51
STOLEN BIKES - BURGLARY
- SUICIDAL THOUGHTS

The date was 7-21-78, one of those nice easy summer nights. Smooth, nothing to worry about tonight. It's already 12:30.

Then we received a call, nothing much, just a bicycle stolen. A man coming to work at Glen's Super Valu went into the store leaving the bike outside. Going back out a few minutes later, he found it was gone.

Twenty minutes later we received a complaint that a second bike had been taken. This one a few blocks away by Forest Lake. A boy coming in was asked by his father if he put his bike away. Saying no, he went out to put it in the garage. The bike was gone.

We were patrolling around looking for bike riders but saw nothing. Going south on Pokegama Ave. approaching the bridge over the river, I saw a man standing in the middle who started to move toward me trying to wave me down. Recognizing him as an old friend, I pulled to the side of the road. Flip said, "God, am I glad you showed up. I was about to go over the edge. I've been waiting for you." Knowing my friend had been having some marital problems, I told him to jump in and we would talk.

We had but a few minutes when the dispatcher alerted me to the fact that the burglar alarm was going off at the Goldfine's store which was located in the southwest side of town where KMart is located now. Flip was still in the passenger seat of the car as we headed up the hill to Goldfine's. Wondering how to approach the situation, thinking it would likely be me who would be the first one on the scene, I decided to head back to the southwest area of the parking lot over by some trees to cut off any escape route. As we were going by the back of the store, I could see two bikes parked by the fence. Getting into the corner of the trees, I turned my squad car to face the store and the fenced-in area and left the car's head lights on. I told Flip I would be approaching the back of the store in the fenced-in area and he was to hit the horn if he saw anything.

I was half way under the fence gate on my belly when the horn started to sound incessantly. Back at the car Flip was pointing to two boys running west across the parking lot toward the trees. Getting up I started to run after one of the boys. About that time one of our squads was heading after the other one who was going into the woods. They went in after him on foot. As I was running after my target, my forward foot came down on a rock, causing me to do complete splits. I couldn't get up for a few minutes. Kirk Skelly and Bob Hince came out of the woods with the other boy. This boy wouldn't tell us who his friend was. Thinking the bikes were the ones stolen from the north side, I figured the other boy would be trying to get across the bridge. I asked the other officers to use their search lights and to take their time and work toward the bridge. I would get across first hiding somewhere waiting. Just north of the bridge on the left was Swanson's used car lot; I waited among the cars with my lights out. The other patrol cars could be seen on the south side slowly going back and forth like a deer drive. A head came up across the bridge behind a cement pillar. Then he was coming across the bridge at a full run, turning behind the Riverside Motel along the river. I came around the corner fast, not expecting him to be in the middle of the road. Hitting the brakes, I almost ran over him. He stopped. He was done.

We now had both boys secured for the night and the rest would be up to juvenile court and the parents.

Shortly the bikes were returned to the surprised owners. I had a good talk with Flip, my suicidal friend. He thought he had enough fun for the night and he would be alright.

So much for a night when nothing was going to happen.

~

52
MOTEL WINDOW (WRONG EXIT)

1-20-86 Gene Bennett-Greg Hopkins-Harvey Dahline

Our department was notified of a break-in at the K&K Farmers Market which is located on Hwy. 2 N.E. just short of the 7th St. Bridge. Four businesses which shared the same building had been entered. The meat market had the largest loss. The wall clock had been knocked to the floor, stopping at 11:30 pm. There were also some footprints on the freshly scrubbed floor that we were able to photograph. There wasn't much else so we were back in the police department by 11:00 A.M.

While we were there one of our officers received a call from the Super 8 saying that they rented out a room to a couple men the previous night. In the morning the maid was a little perturbed stating she had done a very clean job on the room the day before and could tell by the dirt on the radiator and window sill someone had climbed in and out during the night. We were thinking we knew why.

We went to the motel and checked with the clerk who had checked them in. We got their descriptions and checked the car license on the sign-in sheet. Asked if that was the correct number, he said it was because he checked all of the cars before he left. With this information we contacted the State on ownership of the car. Coming back, the name was Coleman and home address was Duluth. From the detective squad in Duluth we learned that this person was a known burglar.

We gave the Duluth officers all the information: car license number, type of car, color and so forth and the fact that they had just left Grand Rapids which is 80 miles from Duluth. We estimated the time they would get there and asked the officers to look for a large sum of money and a certain type of footprints.

A couple of hours later we received a call stating they had been waiting a distance away from this person's residence and that the car had come into that area but then left. The police had left but came back a short time later, parking their car in a hidden spot. The suspect's car then showed up again. They were able to search the car, finding a large sum of money in a brown paper bag with a WW written on the outside. We could not figure out what WW meant but Hopkins said maybe it meant MM for meat market.   We then drove back to the K&K Market to talk to the manager. We asked him to describe how his money was put away. He then told us the amount and that he had put it in a brown paper bag and had written M&M meaning meat market and then put the bag in the safe.

The two men ages 24 and 26 were arrested, brought back to Grand Rapids and charged with felony burglary.

This teaches burglars to wipe their feet off at the door.

~

53
RECEIVING STOLEN PROPERTY

In early November 1983, I became aware that Paul Gregory, age 32, had come into possession of some papers that he had no right to.

The papers had been in the custody of Chalupsky, Nyberg, Hawkinson, LTD offices in Grand Rapids during the Thanksgiving holiday weekend.

I was aware that Paul Gregory had just gone through some legal troubles concerning his house and driveway. He had lost his house by order of the court. Now he had somehow gotten the legal papers, been to the court house and transferred the house back to his name.

Knowing Paul Gregory from the past, his father had contacted me saying that his son had stolen his old check protector and was cashing checks on the father's account.

I contacted the law offices and was able to check for any signs of a forced entry. I was able to determine someone had entered the back of the building through a window. You could make out where the dust had been disturbed over some metal pipes. Kent Nyberg had checked and the legal papers we were talking about were missing. He hadn't given anyone permission to take them. Later I did talk to Paul Gregory. He told me he had come out of his father's place of business one day and all the papers were in the front seat of his car, that someone must have put them there knowing he was having troubles.

Paul Gregory, 32, rural Grand Rapids was sentenced by Judge William E. Kalar in Itasca County District Court Friday to serve 90 days in jail following his jury conviction March 22nd on a misdemeanor charge of receiving stolen property.

In addition, Paul Gregory is to pay a fine of $700, a $70 surcharge and a $3 library fee. The court agreed to credit Paul Gregory for the time he had served in jail and that he may be released from custody during the day under the Huber Law if it was proven to the court that he is legitimately employed.

Gregory was originally charged with five felony counts after his arrest Dec. 1, 1983, in connection with the burglary of the Chalupsky, Nyberg, and Hawkinson, LTD law office in Grand Rapids during the Thanksgiving Holiday weekend. He was charged with two counts of aggravated forgery, uttering, one of forgery and burglary.

The jury, however, would find him guilty only of one misdemeanor count and returned verdicts of not guilty on the other charges.

While convicted March 22nd, Gregory was not sentenced until Friday to allow time for a pre-sentence investigation.

Judge Kalar told Gregory he believed that he knew the checks and documents were stolen when he gained possession of them. He said Gregory used the documents to his own advantage and did not seek to rectify the situation before his arrest. Gregory was remanded to the custody of the Itasca County Sheriff.

You cannot tell what a jury will do; our job is to enforce the law not to judge.

I have heard Gregory has moved to another state and had further problems in which he was not so lucky. Some names have been changed on the advice of counsel.

Herald Review December 1983
Scrapbook, Harvey Dahline

~

54
THE BARKING DOG

I really had some great people to work with over the years. Kirk was one of them and a lot of fun.

Some of the time when it was time for an officer to come on duty, as it is a small town; we would just drop by the house and pick them up.

One night I will always remember. I had just picked Kirk up. We were on the Golf Course Road and making a left-hand turn onto Pokegama Ave. which is on the lower part of the hill. There is a gradual rise to the top of the hill, about five blocks. At the top of the hill on the right hand side was a root beer stand. After making the turn I looked up the road about four blocks and could see a yellow Cadillac that had been coming my way making a left turn into the root beer stand, I thought---to be blunt, I was not looking up my side of the road, I was talking to Kirk and looking at him.

All at once he seemed to get highly agitated, swinging his right hand up to the windshield and saying in a high, shrill voice, "harf, harf, harf---harf, harf, harf." I looked at him and said, "What are you, a barking dog?" Then I looked up the road and there was the Yellow Cadillac on our side of the road maybe a hundred feet away. I swerved hard to the left into the other lane; I really don't know how we missed that car. It was being driven by a very drunk woman well known to us. She was arrested for drunk driving and placed in the lockup for the night.

Kirk never barked again, but if he said something, I listened.

~

55
THE WIFE WAITED

In the early 1960's there was a farm beyond the cement plant in LaPrairie. It was on the right hand side of an old road that led to an aged, steel bridge which crossed the Prairie River. The farm's owner had a herd of cattle which he tended to every day, going out personally to take the cattle to the river to drink. He and his wife were getting well up in age.

One winter day I was asked by the sheriff's office to check out a concern that had been called in. The wife of the farmer was very concerned that her husband was over an hour late from watering the herd and since the farm was right on the edge of town, would I check the situation out.

I went to the farm house and talked to the wife. She explained what his routine was and where the water hole was.

I walked along the river some one hundred yards or more north of the house and found the hole in the river ice on the lower part of a downgrade. The hole was five to six feet across and a few feet from shore with very slippery ice all around it. There were a lot of cow tracks on the edge of the river. Getting as close as I dared, I could see what had happened. The farmer had gotten on the slippery downgrade and slid into the water hole. You could tell by the finger scratches and blood all around the hole that he had been there for some time, probably almost making it out by the marks on the ice, but the cold and wet clothes along with a three to four mph current must have finally dragged him down.

I called the sheriff's office with the information. Tom Montague, an experienced diver, found the man under the ice 75 feet downstream.

Following my call to the sheriff's office, I then talked to the farmer's wife. Her fears had been well grounded.

A little sad history of the area.

~

56
THE ESCAPEE

On a warm, late summer night, the Nip & Sip bar was no more. The new Blandin building was being built where it once stood. The construction was now two stories high but you could walk in or out almost any place. Across the street where the Coast to Coast building once stood is an empty lot.

Officer Tom Roy had called saying a prisoner had fled from his squad car in the downtown area. Being in the area of the Blandin construction, I looked around under the new building. Coming out on the east side facing the old Coast to Coast a block to my right, I saw a man running straight to me while looking back at the squad car around the corner a half block away. I hit him with a football tackle, picking him up and putting him down on the tar.

He was dazed for a bit and when he got up I asked him what his name was; it was Virgil Dam. Never forgot that name. Tom came and took him into custody.

Noticing my right cheek was still hurting the next day and remembering I had tackled Dam, hitting the right side of my face on his hipbone, I went to the doctor. Surgery rearranged bones. You would think that would be the last time I would tackle someone that way. It wasn't.

~

57
HIGH SCHOOL SHOOTING - OCT. 5, 1966

On October 5, 1966, at 7 A.M., I was picking up my first student on my school bus run on Pincherry Road a few miles past Cohasset. This is something I had been doing over the last 11 years. My regular job was with the Grand Rapids Police Department. Most of the other men and I on the force drove school bus and held other part time jobs to supplement our pay as most of us had families and could not make it solely on our police wages.

This morning was sunny and started out routine like hundreds of other mornings: pick up your bus, ride alone enjoying the solitude until your first pickup, and judging your speed, always trying to make each stop at a precise time so your students can time your arrival.

There was no way of knowing this morning was going to be unforgettable as a police officer. At close to eight A.M., I was driving the bus north on Pokegama Ave. heading for the Grand Rapids Senior High a few blocks up the road. Approaching 7th Street N., Highway Patrolman Lloyd Olsen flagged me down saying there was someone shooting every one at the school. I then drove my bus behind the convent where the nuns lived. Using this as a safe place for the children, I told them to stay in the bus, not to get out.

I had been a police officer for 11 years as well as serving time in Korea so this was not the first time in my life to deal with something involving guns. Getting back to the road, I again talked to Olsen, asking him if he had an extra gun. He gave me his .38 pistol and he got his shotgun from his patrol car for himself.

As I approached the intersection of 8th St. just before the school, I saw a squad car was parked across the middle of the intersection blocking it. Dale Fox, a village patrolman, was crouched down behind the car with someone else. Dale said, "Am I glad to see you!" I asked him where the person was with the gun. At this time there was a lot of open space on the block in front of us. To my left, there was a hockey rink and a big oak tree which was in about 30 feet. Dale pointed to one area open to the right of the hockey rink maybe 150 feet away and I saw a boy moving slowly with a gun. He was hard to pick out as there were so many students milling around in the area.

Up to this point I hadn't heard any shots fired but Dale said he had been shot at twice. I moved over to the big tree and stopped behind it, assessing what was going on. Then, I spotted David Black again, standing holding a gun. I could also see 50 to 100 kids in a half circle behind him. I actually was an excellent shot being on the Police Pistol Team. However, David was between the kids and me. I had someone else's gun that I had not sighted in. If I missed him, I could hit a student, or even if I hit him, the bullet could go through him with the same results.

The time had not come to shoot but to get closer. I stepped out and started to walk slowly toward him in a non-threatening manner trying to defuse the situation, my gun half up but pointing to the ground. All this time, I was telling him it's going to be alright. He saw me, started to lift his gun but did not point it at me. I was aware Olsen and Fox were close by. I kept on walking and talking, getting into around 15 feet and I stopped. I told him to put the gun down; he dropped it but there was something in his right hand and up his sleeve. It was a knife, and I told him to drop that too and he did. He was taken into custody and the gun and knife were given to Fox.

The last thing David said to me at this time was, "I didn't get as many as I wanted. I'm a damn poor shot. I guess I should have brought more ammunition. How many of them did I get?" He also told me that his intentions were to use the knife on me when I got close to him.

Soon after my bus run, I talked to David at the Itasca County jail. Giving him his rights first, we then talked about his family life. During this time he repeated several times that he had shot Mr. Willey, the school superintendent, Kevin Roth, a student, and also shot at Robert Camilli, another student. He also kept repeating, "How many did I get?" and that he was going to kill as many as he could. He mentioned the Speck "Chicago" murders several times about a man who had killed 13 nurses (actually 8) in one night. He also brought up the tower sniper killings in Texas. These were his heroes.

He stated that he hated his father who had been making moonshine and added that his father did not treat him right. He said he had asked his mother the night before how to load a gun and she showed him. The gun belonged to his father. I asked if he thought there was something wrong with him mentally. He said, no, that he knew what he was doing. He had been planning it for some time.

Here is the order of events as I understood them at that time: The shooting of Kevin Roth in a hallway in school and then the attempted shooting of Robert Camilli. Next, Forrest Willey, the School Superintendent, came out of the administration building and confronted Black, demanding the gun, and Black shot him two times. During this time, Nobel Hall, who was a teacher and a football coach came upon the scene and seeing that his friend, Willey, was wounded and down, walked up to within 20 feet of David, picked Willey up and carried him away for medical help. While I have great respect for the officers and Mr. Willey, a hero no doubt, to me a hero not mentioned was Nobel Hall. He saw a friend down and had to know the dangers and still did what he did.

Within a few days Mr. Willey died; Kevin Roth lived but had surgeries and a long rehabilitation.

If you were to look at the location of the shooting now, it is all so different. The school is gone, Gym 400 is gone and the hockey rink only a memory. The whole area is now a housing project. The location of Mr. Willey's shooting is house 808 on Pokegama Ave. N. and where David Black was picked up is 803. The hockey rink for many years was just east of there.

Black was found guilty and sentenced to prison. I have heard he had gotten out in a few years but has had a lot of problems since.

History as I remember it.

I have been told that this was the first recorded high school shooting with a fatality in Minnesota???

Scrapbook-Page 7
Herald Review-Oct 6, 1966 Boy Seriously Injures Two at High School ~

Herald Review-Oct 17, 1966 Educator Dies of Gunshot Wounds

Epilogue

I have now been retired since 1995, some 18 years, but my thoughts sometimes wander back to that day 47 years ago. I can see a picture in my mind of a young boy standing there with the gun, looking bewildered and all those students who should have been running just stood there, staying to see what was going to happen.

The tragic incident that had taken place almost seemed to have been swept under the rug with the school principal saying, "The best thing we could do was go back to our normal life."

I had interviewed David Black shortly after the shooting; it seemed in just a short time he had been sentenced through the juvenile court system and gone. Through the following years very little was heard of David.

I had not seen, heard or spoken to Kevin Roth nor had I spoken to anyone connected to the case in all those years. Then, one day I received a call from a young lady, Rachel Bledsoe, in early September, 2013. She was working on a project to help eliminate bullying, "But Be the Solution, Not the Problem." To my surprise she had contacted Kevin Roth to get his side of the school shooting so many years earlier. Now she would like to talk to me and get information on the incident.

Part of her campaign would be a presentation of a memorial to honor Mr. Forrest Willey who may have died in 1966 because of a teasing, bullying incident.

Within a few days of talking to Rachel, my phone rang early one morning and it was Kevin Roth. To say it mildly, I was dumbstruck. Never in my dreams did I think this young man would call me.

As we started talking it reminded me of my long-lost brother at last coming home.

When I am on the phone, I often am at a loss for something to say after a few minutes; we talked for almost an hour and a half. Some times I felt like I was talking to a 14-year-old boy who was listening to every word I had to say. This was a man with the world on his shoulders, taking and accepting full blame for the shooting death of Willey. I could feel the pressure inside of him, the tears so close to coming.

As we talked, I began to understand. He was a 14 year old boy, 110 lbs, hanging with a group of older boys. Lying in the hospital in shock with a bullet in his chest, thinking he was going to die. People were pointing the finger at him. The word was, "Willey died because of his teasing," He was to blame. Right there he took full blame and carried it to this day.

Kevin had never talked to anyone who had as much information or was as close to the full truth as I was able to put together.

I explained to Kevin that David had deep psychological problems before the morning of the shooting. David also told me that he didn't think he had any problems but had been planning the shooting for some time. There were other stories he told me that convinced me of his deep psychological mind-set that I'm not going into here.

As Kevin and I talked, you could feel some of the relief of the burdens this 61-year-old man had been carrying.

On Sunday, Oct.13, Kevin, Rachel, my wife, Dorrie and I sat down for dinner at the Forest Lake Café. Some of the pressure was still there and the tears were close, Kevin saying at this time that he was healing, that at last Jesus Christ was setting him free, and thanking me for our talks and understanding.

Kevin was to be spending the next week talking to area schools on bullying and teasing and what it can do. I was honored to be a participant with him on some of these talks, giving an overview of what happened on that day of the shooting as a law enforcement officer that was there.

After one of the presentations we went for lunch at Bridgeman's. As we sat there, Rachel looked over at the booth next us and exclaimed that the person sitting there was Forrest Willey, Jr. Kevin became apprehensive
thinking Mr. Wiley's son might still be holding some of this against him. After our meal was over, I stood and motioned for Kevin to follow me. We walked over to the booth and I introduced us to Forrest Willey, Jr., and they began to talk. Soon these two older men were hugging each other. And yes, there were tears.

The last I saw of Kevin after the presentation at the Ground Floor, a hangout for teenagers, was on a Friday night. We hugged and he told me, "Harvey, at last I am free." We exchanged addresses and phone numbers. I am sure we will be talking. What happened on those school grounds so many years ago will never be forgotten.

Grand Rapids Herald Review
Thursday, Oct 6, 1966
Monday, Oct 17, 1966
Harvey Dahline-Scrap Book
Kevin Roth

~

58
LURKING IN THE DARK

Driving late at night by the old Rapids Tackle building located next to the Rialto Theater, it did not surprise me that my car came under direct attack from a barrage of tomatoes, squash and cucumbers as it had been a very good growing season. This bunch seemed to want to share.

I continued driving as though nothing had happened but also noticed what was on the road; they had been sharing their produce with others. Continuing south over the bridge and disappearing, I thought I would like to have a little fun.

Swinging over to the 7th St. Bridge east and cutting my lights, I was soon within a couple blocks of my tormentors. Leaving the car, going behind the Pokegama Hotel and out of sight, I climbed up the back of the Kleffman Insurance building. My friends were out front sharing.

The first man was quite surprised as I cuffed him to a metal light pole. The second man had taken off and I followed. He jumped around 15 feet to the sidewalk below between the Rialto and Rapids Tackle. I started to jump too but he was just disappearing out of the alley on the far end. Then I thought, "You're not too bright but you're not stupid, "so I went back to my sure catch.

After charging him with the crime of "lurking in the dark" with the intent of committing a crime, he appeared in court and pled guilty. This may no longer be on the books. Too bad. Another side to this event, the young man was a relative of the assistant chief.

Some years later I was walking the beat and walked into the Dutch Room bar and was talking to some of the fellows and I saw a fellow nursing a beer, scowling very strongly at me. It was no other than my friend from the roof top. Laughing I went over to him saying, "Lurking in the dark." I kept on and said, "I'll buy you a beer." He then started to laugh and said "OK".

Haven't seen him since but I still have to laugh. Lurking in the dark.

~

59
REED DRUG FELONY THEFT

Ernie Jacobson, co-owner of Reed Drug, came in to see me as much as two years before saying, "I have a real problem and I don't know how to pin it down. We have so much product coming into the store so it has to be going out. Now, our figures show we should be showing a certain markup but they are not. The figures are way below what they should be. We have a large leak somewhere either in cash or product walking out the door." This had been going on for some time but he could not get a handle on it. Over time there could have been loses in the thousands.

It was decided to install cameras hidden over each cash register in the store with permanent tapes made of each one. On 4-1-1981 Ernie came in and said to me, "We are ready to move." He and his partner Wade Salisbury had watched several tapes on TV of the cash register operated by "Gale" in the front of the store next to the front door exit.

She made sure there was always something covering up the front of the cash register so the customer couldn't see how much had been rung up.

Here was her method of theft:

1. She had a piece of paper in her pocket to keep track of the amount going in and out of the till.

2. She had a small calculator so she was always giving the correct change. Later she removed the difference between the sum she charged and that recorded on the till.

She was observed taking money from the till on several occasions by watching which slot she was taking the money from. So many $20's from the 20 dollar drawer, so many from the $10 drawer, etc. By watching the tape you could count the money amount as she took it, folded and slipped it into her pocket. In one four day period she had taken $675.00.

Just a short time before her shift was done, she would tip her head back while fluffing her hair as she would be checking all around to see if anyone was near. Then her right hand would go into her right pocket and bring out her list of numbers for the day. This particular day that I was watching it was $200.00 and she counted it out and pocketed it. I had been in their private basement offices and we decided it was time to move.

Wade was to go up and ask her to come to the downstairs office because he had a confidential matter to discuss with her. He was to walk behind her keeping a good eye on her. Shortly Gail was in the office. Ernie then ran the full tape for her to watch including taking the money from the till and putting it in her pocket. At this time I asked her to remove the $200.00 from her pocket. She got very defensive, stepping back, saying no, and that no one was going to search her. She was then informed that whether she liked it or not, I had probable cause to search her and would. There was a woman present but if I had to, I would remove her jeans. Just because she was a woman gave her no protection against a reasonable search. She thought about it for a moment, reached into her pocket, took the money out and handed it to me. It counted out to be $200.00. A further search found she had a controlled substance in her possession.

She was then arrested and charged with felony theft and possession of a controlled substance obtained through subterfuge by presenting an altered prescription for another person. It was said that she and her boyfriend had a nice lake home, an airplane and had been traveling extensively.

At the time of her sentencing she was ordered to make some restitution. It came nowhere near the hundreds of thousands of dollars that were thought to have been taken over the years. She spent a short time in jail.

I don't think she ever went back to work for Reed Drug nor were they ever asked for references.

~

60
A MOTHER WAITS

In early March 1979 we received a call that there was an upstairs apartment on fire next to the Janicke Bakery.

Arriving with Officer Bill Litchke, I could see that the room upstairs was totally engulfed in flames.

There was a door to the upstairs facing 1st Ave. Opening the door there is a set of narrow stairs going up. There was very little smoke at the bottom of the stairs. Having seen the inferno in the room, I knew no one could be alive there. Thinking there could be someone in the other rooms; I took a deep breath and went up the stairs. At the top of the stairs I had to crawl on my hands and knees. There was very light smoke around three feet high but black smoke above. I reached the top of the stairs where there was a hallway to the right. Down the hall there was a door with flames roaring out. Going forward down a short hallway, I was in a kitchen and living room. I could see no one. It was time to get out as it was getting harder to breathe, so I went through the kitchen and out the back door to the roof. I walked to the edge where I could see Bill. Also, the fire department had arrived.

We thought there could be a young lady in the bedroom where the fire was. After getting down I learned the mother, whom I knew, was sitting in her car waiting for word about her daughter. It would be some time as the fire department was doing its job. I believe we have one of the better fire departments in the country as I have worked with them many times. In time they let us know what they had found in the bedroom. The young lady had not made it out.

The waiting mother had to be told. Knowing the mother made it much harder but it had to be done. With sorrow, she was told. She said she had already known and just waited.

~

61
TWO FAST CARS - SPELL DEATH

When first taking the job with the Grand Rapids Police Department in 1955, it didn't take long to realize that with a wife and growing family, we were going to need another source of income. We were making about $4,300 a year.

Dorrie, my wife, tried working but by the time you paid a baby-sitter, you were breaking just a little better than even. I was looking for side jobs that could be worked in. Soon I was driving school bus, digging graves, setting head stones, shoveling roofs and driveways during the winter, putting up TV antennas and anything that brought in a little more. This is information that sets up why I happened to be where I was at the time of the following event.

Just short of Ball Club Lake, about a half mile on the lake side coming from Deer River on Hwy 46, there stands a brown house with attached garage. On the back side of the garage is a TV tower that I was installing one early afternoon. The tower stands 40 feet tall and I was near the top. Looking out I could see and hear two cars coming down the road side by side. They appeared to be like models and brand new. Possibly 1966 Chieftains. They went by better than 100 mph. Within a minute I heard a tremendous explosion. I knew what it was. Climbing down I ran to my car. Throwing my ladders, which were lying loose on the top of my car to the ground, I went tearing down the road. I knew it was going to be bad.

There was a car sitting on the right side of the road with a man slumped behind the wheel, but as I remember, the top of the car from the frame up was gone. Two women, one on the road and the other on the side of the road in the dirt. A Pontiac was on its roof in the left hand ditch, burning, and with a man's legs under the car. I didn't see the other car right away.

What happened was that there was a car coming out of the driveway of what I will call the Ball Club Store. The two racing cars broadsided this car. This car was owned by the Ryder family who owned Ryder's Store just a short distance down the road.

At this time there were 30 to 40 people in the area not doing anything except standing around and looking and some smoking. This wasn't a good combination with gas running out of the vehicles. I ran up the road to the women. A woman identified as Mrs. Ryder had a severe head injury and it was obvious she was gone. Then going to the other one, her face was in the dirt and her mouth full of it; I cleared that out and headed for the burning car. Getting some help from bystanders we rolled the car over so the man could be pulled out. Going back up to the car without the top I decided, in spite of some protest, that we were going to move the driver as there was a running gas leak under the driver. The second racing car was in the ditch a hundred yards down in the left ditch as was the driver. The authorities had been called as well as the ambulance.

Mrs. Ryder died and the other four survived.

Both of the Larson brothers later appeared in court on various charges.

~

62
SOME CALLS "HIT HOME"

You go through your work as a police officer handling other people's problems, never expecting that the next call you get is going to hit you in the gut.

I had a twin brother, Harry, who lived on the LaPlant Road near Pokegama Lake. We had gone through orphanages and the service together and were very close.

On this day I was told that the ambulance had just received a call that a Harry Dahline had been shot in the head. Would I ride with them to show them the way? A short time before this I had handled a suicide and seen the x-ray of the man and knew what a .22 caliber bullet could do. The man lived only a short time.

Arriving at the scene I was very surprised to see Harry was up and coherent. The bullet had entered almost in the center of his forehead.

When asked what had happened, he replied that his friend had been practicing his "quick draw" from the holster and was a good shot but hadn't meant to shoot him.

He did end up in the hospital for a short time. The x-ray showed the bullet had fragmented upon entering and that it would be too dangerous to operate. He had headaches and seizures causing him to have to take blood thinners but Harry still had a good life for many years.

The bullet did its work after 35 years.

~

63
A MOVING OBJECT

When I think of this incident, I know there is a law of physics that hits it right on the head. I now fully understand: A body in motion tends to stay in motion; a body at rest tends to stay at rest.

I had been told that a wanted person I was looking for had been seen at the Country Kitchen. I had just left there without any luck. Going down Powers Hill and heading back north on Pokegama Ave., I saw a figure dart east between some houses and I realized this was the suspect.

Driving down the hill, I kept going as though I hadn't seen him. After driving on for several blocks, I made a right turn, going back behind the Downtowner Hotel with my lights off. Sneaking over to the bridge and hiding behind a large pillar, I waited. In a short time there he came on my side, full speed. I wait then stepped out into his path to execute a beautiful football tackle. He ran right over me, knocking me right onto my ass to the cement. I now understand a body in motion tends to stay in motion.

Getting up, it took me almost two blocks to attempt my second tackle. A body hitting concrete tends to stay. I still have to laugh at what happened to me.

~

64
BEER KEG INTO THE WOODS

Beefy Lawson, a deputy of quite a few years working for the Itasca County, called me saying he had reports of a keg party going on behind the Old Soldiers Cemetery and would like a hand.

At this time there was six-eight inches of snow on the ground. We followed the car tracks to a small clearing. We stopped the car on the edge and the kids ran in all directions. Beefy and I zeroed in on three boys running with a beer keg on their shoulders, but it was heavy and also a challenge with that much snow on the ground. It did not take them long to drop their beloved keg.

It must have been close to 11 P.M. and quite dark, but with the snow we were able to track them. We ran them through the trees for around 10 minutes and then a set of tracks veered off from the rest. Beefy and I were in good shape and they were breaking trail so after a while the two boys gave up.

Walking back with the boys, I told Beefy that I was going to go over to where we had lost the third boy. He said he would go over to the squad car and wait. Picking up the third boy's trail, I ran it for some 20 minutes. Coming to a fallen tree 10-15 inches thick and twenty five feet long, I followed it to the other end but there weren't any tracks there. Going back to the other end it did not look like anyone had back-tracked. Looking back over the fallen tree, I noticed a 10 inch jack pine near it with small branches and standing around 30 feet high. I couldn't see anything up there so I stepped back about 10 feet, and looking up I could see what appeared to be an orange jacket. I said, "Do you want to come down or do I shoot you down?" He said he would be right down. I still don't know how he could get up that tree. Looking across a small bog, I could see the squad car with the other boys.

The boy with the orange jacket became a fan of mine as he was on the track team and seemed to admire someone that could stay on his trail so long.

He eventually got into drugs and moved to another state. One night there was someone at our door. I checked and there was my orange coat friend. He was not talking rationally; the drugs had taken their toll. He decided he was going to stay with us but that was not to be. He still has his problems but he's still my friend.

~

65
THE BOY CAUGHT MAKING THE PIE

A note I left on the kitchen counter for my son to read:

I got up last night for some reason, walked into the kitchen as the lights were on. There, of course, was my son who was visiting us.

As usual he was putting final touches on some cooking. A superb split pea soup. We had some casual conversation, I and this son of mine whom I love dearly. But being old and crass, I don't believe I probably have ever done a good enough job of saying so. So I'll have to do that sometime.

But as I was leaving the kitchen to go back to bed, I looked down and could see the hot elements were on in the oven. I said, "What are you cooking now?" He got a funny look on his face. Being a police officer for forty years I have seen that look before. He replied, "Nothing, I just had the oven on." I looked at him and let it drop and went to bed.

This morning the evidence was found. A blueberry pie.

What a quandary. Do I arrest him or let his mother do it?

January 3, 2012   Chief of Police   Harvey L. Dahline

The note my son added to the bottom of my note:

I know the thought behind it.
Thank you, Dad

~

66
MY FRIEND - PEACE OFFICER DOWN
OCTOBER 29, 1981

How do you go about writing a story about Robert "Beefy" Lawson murdered 31 years ago?

He was a special friend over the years having worked many criminal cases together. His work ethic was beyond comparison. Getting onto a case, he thought the work day was 48 hours.

Honest, admired and respected, he helped send many a criminal to prison. Yet one of the first persons they would look up when they got out was Beefy.

You will always hear fine things said about someone after they are gone. But, I worked with the man. I also spent 40 years as a policeman in Grand Rapids. Robert Beefy Lawson and Pat Medure would be in the top three investigators in all that time.

What follows is information I gained both before and after the eighteen hour stand-off on the morning of October 29. 1981, when Itasca County Deputy, Robert Lawson was shot to death in the Swan Lake home of Audie Fox's parents.

Fox, who was separated from his wife, Pamela, and had been living in Colorado, had demanded to see his son, a five year old. His two children were living in the Pengilly area with their mother.

Lawson had been called by Pamela Fox to see if he would pick up Andy Fox at Audie's parent's home as she was hesitant to do it herself. The deputy who was on vacation at the time called in and volunteered to take the call.

Debbie Shaw, Fox's girlfriend, said that when Lawson walked in the door, Audie Fox came out from behind a partition, holding a .357 revolver with both hands. She said he twice ordered Lawson to get down on the floor and Lawson refused both times. Lawson finally complied when Fox cocked the hammer of the gun.

It is said Fox asked Lawson where his wife was, but Lawson refused to tell him and was given the count of three. Shaw said she took Fox's daughter into the living room and heard Fox count to three and then heard a loud noise.

Officer Beefy Lawson was to lie in the entryway of the Fox house, deceased, for some time. Sheriff Russ Johannsen and Chief Deputy Bob Serich had negotiated by phone with Audie Fox, the shooter. Then Don Irish, without weapons and alone, was allowed to enter the entryway to remove Deputy Lawson's body, bringing it out to his squad car, placing it on the trunk of his car and driving it out to the main road. This took place in the early afternoon.

Looking back in time trying to remember, I thought the best way to cover that day was to use my officer's investigative report. Hoping it is accurate and factual as to my point of view at that time.

Investigative Report by Officer Dahline:

Officer Harvey Dahline doing an investigative report on one, Audie Fox, today's date is 11-2-1981. This incident took place on Oct. 29th and 30th, 1981 in the Pengilly area.

On approximately 11:00 A.M. on Oct. 29th I became aware of the fact that officer Beefy Lawson had been shot in the Pengilly area. As the day wore on we realized this might take some time, but we (the Grand Rapids Police Dept.) did offer our help.

At approximately 8:00 P.M. I went over to the Pengilly area where I met Tom Peltier at a house that was set up as the headquarters for as long as this incident was to take place. I did talk to Tom and he gave me the general lay out of the land, the houses, etc., an idea of what was going on, and what they were trying to do at that time. I asked Tom where I could be of assistance to him at this time, and he told me that there was a point of the house that was possibly a little weak where no one could see the basement windows very well. He did take me over there and showed me the area that he would like me to watch. With me was a Deputy Sheriff from the Hibbing office and his partner, Officer McKinsey. We did place ourselves in an area where we could watch two sides of the house and also the basement windows. This would be approximately 40 feet toward the main highway and to the back of the house; there is a trailer house also located in this area. In the trailer house were a couple of officers also. Don White was at the corner of the trailer house, and these other two officers were with me.

In the location where I was located we were to spend approximately an eight hour period, from 8:00 P.M. until approximately 4:30 A.M. the next morning. During this time I did see Mrs. Fox, Audie Fox's mother, leave the front door of the house area, go up the road with a flashlight, go up the middle of the highway, down to the head-quarters house and then back. One of these times was approximately 3:00 in the morning; the other time must have been possibly 11:00 in the evening. During her walk at 3:00 in the morning shortly after she had left the house, I did see a basement light come on in the far right or what I learned later was the furnace room of the house. That light was on for approximately a four to five minute period. I thought to myself at that time, due to the fact that I had not seen any light movement in the house, that conceivably some body might be trying to hide something in that room at that time. This I passed on to Deputy Herschbach from the Sheriff's Office at a later time.

Around 11:00 P.M. I went back to the headquarters area to get a blanket and some gloves and some jackets that I had in my vehicle as some of the guys around my area were getting pretty cold. When I came up to the main road, I walked with Mrs. Fox as she was going back to the Fox house. On the way up to the house she said that she thought she would need God's help to make these things turn out right, and I wished her luck. She then proceeded on down the road back to the Fox house.

At about 4:00 A.M. on Oct. 30th, the word was coming out that there would be no shooting and that Fox was supposed to be coming out with his children and his mother. About this time Deputy Bob Serich arrived in my area and with him was a Gary Jacobson, a BCA Agent. They told me that there was to be an ambulance going around to the front into the driveway. About this time an ambu-lance did drive down the main road, turned into the driveway and parked facing the house, approximately 50 to 60 feet away from the house. Getting out of the ambulance was Officer Don Irish and Officer Sacherman, both in blue uniforms. They both walked up into the driveway towards the front of the house until they got about 20 to 30 ft. from the steps; this was in a lighted area. They at this time spread their clothing and showed Mrs. Fox that they weren't armed. I believe that Sacherman did go into the house momentarily and then came back out.

Shortly after this I heard that Audie Fox was demanding that a car that was to be the transportation for his family be brought forward. Bob Serich said that this was not part of any deal that they had worked out so far. He at this time asked if I would take my van and bring it around to the front. I went down the road about a block and got my blue and white '76 Chevy Van and drove it up to Deputy Bob Serich and asked him what he would have me do with it. He said to drive it to the front and park by the ambulance so they could get a good look at it, this I did.

Deputy Bob Serich, the officer in charge, seemed to have things well under control and well planned out.

I did take the van and park in the driveway alongside the ambulance; there was no response to my being there at that time. Mrs. Fox was standing in the doorway and the door was open. I could see Audie Fox inside the door on the phone, sitting down about 10 to 15 feet to the left inside of the kitchen. At that time he had a phone to his ear and it appeared that there were two young children on his knees or in his lap. I did not see a weapon. At this time I was down approximately six steps from his level. There was some small talk done of some sort and then about this time Audie Fox started doing some hollering, and the mother said that he thought we were armed. He did not want us around and also demanded to see his wife. He was hollering and so forth at this time, but he seemed to have his senses about him and knew what he was doing; and he was also giving orders in his own way at this time.

We then held a conference around the corner with Jacobson, Irish, and Sacherman and me as to whether to break off contact or not because of the demands that he was starting to make and the frame of mind that he was working himself into. It was decided during this conference not to break off contact because this was as close to the door as we had been able to get, and as long as we had contact we would see what we could do. We then talked over the possibilities, and Deputy Bob Serich then gave me the go ahead to see if I could talk my way to the door. If I thought I could then proceed, I was to, but if I thought I couldn't, then I was just to break contact. Irish and Sacherman were to back me up and were to be close to the steps. Serich and Jacobson were to be close by the corner, and they were to follow me in as soon as possible after I went in. The key at this time was whether we could get Mrs. Fox to stand in the doorway with the door open and talk to me.

As I was standing in the driveway about five minutes, Mrs. Fox came out and said, "He does not like you here because he thinks you have a gun." I told her that she did not have to worry as I would show her that I did not. I then removed my hunting jacket and placed it on the ground along with my gun belt and empty holster. I then proceeded up the steps, spreading my light coat so that she and Audie could see my waist. She was holding the door at the time. I then took a step past her and pivoting, putting my back to Audie, raising my coat in back so that he could see that I did not have a weapon. At the same time I continued to pivot and dove for him; I caught him around both arms with the two children squeezed between us. Within a second or two, Irish, Sacherman, Serich and Jacobson were all assisting me. Audie at this time was still resisting and trying to break free. We were all carried outside, away from any weapons. He was searched and handcuffed. I removed his boots and socks, somebody else removed his shirt in a search for any weapons. Deputy Serich then took over on what he would like done.

As Audie was being taken, his mother went to pieces and had to be removed from the scene, hollering, "They are going to kill him!"

The boots and socks I later turned into the Sheriff Office to Deputy Serich.

Just inside the main door to the Fox house was a great pool of co-agulated blood. Fox was then taken in the Sheriff's car to the Itasca Co. Jail.

Saturday morning about 10:30 A.M., I was at the Sheriff Office and Bob Serich told me that they had not been able to find the weapon, a .357 Magnum that had been used to kill Beefy Lawson and said that he was making up some search teams. I told him if he could use me that I would be happy to assist, and he asked if I could go at 1:00 P.M.

I started for the Fox house at approximately 1:00 P.M. on Oct. 30th, 1981. Deputy Wally Herschbach met me there, as he was in charge of the search and had the search warrant. I started a search of the house keeping in mind having seen the lights go on in the base-ment about 3:00 A.M. that early morning of the incident. In about 10 minutes I found a .357 Magnum, chrome plated or stainless steel, stuck up in a clean-out for a chimney. This was a 6" X 5" shaft, smooth sides with no ledges inside, filled with creosote and soot. I felt up that shaft as far as I could reach and felt something like a barrel; the gun was wedged in the chimney. I had hold of the bar-rel and chamber when I pulled it out, since that time I was careful about touching the gun. I then scratched my initials on the lower left in the back of the chamber of the weapon for identification purposes. Since this time the gun has been turned over to Deputy Wally Herschbach of the Itasca County Sheriff Dept. immediately after the weapon was found.

End of this statement. Submitted by Officer Harvey Dahline, Grand Rapids Police Department.

I must say that I have to commend Sheriff Russ Johannsen and his Chief Deputy Bob Serich for the professional planning and coordination of the safe and successful ending to a very difficult situation.

Audie L. Fox appeared before Ninth Judicial District Court Judge John Spellacy in District Court Monday, November 2 around 8:30 A.M. It was his first court appearance and he was arraigned. Prosecuting attorney was the most respected Bernard Bodien. Fox was charged with two counts of 1st degree murder. No bail was set. Fox was represented by Duluth Attorney Richard C. Hansen.

Fox was no stranger to Lawson or many other law officers. He had been found guilty of two counts of felony theft in August of 1976 and sentenced to two consecutive terms of 0-5 years at St. Cloud State Reform School, serving 1 1/2 years. Beefy Lawson had been the investigating officer. Most recently Fox had been wanted for the theft of a $5,000 motorcycle. Again, Lawson was the investigator. Fox was also wanted in the Twin Cities for theft, assault with a gun and possession of stolen property.

Johannsen reported on Monday, November 2, that the search of the Fox house resulted in the seizure of 41 guns. One firearm belonged to Officer Lawson and had been found in the sump pump. Another was the alleged murder weapon found in the chimney. Also found was 3,100 rounds of ammunition.

Fox was convicted of murder by a jury of 10 women and two men on Monday, April 26, 1982. Judge Warren Saetre sentenced 27 year old Fox to life in prison in the Stillwater State Penitentiary.

In 1995 Fox was to come up for a parole hearing. Many others and I wrote letters of opposition. The following is my letter to the parole board:

Office of Adult Release:
Ref: Audie Fox

In 1981, Beefy Lawson's life was taken in a deliberate execution. He was on the floor face-down, a gun put to his head by Audie Fox, threats were made, and a trigger was pulled.

Left dead was a police officer and a personal friend of mine.

Beefy was known throughout the area as a friend to everyone and an honest, hard working deputy who went beyond the call of duty to help not only citizens but also law breakers to get back on the right path.

Beefy would work hard to send someone up for breaking the law, but the first person they would look up when they got out would be Beefy and then thank him.

I have been a police officer for over 40 years and it seems inconceivable to me that the State could even consider parole for Audie Fox. This execution was planned and deliberate. Fox got a life sentence, but he deserved more. I think this is a good illustration of what is wrong with our judicial system.

Don't you think it is about time we start meaning what we say: 40 years is 40 years and life is life? What kind of a message are we sending? Audie Fox should never see the light outside of a prison. I know Beefy Lawson never will.

Respectfully,

Harvey Dahline
Chief of Police
40 years in the Justice System

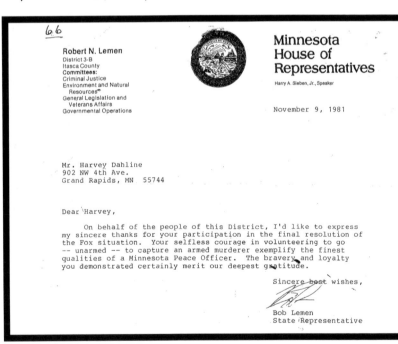

66

Robert N. Lemen
District 3-B
Itasca County
Committees:
Criminal Justice
Environment and Natural
Resources
General Legislation and
Veterans Affairs
Governmental Operations

**Minnesota
House of
Representatives**

Harry A. Sieben, Jr., Speaker

November 9, 1981

Mr. Harvey Dahline
902 NW 4th Ave.
Grand Rapids, MN 55744

Dear Harvey,

On behalf of the people of this District, I'd like to express my sincere thanks for your participation in the final resolution of the Fox situation. Your selfless courage in volunteering to go -- unarmed -- to capture an armed murderer exemplify the finest qualities of a Minnesota Peace Officer. The bravery and loyalty you demonstrated certainly merit our deepest gratitude.

Sincere best wishes,

Bob Lemen
State Representative

~

United States of America.

A SENATE RESOLUTION

COMMENDING CERTAIN POLICE OFFICERS FOR
THEIR COURAGE AND DEDICATION TO DUTY

WHEREAS, on Thursday, October 30, 1981, Robert Lawson, an Itasca County Deputy Sheriff, was shot and killed near Pengilly, Minnesota, while attempting to serve legal papers on Audie Fox; and

WHEREAS, by holding his children hostage, Fox then held off other officers from entering the house; and,

WHEREAS, Don Irish, assistant Police Chief of the Nashwauk Police Department, entered the house without weapons in plain view of Fox and removed the body of Robert Lawson; and,

WHEREAS, after eighteen hours of fruitless talking, Officers Peter Saccoman and Harvey Dahline rushed the house without weapons and captured Fox and freed the children unharmed; and,

WHEREAS, the actions of the three officers exemplified the bravery and dedication to duty which police officers are frequently called upon to display; and,

WHEREAS, the police officers put their lives in jeopardy in order to save the hostage children; and

WHEREAS, the officers' bravery and dedication should be recognized by the legislature and people of Minnesota; NOW THEREFORE,

BE IT RESOLVED by the Senate of the State of Minnesota, on behalf of all Minnesotans, that it commends the bravery and dedication to duty of officers Don Irish, Peter Saccoman, and Harvey Dahline.

BE IT FURTHER RESOLVED that the Secretary of the Senate is directed to enroll copies of this resolution, and they be authenticated by his signature and that of the President, and presented to Don Irish, Peter Saccoman, and Harvey Dahline.

Jack Davies
President of the Senate

Patrick E. Flahaven
Secretary of the Senate

Bob Lessard
State Senator, District 3

67
THOUGHTS

When I first started on the police department in 1955 we were not allowed to have any radios in our cars, AM or FM, 2-way police radios were not available.

Most of the time you were in a one-man patrol car. Some of the time, more so in the winter in the middle of the night you may drive for hours even in snowstorms and not see a moving soul. Things could get very monotonous, sometimes I would get thoughts.

I started to pull over and jot them down on little pieces of paper. As the years went by I put them on a yellow note pad and kept them in my locker at work.

Not letting anyone see them, they were some of your innermost thoughts. Now I have taken them out:

Have you ever walked in the warm sunshine
and felt the fleeting coolness of a shadow?

Have you ever walked in the morning dew
and felt close to the One that created you?

Have you ever seen the wind in the tops of the trees
and felt your heart flutter to your knees?

Seen the birds, the bee, and the howling wind
and know that someday this all must end?

Seen the cricket and heard the chirp
had a love that didn't hurt?

Seen the clouds scuttle across the sky
felt the teardrop in your eye?

Felt the embrace of man
or the love of a child in your hand?

Knew the coolness of an evening breeze
or the rays of sunshine through the trees?

Felt the water upon your feet
where the sand and Mississippi meet?

Looked across the fields in the morning mist
and seen destiny. the shadows of love?

Have you ever dreamed that you could fly,
slip through the wind like a butterfly?

Have you ever tried to pick a dewdrop from a leaf,
evasive crystal clear, a minute to cherish then it's gone?

Climbed a tree looked at the sky
felt your heart beating and wonder why?

Felt your heart skip a beat, then she was gone,
never to know her, never to care
but the magic of that moment will always be there?

Seen a snowflake fall, felt the warm love of it
seen a rabbit run then wonder how it all begun?

Have you ever been to Remer in the summer, felt the sun,
walked in the fields, ate the berries, played in it's streams loved?

You grew up there, loved a lifetime, all is done...listen
Life grew with us then, can we ever go back to our youth? Perhaps not,
but we will be forever richer for it.

Sometimes I feel so full inside, I cannot speak.

Can you take the petals from a rose and still have a rose?
The sweetness from a flower and still have a flower?
The love from my heart and still...

The moonbeams slash through the night with vivid dreams
Can you make a dream come true?
Are dreams real or are they make-believe wishes?
They are real.

Have you ever run in the rain on a warm summer night
while the lightening flashed around you and the thunder rolled?
I have.

Tested, you thought it was real, then it was gone
Love can be a warm tender feeling.

Have you ever sat and watched the Autumn leaves fall
and felt the loneliness of the moment?

Locked within all of us is a little bit of joy, sorrow, love, and loneliness
but tomorrow when the sun comes up, it is a new day?

They say it is better to have loved and lost than never to have loved
at all
Perhaps, but I have never heard one that has lost say it.

Have you ever watched a falling star
Was that the end? Where was the beginning?
Or was that just your moment?

Have you ever walked down a lonely road at night
and felt the shivers run up your back?
Nothing there, but you don't look back.
Home at last, you'll always wonder, was that a tree?

Why is it a river always looks so cold and lonely at night
but a warm rain is like a love?

Have you ever looked into a pair of eyes
and been able to look past the moment,
Knew that when the circle ended
that this may be your beginning, gentle as a velvet wing?

More Thoughts:

There was a lady I wanted to meet
Her age was 90
She was not sure
So I sent her a dozen yellow roses
She had not known nor had I
That she was my sister
What is destiny

The stones like sentinels rise
Through the morning mist
There is pink in the east
And dew on the fresh mound of earth
70 years they were together
Now he is at peace
My friend

When I am sad and weary
And my eyes they need to smile
And you my darling come
Sit beside me for just a little while
Then I am filled with laughter
And my heart with delight
Then all my troubles
Seem to vanish with the night
For you can lift my troubles
And you can lift my fears
And with you I am so lucky
For we have so many years

More More Thoughts:

Just Remember

Just remember how you
miss her when she's gone

Remember how those hours
seem so long

This will help you stay true
although you're awfully blue

Remember how you
miss her when she's gone

On Pokegama South they went with a roar
Those motorcycles were going 70 or more
When a pickup making a U-turn came into sight
Those two young boys never made it home that night

—

They met at school and it was push and shove
Then it was on to the roller rink and the moon above
Now I'm thanking the Heavens and the Lord above
60 years later and we're still in love
(and looking for more)

~

68
THE GIRL BEHIND THE FENCE

Central School was a well known landmark in our town and was right across the street from the police station. Since it was right in the middle of town, there was a very high fence around the whole school back then.

Walking by the school one day there was a very young girl looking through the fence. She smiled a smile that covered her face from ear to ear. Smiling back I said, "My name is Harvey, what's yours?" She said, "My name is Susie." "Do you go to school here?" "Yes, I do."

Many times I walked by that fence and she always seemed to be there smiling. Susie always knew my name. "Harvey," she would say, "how are you?"

The years have come and gone but I always knew she would be around the corner at Walmart, the YMCA or maybe the show. She is a grown lady now. That smile and hugs are still there and the willingness to always say, "Harvey, how are you?"

Young old friends at my age are very much appreciated.

The fence is gone now.

May 31, 2012, I met Susie at her father's funeral. She smiled and said, "Harvey, how are you?" and gave me a hug.

~

69
SAYING THANKS

Receiving a call from the Dutchroom located on 4th St. N.W. at around 1:00 A.M., I was told they had three men there that already had a few drinks before coming to their place of business. Thinking the men had as much as they should; they were refusing to serve them.

The men were large, in their forties with loud talking and challenging attitude. After talking to the owners I was told that they wanted these three men out. The place was full of other customers. The men were told they would not be served due to the fact that they appeared to have had too much already. At this time I was standing facing all three of them six to eight feet apart. One man said something to the effect, "And who do you think can put us out?" I had been standing alone a few feet from the crowd. About this time a person stepped up on my left: Richard Peck, six foot three, probably around 230 lbs, a former Golden Gloves boxer. Stepping up to my right was a friend of Peck's, a brawler in his own right.

The men looked at us for a moment and walked out.

My sidekicks had their little problems in the past but I always treated them fairly. I think this was their way of saying "Thanks".

~

70
THE MEAT CARVING KNIFE AND THE RIFLE

In the autumn of 1975 I was called to talk to a woman on the 800 block of 14th St. N.W. just west of the football field.

When I arrived there, a hefty woman around 40 years of age proceeded to tell me she was having a fight with her husband, Raymond. He was threatening to kill her and she was afraid for her life. He had a .22 rifle and a meat carving knife in his possession. She said all she wanted to do was go into the house, get some clothing and get out. She pointed to a low roofed pink shack some 150 feet away which was not in the best of repair.

Looking down I could see a man standing in the house behind a screen door. I told the lady to stay put and that I would try to talk to him. Approaching the door, I could see Ray indeed had a .22 rifle in his right hand and a carving knife in the left. He appeared very agitated. He was not a pretty man, standing somewhere around 5 feet 8 inches, weighing 230 lbs with a bullet head, thick neck, dark hair and with one eye looking in a different direction. His wife had told me that he had worked in a meat packing plant in Albert Lea. One of his jobs was sticking hogs with a knife.

I told Ray that all his wife wanted was some clothes. He said no way and didn't know what the police had to do with this and before the night was done he would be killing a cop. I spent a few more minutes talking to him, telling him that I thought this was a family thing and that maybe we could sit down at the table with a cup of coffee and work it out.

He seemed to think it was a good idea. I asked him to make some coffee and said that his wife and I would be there shortly and we would talk.

As I walked up the road to where his wife was, more policemen were showing up including Dave Bennett and Russ Johanssen. One thought we should just shoot him, but I told him I thought it was a little early for that and added I would be going into the house with his wife.

I had seen the layout of the inside. At the door was a small living area and to the left around 15 feet in was a table next to a big window which was the kitchen area. I was going to make sure the wife was in a chair close to the door. I told her that if anything happened she was to head out the door.

The wife and I walked to the house and Ray had the coffee ready. I made sure the wife sat in the chair to my left closest to the door; Ray was to my right. He had three coffee cups on the table with spoons and sugar. He still had the knife in his hand but had laid the rifle on the table in front of him, barrel toward the window, the butt toward my side of the table. About this time I might have said the most brilliant thing I have ever said in my whole life. "Do you have any cream?" He said, "Yes" and stood up. I then realized the refrigerator was back behind me to my left. He then walked behind me to the fridge with the knife in hand. Needless to say, I could feel where he was every step of the way. He came back and set the cream on the table and sat down. I did thank him for the cream.

We then had somewhat of a lengthy discussion about what the troubles were between them. At this time he would emphasize a point by using the knife with his arm outstretched, almost going past my right knee. He did this several times. All at once things seemed to be getting out of hand fast. I thought that if he pointed the knife past me again I would chop his wrist. He pointed past me again and I did nothing. I said to myself, "Are you chicken shit?" He pointed the knife again and I snapped my right hand onto his wrist. The knife stuck in the floor between my feet. Standing up I hit the butt of the gun driving the barrel through the window. He was coming out of his chair for me. Getting my arms around him with my head under his chin, we spun and danced in the living room. Keeping my elbows out to block his arms as he was trying to get to my gun, I drove him into the glass of a hutch in the corner.

As soon as I had hit the knife into the floor, the wife was up and gone. She reached the outside door just as the officers did. She was like a bowling ball; they had to back off to let her out before they could get in.

Just as I drove Ray into the hutch my head still under his chin I felt a gun barrel slide over my head from behind right in the middle of Ray's forehead. Dave said, "Move, you SOB, and I'll blow your head off." It was like you let the air out of a balloon. Ray just slumped. He was taken to the county jail.

Later as I was doing some paper work at the jail, a jailer came up to me and said, "This guy is really up in the air, threatening what he is going to do to your family as soon as he gets out." Thinking for a moment and taking my gun belt off, I had the jailer let me in the cell with Ray. I said to him, "Just a moment, Ray, and then you can swing if you want to. Tonight you told me you were going to kill a cop. Now if you think about it, I took a hell of a chance coming in doing what I did. You saw the other guys come in the door; some just wanted to shoot you outright." He just stood there for a little while and surprisingly put out his hand saying, "You are right. If you ever have any trouble with me, remind me of this."

About three months later I got a call that Ray was sitting out in the street with a rifle on his car dash. Walking up to him I said, "Do you remember what you told me in the jail cell?" He said, "Yes, I do," and handed me the gun.

You may think this is the last time I saw Ray, but it was not. Maybe a year went by and our door bell rang very early in the morning. My wife said, "I'll get it." She came back to me very wide-eyed saying it was for me. Ray was at the door and still not a pretty sight. The marriage problems were continuing and he wanted to talk them over with me and we did. I haven't seen Ray since, but in my heart I hope he ended up having some happiness in this world.

My wife no longer answers the door in the middle of the night.

~

71
THE PICTURE

In the 1990's I was riding my bicycle on Hwy. 2 west preparing for a triathlon. It was around 5:30 P.M. Approaching the dam area on the left just up the hill from the Mississippi River, I could see an older model brown car parked off the road facing east. The trunk was open with the right rear up in the air, a jack under it. There were two tires lying on the ground.

There appeared to be three Indians lounging there. One was sitting on the bumper, one lying on a folding lounge chair and the other sitting in the grass. One was quite a bit younger than the other two. They appeared to be very relaxed, enjoying the beautiful summer evening without a care in the world.

I rode by heading for Cohasset where I turned around and headed back toward home. I could see that the car was still there. Nothing had changed.

Riding up and stopping, I could see the two tires on the ground were flat and in bad shape, probably beyond repair. I talked to them a few minutes. No one seemed concerned over their situation. They seemed quite happy and easy to talk to. After looking at the size of their tires, I told them as soon as I got home I would be back with my car.

Upon arriving home I looked in the garage and found two tires in good shape and the same size as they needed. I took them back to their car and picked up the tires because I needed the rims and drove back to the Standard Station, had the tires put on the rims and pumped up. Driving back, I did get some help putting them on their car.

They all seemed very grateful and were on their way. I thought I would never see them again but it wasn't the last time I heard of them.

Perhaps a year or so later I was admiring some prints at the Home Show at the Grand Rapids arena. A well known local artist, Jackie Dingmann, who was also a personal friend, was exhibiting some of her art work. She highlighted the Indian culture in most of her paintings. As I was looking at one that seemed familiar, Jackie said, "Do you recognize the person in the print?" It was a young Indian warrior dressed in buckskin and feathers. The title on the print was "Roots of the Forest". I said that he looked familiar but I don't know him. She said, "Yes you do. Do you remember helping out some Indians by the dam whose car had some flat tires?" She said that was the younger man of the three you helped out and his name was Michael. She said that he was her main model when painting young Indian males.

She then insisted that I come to her studio and pick out a framed picture. She really wanted to show her appreciation over the way I had treated her Indian friends and not charged them. I did pick out a print I had been admiring at the Home Show, "Roots of the Forest", Number 252-500. On the bottom she wrote, "To Harvey, friend of Michael, Roots of the Forest", you're a true Indian's friend. By Jackie Dingmann."

This painting still hangs on our wall—Jackie went home to be with the Lord some years ago but not before leaving a legacy of some beautiful artwork.

Portrait by Jackie Dingmann

~

72
SCAMMING THE PUBLIC AND INSURANCE COMPANIES

On or around January 17, 1982, I was approached by Officer Gene Bennett. He stated that he was looking into a house that was reported burglarized in the south side of town. Now Gene has been around the block, and when he told me that he was very suspicious of this case, I agreed to look into it with him.

We were both aware that this person, Howard, had reported this invasion and burglary from his winter home in New Port Richey, Florida. Two years earlier on April 17, 1980, Howard had reported a similar burglary at this same address in which he had reported a loss of more than $5,000.00.

We did a visual inspection of the home, looking into all possible entry points. Windows, doors, garage, etc. We found some marks on the back door but we both agreed that there was no way entry was made this way. We then wondered who would have a key to the house or the garage door opener. We learned that a relative had a door opener for the garage.

Howard requested we go into the home and investigate. Gene and I had the relative who had the opener and was in charge of keeping an eye on the place while they were away for the winter open the door for us. We went through the house looking for anything suspicious and finger printed the necessary spots.

One of the first things we saw was a glass gun case that had held rifles with the glass broken in. It was empty of all guns including the reported stolen ones. On the bottom of the gun case all of the broken glass was evenly spread across the bottom. If this would have happened the way it was reported, there should have been a pattern of where the gun butts had been. Further searching revealed several rifles and shot guns under the mattress in one of the bedrooms.

Opening the attic door and while standing on a step ladder we were able to search through a couple of feet of the attic insulation. We found several more guns.

In the corner of the living room was a hutch with glass doors. With the use of a chair we found a lot of paper work on top that substantiated his report from the 1980 loss to the insurance company. Also included was a long list of items purchased from Mager Music all carefully itemized and their value listed at several thousand dollars. These also had been turned into the insurance company as proof of loss.

When this list was later taken to Mager Music, we were told that Howard had brought them a list and wanted a quote as he was looking to buy these items. They had given him the list but he never bought them.

At this time we were starting to realize we were getting into a case that would take us months to follow through on.

We contacted the ATF and US Treasury on serial numbers and types of guns stolen. This report came back saying in some cases that no such serial number existed or no such guns were ever made with those serial numbers. Howard, not knowing we had found many of the items, had made a claim to the police department of $15,869 but one of $30,012.60 to his insurance company. This case took many twists and turns.

How was Howard able to dupe the insurance company? He would give them reams of paper work all appearing to be legitimate. Through our request we got some of the paper work. What we got in one case was a stack of paper nearly two inches thick with five to six copies of supposedly legitimate checks on each page. No one has time on their hands to follow through unless they have an idea of what they are looking for, so he snowed them under with paper work.

We were talking to two insurance companies on the phone at the same time, one from Duluth and the other in Red Wing, about a check written to Ray's Sport and Cycle in the amount of $2,350.00 for an electric generator which was one of the checks in the stack used as proof of loss. The lady in Red Wing said that there was something wrong with that check and we asked what she meant. She said if you look at the numbers under the signature you will see the amount paid out on the check. The amount was $23.50. However, the check itself was written for $2,350.00. Also written on the check was that it was for an electric generator. The next day we went to Ray's and asked to see a generator for over $2,000 and they replied they didn't carry any for that much and never had. Asking if they could explain the check, they said they could. Howard had bought a pair of gloves for $23.50. He signed the check then started to leave. As he was going out the door, the clerk had hollered at him and told him he hadn't written in the amount. He hollered back saying, "Hell, it will go through anyway," and left. We later got a search warrant and got a copy of the check as it went through the bank. The check going through the bank did not have "generator" on it or the amount written in. This had to have been altered and then copied on the stack given to the insurance company.

Just another example of what we were finding was a check for a couple hundred dollars for an electric refrigerator bought from Cole's on the River Road. Cole's made snow fence and had never sold a refrigerator to Howard.

Part of the investigation got into a hunting cabin that Howard reportedly owned. He had reported that he was improving the building by adding on to it. Over the months he had raised its value from around $10,000 to over $35,000 with his insurance company. One day he went out to the hunting shack with a friend. As they were leaving he told the friend to go check on a deer stand down near the road, saying he would pick him up on his way out to go home. Would you believe when they got home they got a call that the shack had burned down? It also had the electric refrigerator in it from Cole's although they didn't have electricity out there, but it was reported in his claim to the insurance company as a loss.

When I talked to the insurance company, they claimed that Howard was talking to someone down state and putting pressure on because they had yet to pay him for the burned out cabin and contents. I told the insurance company to hold off and to check further as it was my understanding that the hunting shack did not belong to him. It was not in his name.

We were also aware over the years he had made several other claims to insurance companies. He at one time owned an eating place. One day he reported the place had been broken into the night before with a loss of several hundred dollars. The same night, having left his car behind the building, it had also been broken into with a loss of $500 worth of his son's hockey equipment.

We also had a report from Howard a couple years before this. His car was left on a downtown street and had been broken into. Several guns were stolen, again a few thousand dollars.

We had reports of other incidents that may have some truth to them. It was said that he was a good basketball player over in the Chisholm area but had blown a knee which ended his career. There was also a report that he was at a camp in the Army Reserves and was driving a Jeep when the right front wheel came off. He was found at the bottom of a ditch under the Jeep with an injured knee. Supposedly a captain had found all of the wheel nuts in a pile but a claim had been made. Another incident that we were told about was that he had made a claim with Workman's Comp at the Coleraine School District. The claim was that he had been standing in the parking lot talking to a friend. The friend had left his car out of gear and the car rolled back striking him in his knee badly re-injuring his "same knee", and that he had been on Workman's Comp for some time then returned to work without notifying Workman's Comp.

Later on I did get a taped statement from Howard at his house. This statement was several hours in duration. In it he told me how he had a promising basketball career but had injured his knee in school at Chisholm. While he was at camp he had injured his knee in a jeep accident, and later had reinjured his knee in a school parking lot in Coleraine.

He also told me in the interview that he was very smart with a high IQ, having obtained the rank of colonel which I believe to be untrue. He said that I wasn't very smart because I had only obtained the rank of sergeant during the Korean War.

He shared that he had been notified by his friend while he was in New Port Richey both times of the break-ins. His friend was a relative. I did not tell him that we had found a lot of guns and had discovered other information and that we knew the break-ins had been staged.

He was very intelligent. He was also very talkative which was nice because everything he said was admissible in court. I know I am not very bright so it was nice to have it on tape so I did not have to remember so much.

And yes, we did go through all two hundred checks, spending long hours and finding many inconsistencies. There were too many to share here in what is supposed to be a short story. It would also be very boring.

This is my recollection of the case some 32 years ago. I have left some names out that could only hurt some very nice people. My opinion of Howard based on my investigation and what I learned about him is that we had only seen the tip of the iceberg.

Howard, age 42, was charged with:
1. Theft by swindle
2. Falsely reporting a crime
3. Attempted theft by swindle
4. Falsely reporting a crime claiming nonexistent losses to insurer

On July 23, 1983

Howard appeared before Judge John Spellacy in Itasca County Court
on two charges of theft by swindle, both felonies. He pled guilty to both charges.

Two concurrent sentences were handed down, one year and one day.
Execution of Howard's sentence was stayed. He was placed on five years supervised probation, served 90 days in county jail and ordered to make restitution.

Re: Grand Rapids Herald Review---Sunday June 13, 1982
Officer Gene Bennett
Harvey Dahline

~

73
THE NINJA GANG

In the winter of 1977 we started to have a flurry of burglaries in the area, the first one at the Itasca Community College on December 19th. Then began a string of burglaries; Jan 14, 15, 18, 24, and 30th. All of these were either at the college, the Grand Rapids High School or the Middle School. Over a thousand dollars in damage had been done in the forced entries. Thousands of dollars of equipment had been taken; cameras, speakers, stereo equipment, and other items. It appeared hammers, chisels and crow bars were being used indiscriminately.

On this particular Sunday morning while working by myself, a burglary was reported at the high school. The blue shop building on 1st Ave had been entered. A large number of tools were missing.

There had been a fresh snow the night before so tracks could be seen going to and from the building.

Getting to the police station, I was writing up an investigative report when a friend of mine walked in. After some small talk, he asked me what I was doing. I told him I was working on a burglary at the high school shop area from the night before.

He said he had been hearing rumors of three boys that might be working with a gang that were doing this type of break-ins. Asking if he knew where they might live, he answered, "One only lives three blocks from last night's burglary." Asking if he knew any of the boys' names, he told me. Knowing the young man's name, I realized who the other boys would be and where the stolen items would be found.

Going back up to the shop building, I walked around looking for foot prints, there were plenty. Also, looking up the street to where one of the suspects lived, I spotted his car parked out in front of the house.

I was wondering what to do next. Someone had to be watching over me as they were being delivered unto my hands. While standing at the curb and looking down but also looking out of the corner of my eye at the car, three boys walked out of the house, got into the car and drove my way.

At this time I acted as though I was following some foot prints across the road and did not see them coming toward me in the traffic lane; they had to stop or run over me.

We were all seemingly surprised to see each other, as the boys were all good friends of mine and my family. When they asked me what I was doing, I replied I was investigating a burglary at the school and following footprints in the roadway. As I was leaning in the window of the car, I could see the shoes and boots the young men had on.

So, I said, "As long as you're here, I might as well look at your shoes to eliminate you guys."

They all showed me the bottom of their shoes and boots. Now I don't know if the prints were right or not, but they sure looked good to me along with the information I had in my head.

I said, "Boys, you have a problem. I'm going to drive to the police station. You can follow me and we'll see if we can work this out."

Meeting them at the office, I split them up and talked to them separately. In less than five minutes the first boy was telling me all about the break-ins. These boys had all been wearing dark, Ninja-like clothing along with Ninja knives during their escapades.

Taped statements were taken from each of the boys, all telling much the same story about their break-ins of the Grand Rapids schools and the Itasca Community College. Other boys and girls were implicated, both in town and at the college.

The Itasca County Sheriff's Office was notified. We were soon working together on all aspects of the case. Eventually seven people, five boys and two girls, were taken into custody, all charged with burglary with a tool and with theft. All pled guilty to the charges. Recovery or restitution was ordered by the court. Most of property was recovered.

They must have gotten their thrills out, as all have gone on to do well in life.

Grand Rapids Herald Review, Thursday, February 3, 1977 Vol 83 No 10

~

74
THE ROBE

There was a little man who was around 40 years old who lived in HaCar Addition located in the Southeast part of town just up over Powers Hill. I was very surprised to see him very late one warm summer night standing on the sidewalk by the First National Bank. He appeared to be crying and looked to be a little beaten up. What really stood out was that he was barefoot and apparently only wearing a terrycloth robe.

After I quieted him down, because he was quite distraught, he proceeded to tell me that his live-in of some years had come in after a social night on the town in somewhat of a bad mood. Not thinking, he had asked her where she had been since it was so late. That was his mistake. She went over to a coffee table, breaking a leg off, and went after him with it, striking him several times before he was able to get in the bedroom, grab a robe and make it out the door.

Not knowing what to do or where to go he had wandered downtown.

The man was well known to me as he had been a TV repairman. He was a very gentle person and this was not the first altercation between the two. The lady, somewhat larger in stature, was also well known to me as she would be again in the future.

Asking what he would like to see done or if he would like to make a complaint, he said all he wanted to do was get home and get some clothes and leave. The night finally ended by my taking him home and her being removed to her father's house for the night.

These events continued for some years with him always going back.

Seems we have heard this story before but with a different twist.

~

75
SHOOT OR DON'T SHOOT

Through the years I have attended many meetings of the Asst. Chiefs and Chiefs meetings throughout the Iron Range which included Sheriff's, as well as other department heads of DNR and BCA.

At these meetings, training of our officers is often discussed with as many as 30 to 40 persons there. One of the subjects being discussed was a training film where an officer would have to make snap decisions on pictures. A shoot or don't shoot option. It could be a person turning around with a broom in his hands. It could be a person with a shotgun turning around. The person could have a child in front of him. It would be a shoot or not shoot decision.

The topic brought up by one chief was that the film should be required and taken as a test by all personnel. If they failed they should not be able to carry a gun in the line of duty until they passed. This discussion went on for some time with no one speaking up against it. I finally spoke up saying that, yes, all officers should take the test but that it was just a training film and nothing more. I said that having gone through a few real life situations of shoot or don't shoot, it is only the officer that can make that decision. Yes, he is putting his life on the line but that is the risk we take. I told them of a situation I had been in.

Some years before I had been walking through an alley downtown early in the morning. At this time the State Bank was on the corner of 2nd St. and 1st Ave. N.W. across from the Paper Mill. As I came into the alley going north behind the bank, I saw an older car parked behind and facing the bank. There was some movement on the passenger side. As the person got out I made a judgment of a man around 6 feet and weighing around 220 pounds. As the man got out with the door still open, he stepped upon the lower part of the car, the car between us. His arm came across the top of the car and leveled down on me with what was clearly a silver pistol. I had drawn my pistol but for some reason did not shoot. Something was wrong. The man stepped down from the car and came walking around the back of it. Then I could see that it was a boy around 16 years of age that lived upstairs in an apartment. His father was a local businessman. The boy was carrying a full size silver cap gun. Needless to say when the boy left to go upstairs he may not have been kicked but he had certainly been well chewed out. Shoot or not shoot.

Officers have to be thinking all the time. How did I get here? What alerted me? Is someone's life at stake other than the officer's? What kind of a weapon does the person have? Is there more than one danger? Is this an immediate threat?

I would not take the right to carry away from one of my men based on a training film.

When you are out there alone making that decision, all of your background and training kick in. You make the decision and you live with it. You do your best.

No matter what you do, there will always be second guessers who were not there.

The meeting did end with the thought that a training film is just that.

~

76
PASSING YOUR NAME ALONG

In the early 1980's I got a call from the Holiday Gas Station. There was a very young couple there from out of state. They were newly married and had some bad luck with their car. They were now broke, hungry and did not know what to do.

After some talking I decided the best thing, late as it was, was to take them home to Mother. Dorrie was always willing to take in anyone I brought home. Decisions could be made later.

We got them something to eat and bedded them down for the night. After breakfast the next morning and some heart warming stories about their plight, we thought they were a lot like us.

It reminded us of the night Dorrie and I got married and with very little money headed for Walker, Minnesota searching for information with the hope that we would get some help in finding my younger brother. He had been adopted out, and we had been searching for him for some time. Walker was the county seat and Ron had been adopted from there. It was raining hard and about half way to Remer our car hit a deep pool of water in the middle of the highway. And the engine quit. Someone came along and helped jump start our car getting us going again.

Pay back time. We found out where they were going, filled up their gas tank, got them a few groceries and enough gas money to get them home. We never expected to hear from them again.

Some time went by and we got a thank you note in the mail expressing their appreciation for what we had done. There was a little add-on telling us they now had a new member in their family and wanted us to know that they had named him Harvey.

Now I have nine grandchildren and none of them are named after me.

This little guy's name was Harvey. He must have been a beautiful dog…

~

77
EVERY KIND OF CASE

Years ago a young couple came to me asking for help on just how to handle a situation they were not quite sure on how to go about.

It seems they had a young son around six years old they had taken to a doctor as he was complaining about being very sore. The doctor after much questioning was able to come to a conclusion. That being, that three young neighbor girls had been trying to find out what the facts of life are at a very young age, and they being older than the boy decided to use him as their object lesson.

The doctor assured everyone that the boy would recover. It was up to me to talk to the neighbor girls' parents along with the girls themselves. As I left I was sure we would have no more problems of this nature.

Many years have passed and the girls have gone on to more advanced studies.

The boy does not appear to have been traumatized, recovering quite well. He is not seeing a psychiatrist, appears to be quite normal and has made no attempt up to this time to sue anyone.

Case well handled.

~

78
THE REDEYE SALOON

The Redeye Saloon was located in the south side of the old Pokegama Hotel back in the Sixties. It was one of many bars in Grand Rapids.

I always thought it dark and foreboding. It had a long and narrow door in the front and one in the back leading to the alley. There was a long, old fashioned, wood bar with lots of big plate glass mirrors. The ceilings were made of decorative metal panels.

One night after the 2 a.m. closing the fire department was called to put out a fire in the back of the saloon. After the fire was extinguished an investigation determined that the fire had been set by persons unknown, an arsonist. After talking to several different people, a suspect's name started to form in my mind. I learned the person had been in the bar earlier acting strangely. He had also been observed at the scene of the fire.

I knew the suspect, Cass, was living at the Downtowner Hotel which was one block south of the Pokegama Hotel. I went to the hotel and talked to the   person at the desk who assured me that he was in. There happened to be a maid who had just cleaned his room and had emptied the waste basket. She had noticed a matchbook in it and would I like to see it? I said I would and she got it for me. It had a horoscope written on it. I then went to Cass's room, knocked on the door and he opened it. I asked him if he would walk up to the office at the police department as I had something quite serious to discuss with him. He said he would and showed up a short time later.

After being seated I asked him what he had been doing and had he been at the scene of the fire. He admitted he had watched the fire department working on the fire. After a short time of questioning, I took the matchbook from my pocket being careful to only touch the edges. I unfolded it, laid it out so he could read the horoscope on the cover. I then told him that he may not know it but using a chemical called Neinhydrate we could now get finger prints off of paper. He admitted he had set the fire, the matchbook was his. He then stood there and watched the fire. He was charged with arson.

Cass was appointed a public defender. Also the ACLU came and talked to me. I told them that I thought Cass had some mental problems and I would be willing to work out something with the court system. Cass pled guilty.

His lawyer later came to me and said that Cass insisted he had to plead guilty because the matchbook had his prints on it. The attorney then asked me why he had never seen the matchbook entered into discovery if it in fact had Cass's fingerprints on it. I then told him I had never told Cass his fingerprints were on the matchbook or where I got the matchbook. What I said to Cass when I had showed the matchbook to him the first time was that by using a chemical called Neinhydrate we could now lift a fingerprint off paper. I never said his prints were on the matchbook.

His own mind told him that.

~

79
THE THIEVES WERE VICTIMIZED

Bill Litchke and I had been enjoying a very quiet spring night in our patrol car. Around 2:30 a.m. we headed west on 4th St. Coming to the Grand Rapids Marine boat dealership located in the west end of Grand Rapids, I made a left turn. We headed toward the railroad tracks with the main building to our left. Just behind the building is a fenced in enclosure with quite a few boats and motors sitting on trailers. Bill was in the passenger seat. As we were passing the open gate, Bill said to hold it because he thought he saw some movement. Parking the squad in the gate entrance, we got out slowly and walked to the back corner. There we came upon two men in their thirties next to a trailer with one tire and wheel removed.

After getting identification from them we learned they were both school teachers from Pine City, Minn. They were heading north to do some fishing and had just got past Swan River on Hwy. 2 about 18 miles from here and had a blowout on a boat trailer tire. Leaving the boat with a 70 h.p. motor on it on the side of the road, they headed for Grand Rapids seeking relief from their dilemma, that being the tire and wheel which they were about to take from the Grand Rapids Marine.

After arresting them for theft and doing some paperwork, we released them. As they were leaving I said in jest that they would be real lucky if their motor was still there when they got back as we have a lot of thieves in this part of the country.

In about a half hour we got a call asking us if we had already known. I asked him what he was talking about. He said that upon getting back to the boat and trailer, their motor was missing.

Would you believe when they were out wheeling a deal, someone was out motoring off with their motor?

~

80
THE SHADOW

She trudges through the snow on a cold winter night pulling her sled, worldly treasures piled high upon it.

This old lady with her clothes all bundled against the snow coming down and the blowing wind, where was she going? I know, having seen it so many nights before. Having abandoned her little old shack in the west end of Grand Rapids, she had a new place in the south part of town where a church now stands. It is over the top of Powers Hill.

This night her treasures are heavy. She stops to rest often then leans into her rope to try again. I watch from a distance. The sled barely moves. She does not want help most of the time but this time she relents. I pull my squad car along side and load her sled and treasures into the back seat and trunk. She gets into the front seat. The frail one seems to have nothing to say. Soon we arrive at her new tarpaper shack. She nods her head and a little smile of appreciation appears. We unload the sled, her piles of old newspapers and rags she had picked up on her journey through the alleys this night.

Come early spring she is not seen often, then in the heat of the summer a call comes in to check on the well being of the little reclusive lady. There was no human response to the knock on the door, but there was a response from three or four dogs, very loud and threatening.

Looking through a side window, I could see that this side of the house was completely covered up to around four feet with papers and garbage. The refrigerator door could not be opened. There were canned goods sitting on top that had rusted through and the contents ran down the sides.

The little woman had made a nest just inside the long windows where she had lain for some time. The dogs had not been kind to her.

The first thing we had to do was get the dog catcher Don with his tranquillizer gun. The dogs were scared and vicious but were soon taken care of.

The house was about 30 feet long by 26 feet wide and split down the middle inside by a partition. Entrance could only be gained from one end. As you opened the door you had to climb up on the four feet of trash. The door to the right through the partition could not be entered since that side was filled to the ceiling with papers, boxes and so forth.

With the dogs gone we had to try to figure a way to get the lady out with as much respect as was possible under the conditions. She was slowly pulled through the side window from her nest onto a gurney, leaving all her treasures behind.

Even though she is gone now, I can still picture her in the dim light of winter with the snow coming down, pulling her sled. I don't know if a son or daughter ever found her but she is still part of my memories.

She died alone no family there
She never spent so there must be something there
They came like vultures they search and they tear
They search through her treasures
But there is nothing there

~

81
AIRPLANE DOWN (KING AIR 90)

Trying to bring back recollections of an airplane crash at the Grand Rapids airport 37 years ago, I knew I needed some help.

I talked to Russ Johanssen, who was sheriff at the time. He said someone who had been in the plane crash had gotten out and walked around and got back into the plane. I had not known this. All that I had seen was an unconscious person in the back of the plane.

I went to the airport and talked to an airplane mechanic who put me in touch with Greg Cartie who had been an airplane mechanic since 1970. Greg called me with some very helpful information. He had also been in on the search and rescue along with Dewey Lundgren. With the information from Greg, I was able to find a date of April 18, 1975, and the time of 12:30 a.m. I also located a newspaper clipping with more information.

I will be telling this from my own recollection as a lot of other people got involved that night and each person will have his own memories.

Early on the morning of April 18, 1975, following what had been a somewhat foggy night, the sheriff's dispatcher called me on my police radio telling me that he had just received a call from the National Flight Service in Hibbing reporting that a two engine Beech King Air 90 may be down in the area of the Grand Rapids airport. The plane had not canceled its flight plan. It was emitting an emergency beacon that would turn on when a plane crashes. At this time it was thought that only the pilot was on board.

The dispatcher requested that I go immediately to the airport and check this out. He would notify other emergency personnel.

Arriving at the airport I drove down the runways and could see nothing unusual. Shortly after, Russ Johanssen, Joe Burt, Greg Cartie and others arrived. Since the plane wasn't found in this immediate area, a snowmobile search was started. Everyone was told to look at the tops of the evergreen trees since a descending plane will often shear them off. After an extensive and lengthy search some sheared off tree tops were located some distance from the airport in a heavily wooded area of ridges and valleys. The plane was found and had cart wheeled onto its side.

When I arrived on the scene the entire plane reeked of fuel. There was a concern that it could catch on fire. There was an unconscious person in the back portion of the plane. I was thinking at the time it was the pilot. I do not clearly remember how I got into the plane as it was lying on its side but believe it was through a front window. Crawling to the person in back while sitting on my butt facing the man, I pulled his back to my chest. Then I crab walked on my butt, pulling the man with me several feet to the opening in the front of the airplane. Sheriff Johannsen, Burt and others took over, loading the man onto some sort of a sled pulled by a snowmobile out to the road and on his way to the hospital. I then left to return to my downtown patrol duties. A few days later I heard the man had died. I was still thinking it was the pilot. After talking to Russ Johannsen and Greg Cartie some 37 years later I found that there in fact had been two men in the plane. The man I had pulled to the front was the passenger, Kenneth L. Nelms, from New Brighton, Minn., who died some hours later. The pilot, Martin G. Swinehart, age 39, Monticello, Minn., had gotten out of the plane at some time and after putting out a small fire had returned to the plane. He spent some time in the hospital but did recover.

Isn't it amazing how you may think you know all about a subject but all you really know is your small part in a very tragic event.

Information:
Russ Johannsen
Greg Cartie
Harvey Dahline
Grand Rapids Herald Review
Monday, April 21, 1975--Vol 81 No 32

~

82
CARIN STREUFERT CASE
SATURDAY JUNE 15, 1991

The two young men sit in their little green car, an old Volkswagen. In their early twenties, they are very dangerous, they both know this. They watch and wait. It has taken them a couple years to work each other into this state. Taking a woman off the street. They were going big time, talking it over and building each other up.

They had started with some small crimes, stealing small things: a boat trailer from Ray's Sport Shop in east Grand Rapids, a couple snowmobiles and this last year a very large boat from T&M Marine on the southwest part of town. These items were being stashed at one of their father's farm up the Scenic Highway toward Bigfork.

Earlier this day they had followed a white car with a young blond girl up Hwy. 38 for 12 to 14 miles and had finally given up. They had a gun in the car if ever the time would come. Around 1:00 to 1:30 another blond girl caught their attention as she came out of the Perkin's Restaurant in the Central Square Mall. Not too late, they still had time. To add to their excitement she was very young and pretty. Not heading for a car but walking north over 1st Ave. toward Ice Lake. She was unaware there was a car following slowly keeping pace with her. Then finally after about 10 blocks they decided to make their move. Driving past the girl who was on their right, they turned into a driveway to the right and blocked the sidewalk. Just as they did this the girl turned right up the driveway before them. The driver got out and said something to her, but she ignored them and continued into the house. The night wasn't going as they had planned.

They headed back to the good vantage point of Perkins again, sitting in the dark, waiting. It was now getting past 2:00 a.m. There she was, walking across 4th Street heading for the railroad tracks and then toward the Blandin Paper Mill. Another beautiful blond girl. They repeated their pursuit, staying at a distance. She headed south on the right hand side of the bridge and turned right. The men crept closer, knowing where this would take her. About a block farther there was a left turn that was fenced in with a big gate. As she got to the middle of the gate, the car stopped, the man in the passenger side jumped out, threatening her with the gun, forcing her into their little green car. He knew where he would be taking her as he had hunted this swamp area about 32 miles away many times. They turned, heading up the hill, turning left on Pokegama Ave, and then turning right heading down the River Road, driving past the place where one of them lived.

What was going through her mind, we can only guess, having just moved back from the Twin Cities to her home town where things like this don't happen. She had felt so safe. We do know she seemed quite calm asking them to take her back and drop her off. At this time she had her camera and reddish backpack with her. She sat and waited.

The men at this time seemed preoccupied with little to say, continuing to drive through Jacobson, turning right on Hwy. 65, heading south, passing Mt. Olive Lutheran Church on their left, driving about one mile and turning left off Hwy. 65 at an angle, going down a well traveled logging road. After a short distance they turned right heading back into a small clearing and driving to the end, made a u-turn and stopped.

By now it was getting quite late and sweltering heat filled the small car. They opened the windows for some air but swarms of mosquitoes came in.

They got out having her walk in front of them through the willow brush to a slight rise. They spent some time taking turns holding the gun while fighting off the mosquitoes.

After some time there was a gunshot. A short time passed, then another.

They walked back through the brush wet from a recent rain and through the thick mosquitoes to their car thinking this had not lived up to their expectations. They got into the little green car heading back to Hwy. 65 to go north and home.

Thinking they had pulled off the perfect crime, they told each other to stay calm and be sure to keep your mouth shut. They trusted each other.

Coming to Hwy. 65 and turning right, one of the men looked

down and saw the girl's camera on the floor. They knew they should not be seen with the camera, so one of the men threw it out the window into a grassy ditch just as they were going around a curve. They then drove to one of the young men's home on River Road where they spent the night.

Around 2:00 in the morning, Mary, the girl's mother awoke and began to wonder why her daughter, Carin, was out so late and thinking they would have a "talk" in the morning.

When Mary and Don got up the next morning, Carin was nowhere to be found. At 10:00 a.m. a call was made to the sheriff's office reporting the missing girl. Sheriff Bob Serich called the police department, and after assessing the situation, it was decided something had to be started now as her parents had made calls trying to locate her without success. Both departments were convinced there was something terribly wrong.

It was amazing how quickly all law enforcement came together. No one asked whose jurisdiction it was. A room was set up as a headquarters to centralize information and coordinate the volunteers and law enforcement in the search.

Anne Huntley helped to get information out. Hundreds of posters were handed out. Searches of the woods and houses plus the river were made by hundreds of men and women. Phones were being answered; it seems everybody had something to do. Pat Medure, a deputy sheriff, and I were following up all leads that were coming in by phone plus following any other leads.

As time went on the next few days, we were running 24 hours a day. Bob Serich was coordinating from his office, keeping men in the field checking things out. The police were doing everything they could by checking tips that came their way. But nothing Pat Medure and I checked out seemed to be very solid.

The two men in their little green car drove around looking and listening. No one suspected.

Sunday the little green car arrived later on in the day at the scene of the crime. They had shovels and a pickaxe with them. The girl had been left above ground. She had to be buried. They were growing tired. Try as they might they had only gotten down a few inches because of the hard dirt and entangled roots. They left her there with her reddish backpack on her body a short distance from a trail on a small ridge.

The two men sometimes drove a cattle truck to market in the Cities. Tuesday in the afternoon they were coming home from one of their trips on Hwy. 65, and as they were coming around the curve into the area where they had thrown the girl's camera they could see a line of searchers walking next to each other near where the camera had been tossed. They both knew in their shaky hearts that these searchers were out looking for evidence. Driving on a ways, they parked and waited. After the searchers had been gone for some time, they went back. They searched as hard as they could, but the camera was gone.

They knew what had happened and what was about to happen. The camera had been found and would be fingerprinted. The fingerprints of one of them would be found. The police would be coming after them.

What to do. They argued for a while but then they had the answer. They ended up at the father's house on the River Road.

Their story would be that they were at the Silver Spur on Hwy. 2 when they were approached by some men and forced to go with them. There was also a girl in the car. They had driven to the little field in the woods past Jacobson. The other men had taken the girl into the woods, and after some time they had come back without her. They were then dropped off back at their car. Since they had been with the other men at the time, they would not be able to go to the police as who would believe them? Swanson must have told his parents a story close to this.

Around 1-2 a.m. Wednesday morning the 19th of June, I received a call from Officer Bill Crotteau from my department saying two men had shown up at the sheriff's office claiming to have information on the Carin Streufert case. I arrived at the sheriff's office a short time later where a number of law enforcement people were arriving.

It was my understanding that two men had shown up, Guy Alan Sullivan, age 25, and James Shane Swanson, age 24, saying that they had been indirectly involved in the case. They said they were witnesses at this time and wanted to give information.

Bob Serich and I along with other participating officers decided that we should be talking to our attorney, Bernard Bodien, to see what direction to take this as the two men were saying they had been forced into going with the other men and were witnesses. Now, anyone being forced to do something against their will, even as vile as what we were hearing, has a right to complain to a police officer, and the officer should listen and take appropriate action.

After listening to their complaint, it was decided that the sheriff would talk to Guy Sullivan and that James Swanson would go with Pat Medure and me if he was willing. We would go over all the steps of where they had been and the route taken during the course of the evening. James Swanson was a very talkative fellow and showed us where he had been when he was supposedly forced into the other car.

In just a short time, as we pointed out the inconsistencies in his story, James decided to tell us where Carin's body was. We told him that he was not under arrest and could leave at any time. We had a tape player recording all of this time. Swanson told us he was the one who had forced Carin into the car at gunpoint. We got into the squad car and Swanson directed us through Jacobson to the little field off Hwy. 65. Getting out of the car, he pointed out a certain area and we went in that direction a hundred yards or less through heavy low brush and trees. One of us saw something out of place. A colored item. As we approached the area, we could see it was a back pack placed on a body lying on its back.

Trying not to disturb any evidence, we noted what information we could. The sheriff's office in Itasca County was notified, and they in turn called Aitkin County as we were now in their county and a murder may have been committed there.

Now we had to wait for someone from that county and the BCA. Shortly an ambulance arrived along with the men we were waiting for. It was not too long and there was a helicopter overhead. The news.

Soon we were on our way back to Grand Rapids. Swanson, Pat and I stopped and had a can of soda. Still having the tape player with us, we picked up a lot more information. Before arriving in Grand Rapids around 11 to 11:30 a.m., we told James Swanson that we really appreciated his willingness to come forward as a witness and help us find the girl. Before reaching the court house, we said we felt he had a little more to do with the girl than had come out. But he was also told if he got picked up later he would probably be given a Miranda warning informing him of his rights and if he asked for an attorney we would not be able to talk to him. But if at any time he made a direct request to talk to us, we could talk to him.

We stopped the car out in the parking lot and gave our cards to him, saying good bye and we hope to see him again, and James walked down the street. Pat Medure and I went to get something to eat.

Within an hour we were notified by the jailer that Swanson had been taken into custody and was requesting to speak with us.

Within one or two hours we went to see James. At this time we read him his Miranda rights. He understood, saying that we had treated him right and he wanted to talk to us. Swanson then told us the whole story. After talking to Swanson we then talked to Guy Sullivan. We talked to him for some time but seemed to be getting nowhere. After some time Pat went to get us all a pop. Pat and I had worked many cases together and we knew how to "read" each other. No sooner had Pat left than Guy started to tell me he had done it. He was still talking as Pat came in the room. He looked a little surprised but joined right in like he had never been gone.

Guy told us everything from beginning to the end. It had been James who used the gun to force Carin into the car. Swanson had also been the first to shoot Carin; then after some argument Guy Sullivan had taken his turn with the gun. Now they were both guilty.

When we talked again with James, he told us how they had been planning this for some time even though Guy had a girl friend and a little boy.

About a week later James wrote me a letter thanking me for professional treatment and taking the time to talk to him. He also said he was sorry for what he did but didn't know why he did it.

Also that he was very sorry for the family of the girl he had killed and that they must be having a hard time. He asked me to thank Pat, too, saying he was sorry but being sorry would not bring the girl back and that they should have thought before they did it. At the end he said, "Take it easy and keep on nailing them." Sincerely, James Shane Swanson.

This letter was given to Tom Roy, a jailer, then given to Harvey Dahline on 6-26-91 at 08:56. The letter was entered into evidence.

Since this is a short story, the important things have already been said.

Both James Swanson and Guy Sullivan were tried before juries in District Courts and found guilty of murder and kidnapping and are serving long prison sentences.

To date the camera has never been found.

The search crew walking in the ditch was not looking for a camera or other evidence. They were simply picking up road trash. That was just the conclusion Swanson and Sullivan jumped to.

Also, the girl they tried to pick up by blocking the sidewalk with their car recognized Swanson in court and testified. She knew how lucky she had been.

This case was a classic example of two departments working together as they should to get the job done.

Also, sometimes a guilty mind can be a policeman's best friend.

Locked up and put away.

~

This is a copy of a letter I received from James Swanson:

Dear Mister Dahline I 'am wrighting you To thank You for Your Profesional Adiroude on the gustaning and Having The Pations To Talk To me.

I 'am sorry for what I did, But dout under stand why I did it. I it hot good at spelling can you tell?

I would like you To Help my famly out if you would, may be Talk To them, it is very hard on my dad.

I very sorry for the family of the girl we killed thay must Be Having a hard time with this Too. for me Death is to good.

Would you also thank Pat Medure for me Too.

I wish I could give my life for the girls But it wount Bring Her Back, I wish it would.

well Thanks for what you did, and I am sorry for what I did But sorry Dont Bring her Back, I should have <u>Thought</u> Before we did it.

well you take it easy and keep on nailing em

Sinsarly your

James
Shane
Swanson

JSS
I.C.J

Harvey Dahline
City, Hall, 420 Pokegama Ave. N
Grand Rapids Minn 55744

To M Roy
From Jailod To Hover
6-26-9   Dahnikon
$ 85¢

83
NOT TO JUDGE

In the early 1990's we were having some burglaries in Grand Rapids and Itasca County, one of which was at Chief Products across from the airport.

My investigations led me to a young man named David B. I had known him for several years. He just could not stay out of trouble. Even though we were on different sides of the fence so to speak, we got along well. He would openly say he did not like cops as he had a prior record and had spent time in prison. As my job is to investigate and solve crimes and not to judge, I always tried to treat him with respect.

The evidence was there and he had given me a confession. He had been given some breaks in the case as he well knew. He had pled guilty and was awaiting sentencing as we knew he would be getting some time. While sitting in jail he wrote me a well received letter:

Dear Harvey. How are you man! Me I am sitting here thinking about all the fun that I had when I was in jail. I would like to thank you and all the other cops to. Their is some things that I do not feel good about doing. But I guess I have to face the time. Tomorrow is going to be the hardest time of my life to face. It is really scary thinking about going to prison. I really did try to stay out of trouble. But when I would get around my friends I would always make rong choice. Harvey I would like to say thank you! I really do not like cops at all but I must say you are one of the best. I really did consider you one of my good friends. Hey, I would like to keep in touch with you! I am not going to live here when I get out but I am going to come back. I have to come back and see you and the other cops. you guys are really good people! If it wasn't for my mom and dad and you and the rest of the people from the P.d. I would be dead right now. Every one would make me happy. Every one took my mind off of things. Well enof of that stuff I really hope when I come back you are still the cheif! I would like to say good buy! keep good care of your self! Well I could not leave with out saying good buy and good luck

David B

Harvey I really am going to change my life around! But I just can't say it I will do it!

David did write from prison, but I have not heard from him for some time. The "David's" I have known remind me of the game of baseball. You go to bat for them, some times you strike out, some times you hit a home run.

I hope David is still swinging.

84
ARMY AND NAVY BURGLARY

On Sept 3, 1964, I drove my squad car through the parking lot of the Army and Navy Store. Glen's Army and Navy was a familiar local store owned by Glen Dix of Hill City. The lot was well lit up revealing a large oak tree growing up on the north side of the building with branches reaching the two story brick building. The building at that time was around 125 feet long and 80 feet wide, the upstairs being used as offices.

As I was coming out onto 4th St. (Hwy 2) I saw a brown and yellow 1956 Pontiac going east around 50 mph. As I was about to follow it, a grain truck got in the way followed by a second one. As soon as I could I entered 4th St but the brown and yellow car was not to be seen.

Since it was almost 1:00 a.m., I decided to take a break and go to Mickey's Café. I was almost done with my glass of milk and piece of lemon pie when a middle-aged man, Henry Bennett, came in saying he had just left the hospital and that a man had just come in with a gun shot to his leg.

Wondering why I had not been called, I went immediately to the emergency room entrance which was located in the back of the hospital. The hospital at that time was next to the river on the southeast side of town and is now a housing project.

As the entrance came into view, I could see a brown and yellow Pontiac, the same car that had been speeding earlier. Upon entering the building I was met by 20 year old William Ballard. I asked him what had happened and to whom.

He told me that he and Eugene Boloff had been hunting deer and Boloff had accidently shot himself in the leg with a .44 Magnum pistol. Asking where the gun was, he said it was under the right front seat. I smelled alcohol on the boy and asked if he had been drinking, but he said no. But something else was bothering me. When he could have given me any story, why did he tell me they had been deer hunting which was illegal at that time of year? Also, as this was in the middle of the night, he hadn't had a chance to think up a good story.

I asked if he would mind if I got the gun and checked for beer. He told me to go ahead.

When I opened the passenger side, I saw that the floor was covered with blood. Reaching under the front car seat, I was able to pull out the pistol and some beer cans. I could see some tarps covering up something at least three feet high on the back seat. Pulling off the tarp, I uncovered a mass of rifles, pistols, ammunition, knifes, shot guns, jackets, a sword, camp stove, cameras, binoculars, jeans and other items probably worth ten to fifteen thousand dollars. I'm not too bright but it didn't take a genius to figure this one out.

I still don't know where it was all taken from, and was also thinking that the boy might take off, I went back to the waiting room. The boy was still there. Standing for a couple minutes, I said, "That wasn't too bright since the tags where they came from are still on some items. Tell me about it," And Ballard did.

They had gone into the Army and Navy store. One of them had climbed the oak tree in the back, entered an upstairs window then let the other guy in the door.

Having loaded the loot into the car, they headed west, but as they drove away they could see a car coming up fast behind them, so they pulled into a parking area just past the big pines around 24th St. West. Boloff loaded the magnum then ran behind a tree, waiting to see if the police were coming. At this time he was hanging the gun down his right side. The gun had a hair trigger and went off, going through his upper calf, between the leg bones and out into the ground.

Having gotten this information, I contacted the sheriff's office to send me some help to transport Ballard. Shortly, Morris O'Brien showed up and Ballard was taken to jail.

At the jail I contacted Glen Dix, the owner of the store in Hill City. O'Brien and I went to the hospital to get the car, and to our surprise the car was gone with the loot still in it. There must have been a third party hanging around outside. For some reason Mr. Dix was mad. I could not blame him.

Ballard would not tell me who the other person was but earlier had been to Patterson's store on Pokegama Lake. It was getting close to 3:a.m., but I called the owner of Patterson's and he said he remembered three men in his place and something was said about a grandfather that lived in Remer, Mn. I then called Red, a Cass County deputy who lived in Remer asking him to check for a brown and yellow Pontiac. He called back shortly. He had located the car next to the grandfather's house but the car was empty.

I headed for Remer. Red showed me where the car was parked next to a small cabin. Walking up to what appeared to be a one room cabin, I shined my light through the window and there appeared to be a bunk bed on the far side. The blankets didn't appear normal and there was a stool piled high with something with a blanket over it.

I tried pushing the window up and it slid open. I went in and found most of the loot which had been stolen and then returned to Grand Rapids and a much happier Glen Dix. A 17-year-old boy was taken into custody the same day in Remer.

At the trial, the defense claimed we could not use the loot as evidence as we didn't have a warrant to search the house. The judge asked me if I had a warrant. I replied that a warrant was unnecessary as it was not their house nor did they have permission to use it.

They were found guilty of burglary and sentenced to some prison time.

The tree is now gone from the back of the Army and Navy store. It is a much larger, modern store, having added hunting and camping equipment.

I must confess something here. When I returned from getting the gun from the car and telling the boy that they weren't too bright as the store tags were still on some of the items, this was not true. I had not seen any tags. I took a chance this would get him talking. And it did.

Information:
Harvey Dahline
Herald Review, Ken Hickman picture
Vol 70 No 71 Thursday, Sept 3, 1964

~

85
COIN THEFT SOLVED

Very early in the morning of October 26, 1970, I was patrolling in the northeast part of town and was on 11th Ave. just going around the corner onto Ridgewood Road heading for the fairgrounds. Some headlights were coming in my direction, and about this same time the fire sirens were starting to go off. I turned around in a driveway to get back downtown to see where the fire was. The oncoming car passed me going east and I fell in behind him. He started to go at a high rate of speed down to 10th St., making a left turn and heading for the cemetery past Dick's Distributing. The road ahead joins Hwy. 2 to Coleraine, but at this time some roadwork was being done and barricades were set up in the area.

As I first started pursuit of this car, I notified Dave Bennett in our other squad car downtown of what was happening and our location. As we approached the intersection of Hwy. 2 and 13th St. N.E., the car I was pursuing made a u-turn onto Hwy. 2 heading back downtown past the bowling alley. I was going fast and for some reason could not slow down. I went through the barriers and tore my police antenna off the squad. Continuing up over the grassy boulevard coming out on Hwy. 2 into town and looking down the road, I could see a lot of activity across from the bowling alley. The Figgins family had a two-story house a hundred yards off to the side that was totally engulfed in flames with the fire department already there. The pursued car was still in front of me. As I looked down the road some distance, Dave had his squad parked across the road as a road block. The car I was chasing went around the front of Dave's car and I went around the back heading west on 4th St. We both continued through town for a mile. As I was pulling along side of the car by the big woods on the west end of town, the driver pulled over. He was the only person in the car.

After getting the 19-year-old man cuffed and in the back of my squad, I checked the inside of his car. There was loose change all over. I then asked him his side of the story. He told me he was surprised we had gotten on to him so fast. When I had turned around behind him by the fairgrounds, he thought he had been had. He went on to tell me he had broken into a house some time earlier that evening by the airport and had taken a coin collection valued between $5,000 to $10,000. The thief was from Riverside, California.

He was charged with burglary, reckless driving and no Minnesota driver's license; his friend that had loaned him the car was charged with allowing an unlicensed person to operate his motor vehicle.

I hardly had the heart to tell him I had turned around for the fire, not him.

Again, a guilty conscience can do wonders for law enforcement.

I learned later that I only had the back brakes on my car.

~

86
ARMED ROBBERY
(DENNY'S NORTH STAR STATION)

At 9:55 p.m. on 12-7-1980, I was sitting in the police dept talking to Wally Herschbach of the sheriff's office when I received a call from a woman stating that she had gotten a telephone call, possibly by mistake, stating that Denny's North Star in the south part of town had just been held up and asking her to relay this information to the Grand Rapids Police Dept. I noticed the Sheriff's office was also on the line and asked them to take the call and get any other pertinent information. I then contacted the squad car with Officer Leigh Serfling and Barry Larson in it and informed them of the possible robbery. They were in the south part of town at the time and they responded. Wally and I were also soon on the scene.

We talked to Renee, the cashier and another employee, Robert Larson. There had been three people there at the time. Robert Larson and one other person were ordered to the floor. Renee was ordered to put the money in a bag and then also to the floor. While demanding the money, the robber had threatened her with a pistol and she was scared.

She gave us a description of the man: 6 feet, 170 pounds and had some kind of a stocking cap on. She felt she may have recognized his voice. The person may have been in at 4 p.m., and he may be staying at a house up the road some times. She agreed to show the house to us.

Wally at this time was out following footprints up the alley in the snow. Serfling, Larson and I saw a young man leaving the house and coming in our direction. We stopped him, treating him as though he may have been involved in the robbery. He had been with the suspect earlier in the day. He was quick to get the notion out of our minds, wanting nothing to do with the situation and giving us some information.

The man we were looking for was identified as Joseph Carpenter of West St. Paul and now staying at the Itascan Motel a few blocks away. As we were talking to the boy, his mother showed up and asked us why we were questioning her son. She stated that the suspect had left their house a few minutes to 10:00 in an old brown car, possibly a Chevy.

About this time Wally contacted me saying he had found a ski mask with holes cut in it for eyes. He picked me up and we went back to where he had found the mask. Getting out and following the tracks in the snow for several blocks, I found some brown cloth mitts.

The young boy then took us back to the Itascan and pointed out Apt. 5B. There wasn't a car in the area answering the description given us. I went to the registration desk and asked who was in Room 5B. He pulled out a card which had the name and the car license plate number of a Ford Ltd. He also told us the man had made a call from the room five minutes earlier and that he had a girl with him in the room.

Wally and Barry went to the room thinking we could end up with a hostage situation if we didn't handle the situation just right. We had Wally on one side of the door and Larson on the other. I was to knock on the door rapidly but not loudly. As I knocked on the door someone said, "Who is it?" with a low voice. I said, "Olson, let me in quick." Olson was the name of the other young man. The door came open and we were all over Carpenter.

He was given his rights, the Miranda warning and informed why we were there. We asked him where the car was. It belonged to the girl, Kim. He was taken to the lockup.

We picked up a pair of boots that were wet yet and had the same prints that were in the snow. Behind the motel was the car we were looking for. A wrecker was called to tow it and it was later searched after getting a warrant. Wally and Barry made the search, coming up with a bag with $1500 in it and also a black .22 pistol.

Upon further checking we found Carpenter was on parole out of Ramsey County. He had been previously convicted of armed robbery.

Barry, Leigh, Wally and I took him into a room at the jail for further questioning. I asked him if we could take some clippings from his hair to compare with hairs found in his cap and he said we could. He then asked us if we had found the money and gun. We told him we had. He then said he would give us a full statement of how he robbed Denny's and all his actions after. He took full blame even though he knew he could get 10 years for this.

Leigh had gotten the pictures of the tire tracks and gathered up other evidence to prepare for the BCA lab.

I think it was a perfect example of what can be done when two departments work together. I must commend the Itasca County Sheriff's Dept for their assistance.

Information:

GR Police Dept Investigation Report-Case No 80003254

Scrap Book Pg 9

~

87
MY UNCLE'S HOUSE BURGLARY

In the fall of 1970 I was called to an address of a very irate man in the far Southeast part of town reporting that his house had been entered while he had been out of town. He had returned that morning and he wanted something done about it.

I realized it was my Uncle Ralph Maness's house, my mother's older brother. A nice man but well known for having a short fuse. Middle sixties, 5 feet 5 inches, 145 pounds but a man you would not want to tangle with.

He walked me through the house he had built, showing me things that were out of place. He then took me downstairs to a side closet he thought no one but his family would know about. He told me that some of his firearms were gone.

Of the three or four guns missing I can no longer remember what they were except one that was his pride and joy. It was a very old shotgun that had killed many a deer back in the 20's and 30's and that he still used every year.

He was fixated on the old shotgun. He had serial numbers on the other guns, but the thing that really stood out was that he had replaced the butt pad on the old shotgun with a piece made from an old car tire.

He thought that I was God and that if anyone could catch this thief it was his nephew. Leaving there I didn't think I had anything to work with but knew I had better do something. I went back to the office and sat down to think.

Only one thing came to mind. It was just before noon so I called the newspaper, the Herald Review, hoping to get something out in the next edition.

Some of the guys thought I was nuts that I would be warning whoever had taken the guns, but I had gotten a Sears tractor back valued at $3,000 this way. I had nothing else to work with.

The article came out in the newspaper a few days later. Nothing happened for a couple days.

Then I received a call from a woman living in Jacobson saying her husband had just acquired an old shotgun like the one described in the newspaper, having a butt pad like it was made from a tire. She was now worried that her husband would be in trouble.

I made arrangements to meet the man in Swan River at a prearranged time. He told me he had been contacted by a man who he had known for some time saying he had some guns at a very good price. They had met in Swan River where he received the guns. He had the guns with him now and was very happy to get rid of the hot merchandise. He told me who he had gotten them from and where he lived in the southeast part of Grand Rapids only a couple blocks from the Maness residence.

Soon I was talking to the man that had sold the guns, and he admitted that he had taken them. He was arrested for burglary. The guns were held as evidence for some time then returned to my Uncle Ralph.

With a lot of luck, a good newspaper and Someone looking down

Harvey Dahline

~

88
A HERO

Some of our heroes don't stand out. This one always went about his job in a casual easy manner whether it was a domestic, car accident or a car on fire. Pete Bibich was there when he was needed.

He and I spent many a night together in the squad car patrolling. We had our yarns to tell and good times, too.

One night it was snowing hard, with the wind whipping. I was turning a corner not knowing that the grader had caught a storm drain, causing it to leave a metal spike sticking out from the drain. I had cut the corner, hitting the curb and the spike and blowing the tire out.

Knowing the first person to tell a story sometimes comes out ahead, I picked up the radio mike, called the dispatcher and asked, "Would you send a wrecker to this location as Pete hit the curb and blew out a tire." Pete grabbed the mike from my hand and said, of all things, that he didn't do it, Dahline did.

The dispatcher came back saying, "Go ahead and blame Dahline, everybody else does!"

Everyone knows that directing traffic at night around an accident can be one of the most dangerous things you can do. People get mesmerized with the red flashing lights, and some times they don't slow down, wanting to see what is going on and not looking ahead at the officer trying to direct traffic and slow it down. This is what happened to Pete.

He was out trying to direct traffic on 169 South, over the top of Powers Hill. In the dark, early hours of the morning, a driver for some reason did not see him. He was critically injured with a severe concussion and other injuries. He was taken to the local hospital where it was questionable for some time whether my friend and partner would make it.

It took Pete a long time to recover. But after a lot of rehab he finally came home.

He had been through a terrible ordeal, but after some time he took a position as a dispatcher at the Sheriff's office where he remained until his retirement.

Some times our heroes are those people that just go out and quietly do their jobs.

Pete now spends a lot of time in his wheelchair, the result of doing his job, but you don't hear him complain.

~

89
WAR IS SO IMPERSONAL

I haven't thought of it for years. Sometimes it's like a foggy dream. It comes slipping back into your mind. The sound in the distance, the tree burst, the shrapnel flying above you, your buddy next to you goes down, a large piece of metal sticking out between his eyes, there's only so much you can do, will he make it? Three months later he's back by your side.

Some mornings you're firing your machine gun over the heads of your troops, taking the same hill that is an outpost for observation as they have countless mornings before. Then you see them coming back from your position high on a hill. They come first carrying their wounded on stretchers, struggling to carry their burdens up the steep rugged hill. You work your way down the hill to help, you cannot believe your eyes. A ROK soldier (South Korean soldier) is stumbling trying to do his share. I look again; there is blood down his left side. There is a tourniquet above his left elbow, there is no lower arm.

Some days all is quiet, nothing, but you are always listening. Then off in a distance you hear it. Thump, thump, thump. Mortars are being fired. Are they coming your way? Incoming, you drop down flat to the ground or into your foxhole.

Land all around you, rice paddies, and trees with only a few limbs sticking out but that's all. Buildings are down, barren land. The mud is every where. Some days you may see lines of South Korean peasants carrying baskets on an A frame strapped to their back. There are sixty pound rocks in the basket. The Americans are trying to build a road in the mud. The rocks are used for a road bed to put gravel over.

If you're lucky enough to get off the front line positions to get something to eat a mile or two back you may see things you don't want to see. Little kids with their arms up to their elbows digging in the slop of the garbage cans for something to eat. A six or seven-year-old boy with burlap wrapped around his knees. He has no lower legs. He has cans in his hands and walks like an ape.

Every day you are building fortifications on top of your higher hills. First of all you have to have a large hole fifteen feet across about eight feet deep. The ground is frozen. Now you use a shaped charge to blow a hole ten feet deep and 20 inches wide into the ground. Then you put a 25 pound satchel charge (which is dynamite) into the hole with wires attached. Then you blow a large hole into the ground. After the hole is blown it has to be shaped with shovels. The next step is to carry logs up the steep hill. Actually you are building a small log cabin in the ground with logs for a roof. It is piled high with sandbags on the top to absorb mortar rounds. In the front facing the enemy is an aperture or window opening three feet wide and a foot and a half high. A platform is made of sandbags. Your machine gun sits on the platform and is fired through the opening from inside. The machine gun is a water-cooled, .30 caliber that can fire 400 to 600 rounds a minute but you have to be careful as you can burn out the barrel which would have to be replaced.

The winters are the same as they are in Minnesota, but if you're living pretty much outside, that is cold. Your feet are cold most of the time as you wear pacs and they are not overly warm.

But the spring comes. The beautiful sunshine is so welcome but the rains come with it. You use your poncho or rain gear that slips over your head but are wet a lot of the time.

One time a friend of mine called. I hadn't had a bath or shower for three weeks. He asked me to come visit him. He was back a couple miles with the 155 Howitzers. The big guns can fire for miles so are in back positions. My friend, Gaylord Kuschel, got me some clean clothes, a hot meal and a shower, but all good things must come to an end. Shortly I was back with my group, the 3rd Division 16th Infantry Reg. Company D.

It was good to be home.

One thing you notice in a combat unit is there are very young soldiers. The army likes young men. Many start out thinking they can't be killed. These are just a few of the things I seldom think about any more. So long ago like a fog out of a dream.

I still do remember, 60 years later.

~

90
27 BURGLARIES SOLVED

Some time during the night of April 16th a downtown insurance agency was broken into and money taken. This was to be the first of many over the next few months throughout the Grand Rapids area. Try as we might we weren't getting any closer as to who or how many were doing this.

Then one night my neighbor's small car was stolen and then returned during the night. This very same night the VFW had a break-in and the safe stolen with $2,700 in it. Thinking it must take at least two people to move a heavy safe like that, I checked the stolen car for any signs of a safe being loaded into the hatchback. Once you knew what you were looking for, it was obvious the car had been used to move it.

Now, I also knew that there had to be at least two people to move the safe from its upstairs location. But something else came to mind, why had they returned the stolen car? The answer was that they know the owner and may also live close by.

During the time I was patrolling, I often stopped in bars and just walked through talking to people and stopped at sports events and chatted. It was surprising what information could be learned. Many times you could steer a conversation in the direction you wanted it to go which was what happened the night I hit pay dirt.

As I was walking back to my car from the Legion ballpark, there was a young neighbor walking to her car along side of me. I just said, "Hi." She asked, "How are you doing?" When I replied, "Not so good," she asked me what was going on. I explained that I was working on some break-ins over the last couple months and not having any luck. She very simply responded that she couldn't understand why they hadn't been caught, "They're so dumb." I thought, "What a nice thing to say" and replied, "We're only as good as the people around us, but from what you said, you must know something, and I would really appreciate your help." She replied that she didn't want to get involved. I told her that anything could help me and that she had my word no one would ever know where the information came from. I was thinking I was going to have to figure out how to approach it from a different angle, but she then started to tell me about two boys. One lived close to the Betts family where the car had been stolen and the other lived a short distance away. She also told me some of the dates and places of certain break-ins and the fact that they had put the car back. I thanked the young woman and it was never mentioned again but I did sing a few "Hallelujahs".

The next night the H&R Tire Company in the east end of town was broken into with possibly some good finger prints which I never got a chance to use.

The next few days were spent gathering all the information I could on the two boys who were under the age of 18. The more you know the more power you have questioning them. Some times you think Someone is watching over you. The next day, I struck gold.

In the early afternoon I was called to a home where a young man had slapped his mother. After a short talk in the house I put him in the patrol car and went back to talk some more with the mother. She was doing her best but could not seem to be getting through to him and asked me to see what I could do. Going back to the patrol car in a short time, I found the boy in tears and losing it. Crying, he asked me to give him a break because he didn't think he could handle jail. As I knew him quite well, I laid it on the line. I told him I didn't know why I should give him a break as he ran with the other two boys doing the break-ins and never said a word. You can not believe how much information you can get in 15 minutes!

Now I knew who, what and where some of the loot was and what they were doing with the money. Some was for buying weed, a small motorcycle and so forth. Also, that the safe was in a lake.

Now what do you do? After thinking about it for some time I went directly to one of the fathers. He found it very hard to believe but there were a lot of facts to back up the story. He had been a victim of the burglaries since they had broken into his business too. He knew as a father what he had to do. He then said, "Harvey, what do you want me to do?" I asked him where his son was and he responded that he was at home. The father was to go to his house and say, "Dahline is waiting in his car outside. Go out and see him.

You know why he's here."

Shortly after the boy came out and sat in the passenger seat and closed the door. We sat there for a few moments not looking at each other. We were facing an open garage door a few feet away. Finally I asked, "Where are the tools?" Not looking at me, he pointed to some tools on the garage floor. Just that fast, 27 burglaries were solved. The boy was very cooperative, never trying to shift the blame, saying what started off as a lark got away from him.

I got Deputy Mike Sande and Kirk Skelly from our department to assist me. We still had to get the VFW safe out of Cavanaugh Lake. Rapids Body pulled it out. It was empty of the $2,700.

Both boys appeared in juvenile court and were charged with burglary and vandalism. Pleading guilty, they were given jail time and ordered to make restitution. Since all of the money had been spent, it was hard to pay thousands back.

I have questioned the juvenile court system. Because they are young, they sometimes don't have to face the consequences of what they have done simply because they are below 18 years of age.

I lost track of one of the boys. The other one has gone far beyond my expectations and succeeded in life.

This time we hit a home run.

~

91
NOT A POLITICIAN

Being Chief-of-Police, I didn't think I was or should be a politician. Some things take strange twists.

Sitting at my desk one morning I could see a man at the counter in the outer offices who seemed to be quite agitated. Sue, my secretary, a very efficient person that could handle almost anything that came along, put her head in the door saying, "Harvey, do you have a moment?"

She proceeded to tell me that the man at the counter was somewhat up in the air, having been rejected on an application to get a permit to carry a firearm and saying, "Before I leave here today I will have one."

Telling Sue I would handle it, I went out saying, "Hey, Lou, It is good to see you, it's been a long time." Touching him on the shoulder I asked him to come into my office so we could talk. He seemed glad to see me and I showed him to a chair. We must have sat and talked for a good half hour about many things. It was getting close to noon and I looked at my watch and said I had a meeting soon and was going to have to go. He got up and I walked him out to the hallway telling him it was good to see him and that he should drop back some time soon.

Going back into the office, I sat down. After a while, Sue stuck her head in the door. Looking up I said, "Can I help you?" She said, "I was curious, did he get his permit to carry?" I looked down for a short time thinking, and then said, "It never came up."

I never saw Lou again.

The Mayor Came To See Me

Sitting in my office, I looked up and here was the mayor coming to see me, saying, "Chief, I would like to talk to you about your men going for coffee." It got no further than that as I said, "Isn't that great." He said, "What?" I said, "Isn't it great our guys have a right to take a coffee break every morning like all employees do, only our guys will take a break with the men from other departments so they can exchange information while on their break and not waste time later. The mayor looked at me and said, "See you later. Harv," and walked out.

I have been here a long time and we did have some pretty good mayors, some smart ones too.

We All Lose Our Cool Sometimes

One morning I asked one of my guys to go to the high school to do something that wasn't out of the ordinary. He must have gotten up "on the wrong side of the bed."

He was standing in the hallway door and he just exploded. Ranting and raving, he said it would be a cold day in hell before he would do what had been requested. He was hollering, and everybody was peering out of their offices. I just stood there listening, and all at once you could see it in his eyes that he understood that he had stepped across a line. He looked at me and turned to leave.

I said, "Hold it, step into my office." He looked at me and followed me in. Shutting the door, we sat for a couple minutes, and then I said, "You know what I'm going to do?" He said, "No" "I'm going to give you this one. You stepped over the line today; it had better never happen again." And it never did. He was a good cop.

Disruption in the Department

Shortly after becoming chief I became aware that a problem was developing within the department.

One of the men was taking sick time off that was questionable. Was he really sick as he was seen at nearby casinos and also coming from that direction late in the mornings? If a man calls in sick it can be disruptive as the shifts of other officers have to be changed.

This morning I was met by five or six officers, complaining about this officer and what was going on. They wanted something done; in fact, some of them wanted him fired. NOW.

I listened to them and they wanted me to tell them what I was going to do. One thing you do not want to do is make rash decisions with five or six men telling you what to do at the same time even though what they are saying sounds right.

I told them I would be thinking this one over and make a decision at the right time. I heard one of them say, "Boy, he sure can't make a decision."

This was not an emergency. As soon as I was by myself, I began to think: was he a good officer, does he do a good job overall, how long has he been here? Weighing his positives and negatives, part of my answer was, yes, he had been a good man in the department for years. In fact, probably better than some of the men who were complaining that morning.

Do I pull him in to talk to him? He has certain Tennyson rights which are rights for workers in the work place. He could have Union rights. From the information I had, could something be done now?

As I had done in the past, I took it to bed with me. Very early in the morning, I woke up with my answers. The next morning, not going through all the hoops, questionings or warnings, I decided I had the information to act now.

I sat down and wrote him an official letter telling him that as he was well aware of that what he had been doing was very disruptive to the department and causing much turmoil within, he would be getting two days off with no pay. Also at the bottom of the page was a paragraph explaining the steps he could take if he did not like my decision.

Later that morning I called the officer in and handed him the letter of reprimand. I asked him to read it which he did. After reading it, he seemed to get tight in his face and a little red. He then opened the door and stepped out. At this time it looked like the door was about to be slammed shut. Then standing right there he stepped back in. Looking at me he said, "You know I've really got this coming."

I then knew I had made the right decision.

This officer and I worked many investigations over the next few years. I have always had a deep respect for him as an officer and friend.

There is one thing I always try to hold to but as the Good Lord knows I have failed many times. At the end of the day it is not how many did I please but did I please myself. Did I call the shots the best I could?

There is something that I have learned about power. The less you try to use it, the more you have. People will follow good leaders.

~

92
A LITTLE ENCOURAGEMENT

We were holding interviews to hire a secretary for the department and had several good applicants. Carol seemed to meet all of the requirements but was extremely nervous. Some of the other interviewers thought due to her nervousness she might not be a good fit. After watching and evaluating her, I felt she was nervous not only because she wanted the job but also because she really needed it. After explaining to the others my observations, she was hired.

After she had worked for a couple months, I called her into the office. I always knew the right thing to say? I said, "Carol, I notice you have been making a few mistakes." You could see her heart jump into her throat; I knew I had not chosen the right thing to start with this time. I continued, "But that's great because it's only if you don't do anything that you can't make mistakes. However you never make the same mistake twice. I have never had anyone come into the office and learn so fast and do so much. You keep it up."

About a month later Carol was standing in my doorway. She said, "I just wanted to let you know that little talk we had gave me so much confidence, you can't believe it. I just wanted to thank you."

Later we lost her to the sheriff's office.

Our loss.

~

93
TWO GUILLOTINES

Its 3:00 a.m., a quiet night. I received a call from our radio dispatcher saying that the night watchman from Blandin Paper Co. was on the phone and had been seeing a lot of activity at the Gambles store. A lot of people were going in and out carrying things.

The Gambles store was located on 1st Ave. NW just up from the paper company and a block next to what is now the New China Restaurant.

I drove down to the paper mill corner so I could see two sides of the block. One officer covered the far corner of the same block. No one could be seen. Then going to the door of the Gambles store, I noticed the lower half of the heavy plate glass door had been broken out, leaving the upper half with a V up the middle just hanging there. We went in and out several times ducking low under the glass.

One time just after we came out, straightened up, turned around and looked back, the heavy upper glass came crashing down like a guillotine.

Seeing that is something to remember.

After making sure there wasn't anyone in the store, we checked the alley of the block and the roof tops. That only left a couple places they could be. Being very quiet as we climbed the stairs in the Miltich building, we got to the landing and listened. After a bit I could hear someone walking around in one of the apartments and then a lot of talking. Going to the door, I knocked. It was quiet for a few minutes. Then a young man opened the door trying to hide the merchandise that was all over the floor behind him. He could not.

Three young men soon appeared in juvenile court.

But this story is not yet complete.

A year or so later I received a call of an accident. A car pulling a boat trailer was going south across the railroad tracks on Pokegama Ave. The boat trailer had come unhitched in the area of the tracks, the car kept on going with the trailer heading for the corner of the McAlpine building, but its right tire hit the curb making it head for Mickey's Café (now Edward Jones) which had a big heavy plate glass window about six feet high and eight feet wide by the entrance door.

The trailer tongue went through the bottom half of the window leaving the upper half in a V shape hanging there.

I was standing talking to a man out on the road some forty feet away when I looked and there was a young blonde-haired boy six or seven years old, bending over looking at the broken glass right under the upper glass still hanging there.

I hollered loud, "Get the hell out of there and I mean now!" The boy was startled and ran to the man I had been talking to, the father. The dad immediately turned to me looking very angry and started to say something. Then we both saw it. The window came down like a guillotine with a horrible crash.

If his son had still been standing there looking?

The father now understood. I talked to him today as he made his rounds. After all those years, we are still friends.

~

94
A BLESSED EVENING - A TRAGIC ENDING

The two young men had known each other for years and were the best of friends. Recently they had gone deer hunting together enjoying the out of doors. One of them had carried on his hip his .44 cap and ball pistol just in case.

Tonight was a new season, a season of joy, and they were looking forward to sharing this Christmas Eve with their friends.

The evening was going well when Mark decided to remove his cap and ball pistol from its glass case. He was looking it over and admiring it when his friend Paul walked by; not thinking, he pulled the trigger on the "empty gun". There was a loud deafening sound in the small room. Paul looked shocked but just stood there. Realizing Paul had been struck by a bullet in the left arm and lower chest, his friends immediately made a call for help.

It was a slow, quiet Christmas Eve in the late 1970's, one I will never forget. I received a call to go to a residence on the NW part of town close to the business area. There was a report of a possible shooting with someone injured. I was only a short distance away in my squad car and knowing the house, I was there in a short time.

While approaching the house in my car, I saw a young man walk by a large picture window.

I walked in and observed the same person I had seen from the car walk over by a stove and sit on the floor. He appeared very alert and rational. It was Paul, and he told me that Mark had accidently shot him with an old pistol. Something he repeated more than once as we were observing the situation. There was nothing we could do for him as we waited for the ambulance.

I talked to Mark while we were still at the house. He could not comprehend that the gun was loaded as he thought he had unloaded it after deer hunting.

Paul was at the hospital around 8:00 p.m., still lucid and appearing very strong. We were hoping and praying for him. After some time he was taken into the operating room.

The wound was too severe. He did not make it.

Who was to blame? All Mark did was "touch" the trigger of an "unloaded" gun and he lost a friend.

Two weeks later, Mark was charged with reckless use of a firearm.

A tragic ending to a blessed evening---

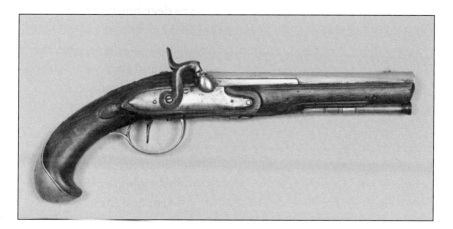

~

95
APPREHENDING A MURDERER

On December 13, 1979, the Grand Rapids Police Department was contacted by the Duluth Police Department asking us for assistance in locating a Bill Helenbolt believed to be in this area. Their department was doing an ongoing investigation in the homicide death of Robert Noffsinger.

They had developed information leading to the issuance of a warrant on Helenbolt for the murder of Noffsinger.

I was assigned to the case and soon was working closely with Robert (Beefy) Lawson of the Itasca County Sheriff's Office.

As I remember, we worked the afternoon trying to find relatives or friends of Helenbolt in the area. Toward dark we had located a house on the airport road a short distance south of the airport. We approached the house and a short time later Helenbolt was taken into custody with little resistance.

Recovered at the time was a large, expensive coin collection which was related to the Noffsinger murder case. He was taken to the Itasca County Jail and the Duluth Police notified.

Shortly thereafter the following letter was received from Milo S. Tasky, the Chief of Police for the Duluth Police Department, February 20, 1979:

Harold L. Snyder, Chief
Police Department
Grand Rapids, Minnesota 55744

Dear Chief Snyder:

During our recent investigation into the homicide death of Robert Noffsinger, we requested and received immediate and extensive cooperation from the Grand Rapids Police Department.

I would especially wish to thank Officer Harvey Dahline for the diligence he displayed in gathering evidence for the Duluth Police

Department. The time and care expended by your department and particularly Officer Dahline, is a tribute to your interest. The cooperation extended by your department in an investigation that did not directly involve your own jurisdiction is in the finest tradition of professional law enforcement.

Please accept my personal thanks and the appreciation of the entire Duluth Police Department. If I can be of any assistance to you or your department, you may be assured of my readiness to cooperate.

Sincerely,
Milo S. Tasky
Chief of Police

Case NO 79000104 Grand Rapids Police Department
Arrested For Murder on 1-13-79
Bill Helenbolt
By Officer Harvey Dahline and B. Lawson

~

96
MY DAUGHTER BETH'S ACCIDENT

Our family was avid followers of the Grand Rapids Indians Wrestling team as I had been on the 1952-53 team. My four sons followed in my footsteps with some doing quite well. My beautiful daughter, Beth, was a wrestling cheerleader back when they still had the Indian headdresses with orange, black and white feathers that went down to their waists. They had matching brown leather skirts, vests and moccasins and were stunning.

Coming back from the Cities in March twenty some years ago after watching the Mn State Wrestling Tournament, something happened that could shake your faith in God.

My wife and I were following our daughter who was driving her car with our grandson strapped in a car seat in the right front. Dorrie was driving while I read a book. About thirteen miles this side of McGregor, my wife exclaimed, "Harvey, look!" We had just come over some very large hills and was about a quarter mile from a large corner going to the right. We were a couple hundred yards behind Beth. Looking up, I could see a tan Pontiac coming at a high rate of speed on the curve trying not to go in the ditch on his right. The snow was flying on the shoulder. As he was sliding, he managed to get his left front tire on the tarred main road. As the tire caught the dry tar, it threw the car into a spin. Now the car was going down the road backwards and across the center line. It was too late for Beth to brake. The two cars came together in a horrible collision. Beth's car went under the Pontiac, pushing the back wheels to the driver's door. As we watched Beth's car go under the other car, we thought no one could live through that.

Then miraculously the two cars snapped apart. My daughter's car stayed almost in the same spot, the Pontiac some 20-30 feet away.

Doris pulled up a short distance from Beth's car. As I jumped out I noticed a small house up the road on the right side. I told Doris to go and call for an ambulance and a wrecker. In the stress of the moment I lost my glasses in the snow. In the meantime, without knowing the extent of anyone's injuries, Doris had driven up to the small house to make the call.

As I ran up to Beth's car, things didn't look good. The driver's door was locked. I told her to unlock her door but she just looked at me in a state of shock. Hoping, I ran to the other side. The passenger side was unlocked. Her 9-month-old son, Nick, was still in his car seat. He had a large bruise on his head and had bitten a small portion off the end of his tongue. The dash had an indentation a quarter of an inch deep and four inches across.

I was able to remove the boy and give him to a Good Samaritan. Why remove the boy? For one thing to be able to get to his mother and the other was fear of fire because the vehicle had driven under the other car's gas tank. After getting the driver's door unlocked I was better able to assess the injuries to Beth. Her knees had been driven into the dash. Thank God she still had her seat belt on. She was in great pain as the seat belt had bitten deeply into her flesh and some contact had been made with the steering wheel. She was conscious, but seemed to be in shock. I thought she had some broken ribs and possibly internal injuries.

Upon returning to the accident scene, Doris could see no sign of Nick and was looking for him, fearing the worst, seeing his empty car seat on the trunk of a car. Soon a young man approached her and asked if she would help his girlfriend with the baby because she was nervous holding him. Nick was screaming and bleeding from his mouth. Doris later told me that the people in the house had heard the crash and had already called in.

The young man in the other car had a broken shoulder as he was going backwards at the time of the collision which pushed him back into the seat.

A highway patrolman showed up shortly followed by the ambulance. The ambulance driver said he would take the injured to the Aitkin Hospital but I said, "No way since the distance is about the same to Grand Rapids." Doris rode in the ambulance holding a crying Nick and with Beth in the back moaning. Arriving at the hospital they were examined by a doctor. Beth had some internal injuries and bleeding. Thank the Lord, she looked like she was going to make it. Today she still bears the scars where the seat belt killed the skin and flesh. Nick survived, losing part of his tongue among other injuries.

For the next two to three weeks Beth and her family lived with us as Beth's husband Jim had to work and they needed constant care. I, with my wife and her husband Jim, were up with them often. For one thing, Nick was still nursing but with a sore mouth was not too happy. Beth needed help even getting up to go to the bathroom. Many were the nights I would hear her very low, "Dad." She had a hard time breathing and I would go to her, my only daughter.

The boy driving the other car did not have permission to have the vehicle and at the time was speeding to catch up with some friends. Later he went home and told his mother some woman had hit him from behind.

I did find my glasses in the snow as we were leaving the scene.

The driver of the other car was ticketed by the highway patrol.

Lesson learned: If you don't have your seatbelt on, it can't save your life.

~

97
TWO NAKED BOYS

Two boys, Ron and Keith, were at Ice Lake fishing off the shore as they had done before. The 12 year olds were always together, the best of friends. The summer had gone; fall was approaching as well as a new school year. Not too much exciting had happened but that was about to change.

They left the shore walking and heading home proudly with a small fish, the catch of the day. At this time Rick and Randy had been tooling about town in their father's car. The summer had gone fast for them, too. They weren't looking to get into some mischief but what could they do? Here it was right in front of them, too good to pass up. Two young boys, younger than themselves carrying their fishing poles and a small fish that should have been thrown back into the lake.

The two older boys pulled the car to the edge of the road, blocking their passage, waiting. As the two boys approached, they stopped them and began giving them a bad time. Pushing the two younger ones around, swearing at them, saying how tough they were as one of them was a wrestler.

One of the two older boys had a jackknife in his hand. Taking the fish, he stabbed it several times and then poked its eyes out.

They thought that the younger boys didn't seem too bright by allowing themselves to be pushed around like that, not fighting back. Well, they had had their fun for the day. Laughing, getting into their car, driving off. This was something they would always remember. The looks on those kids' faces, they were so scared they couldn't even think.

There was something Ron and Keith could do. They ran over a half mile home and soon were telling Ron's mother, Doris, what had happened.

Quickly Mother Bear was on the phone calling her police officer husband, Harvey, home from work. At this time Mother Bear, whose knees were shaking, seemed more traumatized than the boys.

The two boys then began giving a very detailed description of the car the other boys had. They told what had taken place, including the fact that one boy held a knife while they were being threatened. I looked at them and said, "Just one question, did you . . .?" They knew what I was about to ask. Yes, they remembered the car license number.

I arrived at a house later, noting a car sitting in the driveway which matched the description and the license number I was looking for.

My knock on the door was answered by a polite gentleman asking what he could do for me. Could I step in and explain my reason for being here? I explained to the gentleman the situation including the knife. He told me he was the father. They had come home a short time ago and were now out in the sauna. He said he did not condone the actions of the boys and to do what I thought was appropriate. Thanking the father for his discernment in the matter, I was on my way to the sauna. Sometimes, I wonder if they make fathers like this any more.

I thought for a moment, thinking a direct forceful approach was called for. Coming to the sauna door, I pulled it open, slamming the door, stepping into the small space. Two naked boys sat there with fear on their faces, not at first knowing what was going on. One mad cop standing over them, glaring, not mincing any words. Words perhaps better not written here, asking what they had to say. They were speechless. They had gone too far and they knew it. I left slamming the door.

The fear of God can be a great thing, the father was waiting.

Due to the discretion of the officer the two boys did not appear in court. Some boys do learn!

~

98
RUNNING WITH THE HOUNDS

The morning of September 1, 1963, a Tuesday, I became aware of an incident taking place in Deer River. I understood while the Chief of Police Dewey Mattfield, was directing traffic for a funeral at the intersection of Hwy 2 and 6, he heard some kind of disturbance up the street. Tires were squealing, looking, he could see a man hanging onto the side of a car. As the car accelerated, the man fell off onto the street.

Mattfield was to learn later that two men had just robbed the Rendezvous Bar at gunpoint, going outside stealing a car. The owner was hanging onto the side of the car trying to stop them and had fallen off onto the street.

At a later date, I talked to Chief Mattfield. He related to me how he had gotten into his patrol car to give chase up Hwy 6 north at a high rate of speed attempting to get the car pulled over. Lights and siren on, he pulled along side waving them over. They just kept going. One of the men, the passenger, could be seen pointing a large caliber hand gun at Mattfield through the window.

Mattfield had been reluctant to shoot at them still not knowing what had taken place earlier; the robbery or that the car had been stolen, so he had fallen in behind them with his patrol car. At this time other law enforcement in the area were being alerted as to what was taking place.

Approaching the Talmoon area, the stolen car lost control going off a sharp curve into the ditch and into brush and trees.

Mattfield going at a high rate of speed had over shot where the car had gone off the road. Backing up then running to where the two fugitives were disappearing into the woods. Upon checking the car it was found there was blood on the seats, at least one of the men had been injured.

This was to be the start of an intensive manhunt that was to take place over the next four days.

Sheriff John Muhar was asking for volunteers. Highway patrolmen, police, game wardens all stepped up as well as 55 members of the National Guard. This is how I became involved in the manhunt.

We were searching on the edge of Hwy 46 about 3 miles south of

Squaw Lake. It was in this area Sheriff Muhar said that the two men had been spotted at 9 PM Thursday night by the deputies. The deputies had ordered them to halt and shot in the air. Apparently unconcerned the fugitives dashed out of the spotlights into the darkness and thick hazel brush.

A motor patrol was set up immediately around the triangle formed by Hwy 46, the Max Road, and a part of the Dixon Lake Rd.

During this time an attempt was made to alert all persons in the area including fishermen to lock their car doors and remove their keys.

Blood hounds had been brought in from the Cities to help with the search. Russ Johanssen, a game warden, was running with one of the hounds. I was running with another while carrying a 32 Winchester carbine.

The handlers of the bloodhounds each had to have an armed man running with them that could keep up with the hounds as they were always pulling at a running pace and could keep this up for extended periods of time.

Some of the area we ran through was called the Avenue of Pines. Much of it was matted pine needles with large pine trees so the trail we were following was at a running pace.

A couple hours later word came that a fisherman's car had been stolen from a landing at Biauswan Lake two miles west of the center of the search. Apparently the fugitives had crossed Hwy 46 some time during the night, and then finding the car---a station wagon with the back door unlocked, had shorted its ignition system and headed west. It was recovered a week later in Grand Forks, North Dakota.

There is nothing as exciting as running with the hounds.

Somewhat dejected, we headed for home.

There is a story that some years later, George Porter, a deputy sheriff formerly a highway patrolman was told be Ed, a prisoner at the county jail that he and a friend had been the two men that day in Deer River.

By this time nothing could be done as the statutes of limitations had run out.

But of course, this is just a "story".

Oct 30, 2014   ∼

99
HANDCUFFED TO A TREE

In the early 70's we were having a lot of petty break-ins around town. Not a lot taken but it was starting to add up. It seemed to be younger boys as we could tell from the snow prints. Picking up information had not been too good.

While I was talking to a boy who seemed to know something, he started telling some of the things that three boys had been doing. I believe they were 15 to 16 years old. He said they had just rented a room at the Holiday Inn on South Pokegama Ave. and were living it up.

I then went to the motel and asked at the desk about the boys and which room they were in. As we approached the room, a man told me three boys had just run out the back door.

This wasn't bad as it had just snowed and I could see their tracks this early afternoon. Within one to two blocks I caught up to one of the boys but the other two kept going. I handcuffed the boy onto a tree then took off after the others. I then chased the two way back in the woods for the better part of two hours before finally catching them by the river. After I took the two boys to the police station, I then went back to where I had left the handcuffed boy.

I don't know what he was worried about; even though it had snowed it was quite warm. He had started to think I wouldn't be back and he would have to spend the night there. After all that time he seemed happy to see even me.

He was very talkative and soon I had all the information I needed.

Getting back to the police station one of the boy's mothers was there with the father. The Mrs. was a hothead. To put it nicely, she was a very forceful person. Asking why I had her son, she said she knew her rights and that I wasn't going to talk to her son without her or her husband present.

Already having all the facts from the other two boys, I took him into an office to get his side. The boy seemed very willing to talk and get things cleared up. He knew he had been had. But as I would ask him a question the mother would butt right in with the father not saying a word. This went on for a good half hour. Then the unbelievable happened. The man stood up, looked at his wife and said, "Get your hind end out of here and let the man do his job" and took her out. She had the most unbelievable look on her face but she uttered not a word.

The boy and I had a nice conversation. It was over in five minutes. He was then released to his parents knowing he would be appearing in juvenile court.

I did thank the husband for being so understanding. She left without saying a word.

Although I will always remember her name, the names have been omitted to protect the husband.

~

100
FIRE CALL (SOMEONE INSIDE)

Early one morning I received a call from the sheriff's office with the dispatcher saying a fire alarm had gone off at the Rainbow Inn which is located just east of town. Saying he had no one in the area to respond, would I check it out for him?

Arriving at the motel, I couldn't hear any alarm going off but thought I had better be thorough just in case.

But where should I start? It is a very large two story building. The hard part is that each room is set back from the hallway some 2 ½ feet so each room has to be checked individually. I started at the end of the second story, trying to hurry, looking for smoke and listening for a fire alarm in each room.

Getting about half way down the hallway, I saw a man come out of a room and wave to me. Running down the hall to where he was standing, I could see smoke coming from under the door of a nearby room.

I pounded on the door, no response. It looked like a solid door and it was. I hit the door a few times, but didn't budge it a bit. The fellow close by looked solid so I asked him for a little help.

I'll tell you, this is not like in the movies where you flick your foot up and the door goes down. We hit the hardwood door four or five times before it gave way. The smoke rolled out and it was moments before I could see the mattress was on fire on a corner of the bed. There was a large naked man on the other side, around 230 pounds, unconscious.

I tried to move him; it was not easy. He was so floppy, dead weight. For some reason, I hit him on his bare bottom hard with the flat of my hand. He immediately responded by becoming more rigid and easier to handle. By the time we had dragged him out into the hallway, he was more conscious.

We then dragged the mattress outside. It was obvious he had been drinking heavily and smoking in bed.

The Rapids fire department showed up very quickly as they usually do and took over the whole situation, leaving me to return to my downtown duties. Sometime later I was honored at the annual fire department banquet for possibly saving a life.

~

101
SURPRISE WITH A SNARL

The little black coupe slipped into town. No one saw them until they were sitting at the only stop light in town. This was in the early 50's and early in the morning. Cold winds whipped the falling snow through the darkened streets.

Two men could be seen in the little car. What were they doing here? They did not belong, you could feel it. In this snow storm no one had been on the streets for hours.

They turned west on 4th St. driving slowly, seeming to be slowing at each intersection. It was easy to follow at a distance with my lights out having done this many times before.

They drove to Miner's grocery store on the west side of town, then made a left across the railroad tracks, headed back into the downtown business district, and went up and down a couple of alleys.

It was time to show myself, headlights on pulling close in behind the little black coupe in the Marlon block in downtown. I could see the driver attempting to adjust his rear view mirror through the small back window so he would be able to see the police car behind him with the light on the roof. I got their license number and wrote it down just in case.

The car then drove to the main street turning right across the bridge and up Powers Hill going south the way they had come. They appeared to be heading out of town. A half mile farther I pulled the car over. In the 50's this area was a very desolate area with all trees, no buildings or lights of any kind. The snow coming down thick and hard, and having on my long coat with a large fur collar, I got out of the squad car. I had my right hand in a pocket holding my small .38 Cobra, barrel pointed up.

I could see the two men sitting very still with no movement. I walked up to the car which had two windows on the side, a large driver's side window and a very small window where a back passenger seat would be. As I approached the driver's side, he rolled down the window. Leaning over to the window to ask for a driver's license, I was about six inches from the open window when a large German shepherd lunged loudly and viciously with his head out the window from the back seat. Needless to say, I was startled and removed myself with the utmost of speed to a safe distance. They say something like this can raise the hair on the back of your neck. It did mine.

The driver was a very lucky man. At the time this happened my finger was on the trigger of my little pistol and pointed in his direction (this he never knew).

After the driver got the dog under control and I got both parties' driver's licenses, I checked them out as well as the car. They both were a little older and seemed easy to get along with but did tell me they had just gotten out of St. Cloud Penitentiary recently. They were just out seeing what some of the small towns in the north looked like.

Of course, being a small town cop, I believed all of this. But as they drove away, I bet they were laughing about how fast a small town cop could move.

~

102
JUST LIKE ME

They both had strange beginnings in life but were destined to meet.

Sally was a beautiful little girl, dark brown hair, hazel eyes. An impish smile that could take the heart right out of her mother and, of course, dad was taken in as well.

They lived in a small suburban home outside of the Cities with a small pool on a couple acres, a few trees and a small dog. Life was good, they had everything they had dreamed of, and then tragedy struck.

Sally's mother had to go shopping and run some errands, leaving dad in charge. He had always been the most trusted of fathers. After mother left they were doing some household chores. Because it was such a nice day, they decided they would go out and bask in the sun on a couple lounge chairs. Sally drifted off to sleep, dad was not far behind. After some time he woke up feeling it was a great way to spend a day. He then looked over to Sally; she was not there, probably in the house. Getting up he walked into the house, no Sally there either. A little concerned, he thought "No' and ran to the swimming pool. She had been told never to go there without one of her parents. Thank God, he couldn't see her anywhere. Turning to leave he saw something under the pink raft in the corner of the pool. Running and jumping in, pulling Sally up out of the water onto the dry tiles. She didn't seem to be responsive.

Not knowing what to do, he lifted her up, face down. Some water seemed to come from her. Laying her down he tried to do some mouth to mouth. Seeing the phone on the table by the chair and dialing 911, he gave the dispatcher some fast information. Then he was back to giving her mouth to mouth the best he could.

It was not long, although it seemed like it, until the ambulance was there. They took over getting her into the ambulance, heading for the hospital only a short distance away. The mother was called; it didn't look good.

Some time later as they were talking to the doctor, he told them that she had a strong heartbeat. She was on life support. They wouldn't know anything for perhaps a week as she was now in an induced coma; no one knew how long she had been without oxygen.

About the same time the dispatcher was taking the call on Sally, a call was being taken about a car accident and a roll-over.

Ben, a young boy was being driven from across town where the mother now lived. As his parents were separated, the mother had just called Ben's father, saying if the boy wasn't there in half an hour, she was calling the police. The father hadn't sobered up from the night before, having tipped the bottle up a few times also that morning. Ben was sitting in the front passenger seat not strapped in, as his father had no time for that type of nonsense. As they were driving around a long corner, he saw a young man driving like he might come across the center line.

"What is the matter with those people giving out those driver's licenses anyway?" Then his right front wheel was off the road into the ditch and the car was rolling over. Ben's father was still in the car but Ben was found some 20 feet off to the side.

Someone saw the accident and called it in. Soon the police arrived with the ambulance. Unbelievably, Ben's father seemed to be OK. Ben appeared to have a broken arm. It also appeared that he had damaged the side of his head. The ambulance took Ben to the hospital where he was examined and a specialist called in. It was found that Ben would have to have surgery as pressure was building in his brain.

Ben's father was given a breath test which turned out to be .29. He was then booked into the county jail and arrested for driving under the influence. Ben's mother, notified by the police, was soon at the hospital and told he was already in the operating room.

As his mother sat waiting, she started to think, where did everything go wrong? They had a wonderful marriage for five years until Ben had been born. He had been a beautiful boy, easy to take care of, a mother's joy. Something happened to Ben's father. He didn't seem to like his son, saying, "You seem to think more of him than you do of me."

She knew this was not so, but he had started to stay out late, coming home drunk, until at last she couldn't take it any more.

Shortly, the surgeon came out to her saying he had done all he could. The boy may have suffered some brain damage, only time would tell. After Ben's surgery, he was breathing on his own but a lot of healing had to take place before much could be expected. His mother was by his side every moment. Ben's father seemed to be fading from the situation. He called the first day but hadn't been heard from since.

After Sally had been in a coma for a couple weeks, the doctor tried to bring her out. Hours had gone by, her eyes seemed to be making some movement and then they were open. She did not know where she was. Her thoughts---there were some---there was someone by her bed. There was a ---her thoughts---pretty woman.

The doctor said it was going to take time, that she could end up being somewhat impaired. She seemed to be gaining some muscle control over her body but her reactions seemed to be quite slow.

The nurses would be taking her to some physical therapy, but it would probably be a month or so before she would be coming home. She would need lots of care.

It had been some weeks now. Ben, after all he had been through, was doing remarkably well. He would no longer have the use of his arm due to the brain damage but that was expected.

His thought process was slow with a speech impediment. He would be thought of as a special needs person but could still go on and have a good life although with some limitations. He was finally with his mother who would do her best to guide him through his next few years.

Sally's parents were having a rough time of it. As a mother, try as she might, could not get over the thought that he should have been more watchful. This was her husband's fault. They had many a fight over this but were now in counseling. They realized it was going to take both of them to raise a special needs child, one they both dearly loved.

On the day they brought her home, they had a cake and other decorations for her birthday.

So, a new life began for Sally. As time and years passed, she realized she was not like her friends. They all seemed to have boyfriends, but though she was very pretty, no one seemed interested in her. She sometimes was lonely. One time she heard her parents talking, concerned about her future. She was nearly 24 years old and had worked a few jobs but was now working for the ODC (Occupational Disability Center). She still appeared to be quite happy.

As time went on, Ben was growing into a nice young man even though he did have some limitations. He was a hard worker through high school and had been the wrestling team's manager.

Out of school now and having worked for Mann's Theaters for a few years, Ben went far beyond what his mother could ever have expected. He recently had been promoted to manager.

One evening he saw a pretty young lady walk in to get a ticket, hanging back somewhat from her friends. She seemed to be having a bit of trouble trying to get across what show she wanted to see. Thinking he could help, he listened and thought, "She's a lot like me." Starting to say something, he was tongue tied. He backed off. This had never happened to him before.

Sally looked at him and smiled. Getting her ticket, she followed the others into the show.

That dark brown hair, those hazel eyes. Ben could not get her out of his mind. But she could never be interested in him, the way he talked and the arm that was useless. Later, after the last movie was over, he saw her friends walk out. She went to the restroom, and then left the theater.

Ben had his closing to do and then he was walking out the door. Looking up, turning, there was the hazel-eyed girl standing at the corner of the theater as though she was waiting for someone; it was quite late and getting dark.

Ben didn't know what to do. He wanted to ask her if he could help but could not seem to move. She looked like she was lost. Finally he walked to the girl, saying, "I'm Ben, the manager of the theater. Could I help—help—help?"

The girl looked at him for a minute, stumblingly saying, "My name's, Sally, friends---left---me---forgot."

Ben said, "Let's walk to the Dairy Queen---just---just---over there. We could call your parents." At that she smiled. He bought her a small cone while she called the number.

As they waited sitting at the table, she thought, "He's like me." He seemed very nice and for some reason she didn't feel so alone.

As they sat there, they didn't seem to have much to say, glancing at each other once in a while.

Her parents showed up shortly, showing some concern. They

were both nice looking, their hair starting to gray. They hurried over to the table where Sally and Ben were sitting. Introducing themselves they thanked Ben for taking their daughter under his wing. Saying it was getting quite late and thanking Ben again, they headed for the door. Sally, getting up, standing for a moment, put her hand out to shake his good hand. Managing to say thank you, walking to the door, she looked back once then was gone.

Ben just sat there for some time thinking that he probably wouldn't be seeing her again.

As the days went by, he often thought about Sally. Then late one evening the second show was about to start when he saw Sally's parents' car pull up to the curb. She was coming in the door, getting a ticket, and then was heading his way. He just stood there. She made her way to him, stopped and managed to say, "After---ice cream." He answered, "Aah"---he wasn't sure what he had said, then she walked into the show.

Ben was trying to get as much of his work done before the show let out. He was standing wondering what was wrong with the clock, looking at it every few minutes.

Then the shows were letting out and people were standing around. Finally, they were starting to leave. Then there she was with those hazel eyes and a little smile on her face. She stopped before him and looked up, just standing there. By now he knew he should say something, then a little louder than he expected, "Would you like---like---ice cream?" She stood there a moment and just nodded her head with that same little smile.

Ben said, "It's going to take---take me a few minutes to close"; but soon he was back walking outside. He locked the door and they walked to the DQ. This time he bought them both a small cone.

Then Ben found himself trying to tell her what had happened to him, what was wrong with his arm and speech. She just sat there smiling like she knew what he was saying. Then she began talking about a swimming pool and---.

Time was flying. They had been sitting there an hour or more and she had not called her parents, yet there was her mother coming in the door. She walked over, sitting down. She said, "How are you doing, Ben?" Sally smiled and Ben thought he understood.

When Sally left, she said, "Two days" and sure enough, two days later she was walking in the door of the theater. Later as they were walking to the Dairy Queen, she reached over and took his lifeless hand, holding it all the way to the Queen.

That night something passed between them. Not only did this start a ritual for the ice cream cone but he was also starting to come to the ODC where she worked when they were having some events such as a dance with karoke, picnics or a special party.

As time went on, they were inseparable.

One night walking to the DQ, they walked into a special party; finding out it was for them. It was a year to the day he had bought her that first small cone. People had seen and remembered.

That night he told her what he had been thinking. Later at home, Ben told his mother that he wanted to marry Sally. She started crying, saying she was so happy for them. Both of Sally's parents seemed to know this was going to happen.

Some people may say this was a marriage made in heaven and it was.

Soon they had a little apartment by the river and at times you could see them with their little blanket and picnic basket on its banks walking hand in hand. If they ever had a major disagreement, I never heard of it.

I watched the couple for many years, and as time passed by it took its toll but not on their love for each other. Then one day Ben was gone, possibly from his injuries of many years ago.

The other day I was singing with a men's choir at an assisted living home, looking across the room I could see an aged lady with hazel eyes looking my way. I walked over, she managed to get up, and we hugged.

It was not hard to see the picture of Ben sitting there.

This was based on a true love story. The names and some facts have been changed to protect their privacy.

Everyone needs to be loved.

~

103
THE TATTERED BLANKET

How a day can turn around. This was in about 1960 and we had driven to Duluth on a Sunday morning. I was to participate in a police officers' pistol shoot. Doris and I always tried to make these a family affair. We had our four boys with us; they would be playing with other officers' children while the wives visited.

We all know how some children have their "must have" blanket with them to feel the silky edge when they are tired and perhaps need a nap. Ours were the same on this warm day.

Coming back to Grand Rapids around 4:30 to 5:00 p.m., we decided to finish the day by visiting Grandma south on Pokegama Lake. We were driving south on 169 and as we came out of the "S" curve, there was a field on the right side of the road. At first I wasn't sure what I was seeing, it was a newer car some 100 to 150 feet off the roadway with some damage in the windshield area. It was facing north toward Grand Rapids and there appeared to be someone in it.

My thought was that it didn't belong there. The car had also caught the attention of my wife. Making a U turn and coming back, we parked as safely as we could. I left my car and ran to the car in the field, discovering that the engine was still running. A man sat dazed, looking straight ahead. A woman was in the right passenger seat looking like she had taken the brunt of some heavy object that had crashed into the right windshield and into the car doing extensive damage. She showed no signs of life, a lot of upper body trauma.

Finally getting the driver's door open, I reached in and turned the ignition off. Assessing the situation, there wasn't much I could do until more help arrived.

Trying to protect the driver from the shock of looking at his wife in this condition, I ran back to our car asking my wife for a blanket. She handed me a tattered blanket belonging to one of our sons, Ron, who was about six years old. I was to hear more of this later. Back at the damaged car, the driver was still staring straight ahead, dazed. I hung the blanket between the driver and his wife like a curtain.

It was quite obvious from some marks that a large truck tire had struck the corner of the car. Other people were stopping along the road, some with medical experience. I was soon helping direct traffic.

Lloyd Olson, a Minn. State Trooper was soon on the scene investigating the accident and directing traffic. An ambulance arrived; we then loaded the driver of the car and proceeded to the hospital. At this time, I heard the name, King Cress. My wife drove our car home and later picked me up at the hospital.

At the accident scene, a large truck tire had been found. The theory was the tire and rim may have fallen off the flat bed of an eighteen wheeler, bounced off the road, and went through the front window of the Cress car.

As each vehicle could be going 50 mph in a different direction, the heavy tire could have the equivalent speed of a hundred mph when striking the Cress car.

The driver of the truck was never found nor was the tattered blanket recovered as we were made aware, as someone wanted his blanket. He can still describe it in some detail over 50 years later.

Many years later Ron was traveling in the state of Washington when he came upon a bad accident where a truck had rolled and an injured woman was lying in the ditch in a bad way. Taking his sleeping bag, he covered her as well as he could.

He never recovered the sleeping bag. He made a comment that summed it up, "Too much like my father."

~

104
UNCOOPERATIVE

I was driving on Hwy. 2 west, making a left hand turn toward the bridge, when I saw an older model Ford coming my way across the bridge at a high rate of speed. It made a right hand turn onto 3rd St. and headed into the downtown area. It was getting onto 3:30 a.m. At this time the vehicle was still moving fast. The area we were heading into on 3rd St. was where the old Dutchroom beer joint once stood. A two story structure with apartments upstairs, its location is now part of the Blandin Paper Co. I turned my red flashing lights on as the car had been doing better than 45 mph in a 30 zone. The lady pulled over at an angle, parking at the curb.

As I walked up to the car, she rolled down the driver's side window, and I asked her what might be the reason for her speeding. She said she had just left the bar in Cohasset where she had been dancing and had a few drinks and was in a hurry to get home to her husband.

At this time I asked her for her driver's license; she appeared to be around 40 years of age. She was very cooperative, saying, "Just a moment" and reaching down to get her license from her pocket. She then became very flustered, agitated and uncooperative, saying she could not find it.

Knowing she had been drinking, I asked her to get out of the car as she was going to have to walk and turn for me to see if she was sober. At first she refused. After telling her I would be calling a car over and she would be taken to jail, she then consented to get out of the car and show me her driver's license. Right away, I knew what her problem was.

She had told me she had just come from a bar. But the bar had been closed since 2 a.m. She had been seen coming from the "Big Woods" area and the pockets to her jeans were on the outside.

Giving her a verbal warning about her speeding at this late hour, I left thinking she had enough troubles.

Driving away I could see she was learning to dress properly to go home.

~

105
THE INFERNO

It was what police officers described as one of the worst accidents they had ever witnessed, a chain reaction collision with three cars and a 12 yard dump truck on 169 S. near the Grand Rapids Motel, leaving three people injured and four people dead along with an unborn child.

What really happened to start this chain of events may never be known. We do know a car was coming into Grand Rapids from the south on Hwy. 169 at 4:15 p.m. A truck was following a short distance back. Did the car slow to turn? Did the truck driver try to slow down?

We do know the right front tire of the truck climbed the middle of the car's trunk, squashing the trunk down and rupturing the gas tank. The truck with its right tire high on the trunk started to flip and roll to his left high in the air.

There was an oncoming car. The truck, upside down, landed on the incoming car's roof, collapsing the roof and trapping four people in the car. One man was ejected from the car.

The truck continued rolling to the ditch, leaving behind two wrecked cars.

The car with the ruptured gas tank was sitting up grade from the car with the trapped people in it. Meanwhile the gas was spreading on the highway and running under the trapped car. A scrape, something, set the gas on fire, which spread fast.

Two state highway patrolmen, George Brook and Kermit Matyas, arrived on the scene almost immediately. The car up grade was burning fiercely along with the truck.

The car with the people trapped in it was just starting to burn. Both Brook and Matyas attacked the flames on the trapped car with their small fire extinguishers. Both were soon driven back by the heat and a developing inferno with car tires blowing and sending flames for 30 feet.

The police department was on the scene within a few minutes with the fire department close behind. Soon all of the local departments were on the scene but were helpless with the black smoke and flames shooting high in the sky.

The fire department waded in and had the fire under control in a short time.

It was too late for the poor souls trapped in the inferno. The screams and the feeling of helplessness as you can only stand back and watch.

This was a scene one should never have to go through, one you will never forget.

The fire is out and everybody has a job to do. Traffic diverted, bodies to be recovered, ambulances sent on their way. After the investigation the road has to be cleared. The road washed down by the fire department, the wreckers sit and wait.

More information is gathered on the dead and injured. Families are going to have to be notified.

Now you've done your job, time to go home and try not to remember.

Monday, August 2nd 1971
Herald Review Vol 77 Number 61   Harvey Dahline

~

106
THE LOVING SISTER

Jay sits in his car back in the tall pine trees. It's dark, he won't be seen. It won't be long now, where is she? Who is she with?

It's getting late; the lighting is not the best around the 4th Street Station, a local beer joint and eating place located in west Grand Rapids. Most of her friends hang out here, she'll be along, give her time. Who is she with?

Taking the knife from his pocket, sliding his finger over the blade, it's sharp enough to do the job. Folding it, he puts it back. Where are they?

The car is there, its parking. The couple sits there, moving closer, becoming very friendly. He knows what he's going to do, this is his girlfriend. The guy is going to learn a lesson he won't soon forget. If he lives, he won't be going out with her again.

Getting out of his car, the inside light comes on. He hadn't thought of that. He quickly shuts the door, looking to see if they had seen the light. No, they are too engrossed in each other.

Slipping through the trees, he's getting closer. Yes, that's her, she should know better. He's ready, taking the knife out, he is almost there. What will he do if the door is locked?

He walks out of the darkness, they don't see him. Grabbing the handle, opening the door, he is on the man, his arm goes around his neck and he is stabbing and slashing. But, there are clothes in the way and the man is fighting back. No room.

The knife goes in, one, two, three times. The girl is screaming, something is wrong. She's not my girlfriend, it's her sister!

Got to get out of here fast. Running back to his car, Jay throws it into gear and is soon heading out Hwy. 38 north. Got to get home, get some clothes and head for the Twin Cities.

Late in the evening the police are called to the 4th Street Station on the west end of town where there has been a stabbing.

A young man is waiting, describing what had just happened to him. Bleeding from some knife wounds around the neck, thanking God his attacker had just used a small jackknife. The girl in the car also recognized Jay as a part-time suitor of her sister and named him as the attacker.

The young man was taken to the hospital for treatment. His wounds were not as severe as first thought.

The police and sheriff's office are out looking for Jay and his car. It is a futile search; he has been home and gone. A warrant for him is issued.

It will be some time before he is found.

I had known Jay for most of his life, not as a close friend, but just a friend. Having a father who was seldom sober, a tarpaper shack out in the sticks, it didn't seem like he ever stood a good chance in life. Always in trouble, small problems at first but then more serious. As time went on, even though I was a police officer, we seemed to get along well.

Maybe it's that I saw so much of myself in Jay, such a deep hole to climb out of. Maybe that's why it didn't surprise me that when he was picked up in the Twin Cities and brought back to the Itasca jail that word was passed he wanted to talk to me to get some things off his chest.

Arriving at the jail, meeting Jay, we had some small talk. He indicated to me he wanted to tell me everything, knowing what he was about to say would be used in court.

I then read him the Miranda card, which is a card explaining his rights.

Shortly I had my tape player turned on, and reading him his rights once again, we were soon into the incident of the stabbing.

Unexpectedly, a jailer put his head in the door while I was taking Jay's statement saying, "Judge Spellacy wants Jay upstairs in court now!" You may know the respected Judge John J. Spellacy was not a man to be kept waiting. We were just getting into the statement. Getting a good statement with all of the facts on tape may save hundreds of hours of court time later on. I continued taking the statement, and then the jailer was back a second and a third time. Having all of the important facts, I quickly finished the statement. Since it was Judge John J. Spellacy, you can bet we did some fast walking to the Judge's chambers.

Jay was appointed a public defender, eventually pleading guilty to his charges and spending a short time in jail.

I have said this before, you give a man a break, some times you hit a home run but Jay never got past first base.

The drugs and alcohol took their toll. He left us at age 35.

~

107
THEIR MISTAKE - THE INTERCOM

They came to the little town of Grand Rapids, Minn., early in the morning on a summer day, pleased with themselves. They had been working the small towns across the Range, burglarizing a couple bars a night.

It was the time of pull tabs and bingo games, every town had them. The money was always kept on the premises. Also, the small town cops were never a match for them. Coming from the big town of Shakopee, it never took them long to scout out these little one-horse towns to get two good prospects for the night. Driving around town, they settled on two in the western part of town.

Dropping into the 4th Street Station for a drink and something to eat, they were able to walk around and locate a very large safe in a middle room. While standing by a window, they unlocked it for entry upon their return much later that night.

The next step was how to remove such a large safe. It would take some time to enter because the plating was very thick; peeling it would be almost impossible. An idea came to one of them. He then dropped over to the Rapids Body Shop only a block away from the 4th Street Station.

Coming into the Rapids Body Shop, he asked the owner, Roger Hirt, if Pete was in. As this was the dinner hour, Pete was out, so he just wandered around looking. Going to the back he saw what he was looking for, a set of cutting torches with tanks on a dolly. Standing by a window, he was able to unlock it also for later entry.

Having a beer at the Dutchroom, they were able to learn the location of a small safe. Entry would have to be at the back door as there weren't any windows to be unlocked which had become their entry of choice. Now all they had to do was kill time.

Knowing that bars stay open until 1:00 a.m., everybody out by 2:00 so employees are out by 2:30. It would be a long wait.

At 1:30 they were at the Rapids Body Shop, entering by the window they had unlocked earlier. Finding the acetylene cutting torch on the dolly, they soon had it out the back door and loaded it on the wrecker. This would be used later to open the large safe.

In the meantime they had found the key to start the wrecker.

They had to sit and watch the 4th St. Station at a distance. After the last car had left, they could move. A little more time to make sure no one comes back.

One man enters the unlocked window. Going to the backdoor he unlocks it and waits.

Soon the wrecker is backing up to the back door. Unwinding the cable, they are going to need 80-100 feet to reach the room deep inside and get it hooked around the safe.

In a short time the cable was hooked around the safe and the winch was starting to pull the safe to the back, pulling walls and doors down and causing several hundred dollars in damage.

Earlier in the day they had driven west toward Cohasset on Hwy. 2. They found a road about four miles out of town; turning to the right they would be back on the Baker gravel pit road. They would take the safe and cutting torches, dropping them on the far end of the field in the trees.

As soon as the safe was hanging on the wrecker, they headed west toward the predetermined field. Arriving at the back of the field, they soon had the safe and the cutting torches unloaded; then on their way back, they returned the wrecker to where it had been parked by the Rapids Body Shop.

Time was getting short but their night was not done. They still had the safe to get at Madden's Dutchroom. On their way they decided to burglarize Hunter Alignment where some tools and an undetermined amount of cash was taken.

Soon they were at Madden's and forced the southeast back door open. There was now a large plate glass door to be opened. Rather than breaking the glass and make a loud noise, they decided to go over the door frame. One man boosted his partner up, over, and through the hanging ceiling, dropping down on the far side. He then opened the door from the inside.

However, they had not done a good job of scouting the building, failing to notice that the owners lived upstairs on the far end of the building. Also, there was an intercom system downstairs. The lady owner upstairs could hear the break-in taking place and what was being said by the burglars.

Anita was soon on the phone with the sheriff's dispatcher explaining what was taking place. The police and Itasca County Sheriffs office were alerted to a burglary taking place at Madden's Dutchroom in Grand Rapids about 4:45 a.m. Sunday, October 29th, 1993.

When Officers Rod Trunzo, Jim Martinetto and Deputy Tim Oakly arrived at the scene, they saw one person leaving the area. After they had chased the man on foot for some distance, Trunzo caught and arrested him. Valley said another person who was in the building had escaped. The arrested person was taken to the Itasca County Jail.

It was not long before Pat Medure and I were reading the suspect his rights. We had given him a can of Mountain Dew and he agreed to talk to us.   We were having some very casual conversation. After about a half hour, he stopped talking, and then said, "What the hell is going on here? I don't talk to cops! I've been sitting here talking for more than a half hour and I just got out of Stillwater a short time ago." He then brought up the subject of his girlfriend's car. He knew we had confiscated it as it had been used to commit some felonies of which he said she had no knowledge. At this time we told him that maybe we could work something out.

As the suspect was going back to Stillwater anyway, we said if he would cooperate with us on what took place tonight and lead us to where the safe with a large amount of cash had been taken, I would see that his girlfriend got her car back. This he was willing to do, directing us out west to the field where the safe and cutting torches had been dumped.

The next day was busy for us. We got the Rapids wrecker to go out with us to recover the safe and torches. Talking to the Shakopee police department, we learned the girlfriend was in a local motel. The other suspect had made it to the Cities.

Late the next night, Pat Medure and I hadn't gotten any sleep. We headed for the Cities in Pat's unmarked squad car with Gene Bennett driving. Pat and I were trying to get some sleep; I don't think Gene was always holding to the speed limit. It was hard to sleep as Bennett swerved to miss a deer and then had to hit the brakes as a bear was in the road.

Arriving in Shakopee, we were able to locate the girl at a motel. The other suspect had left by this time, going to an address in downtown Minneapolis.

Leaving Bennett with the girl at the motel so that she could not call the suspect and warn him, we headed down town. About half way to our destination, the suspect's car was seen heading back the way we had come.

Pulling the suspect over we found that he was uncooperative. We searched the car but couldn't search the trunk; he said he didn't have a key to the trunk. We replied that he did not have to worry, that we had some large crowbars with us. As we were about to enter the trunk, the suspect miraculously found the key in his pocket.

Now having picked up Gene from the motel room, we were about to head back to Grand Rapids. The suspect told us he had family a short distance from here. Knowing he would be heading back to prison and would not see them for some time, he asked us if we would give him a break. Could he stop to see them for a few minutes and talk to them and hug them without the cuffs.

We knew we were taking a chance but sometimes within your heart, you just know it's the right thing to do. We took him in to see his family without the cuffs on, and, yes, I did see the tears flowing from the child as well.

On the way back to Grand Rapids he kept no secrets.

The young men went through the court system and were soon headed back to Stillwater Prison.

The lady did get her car back. As she had no knowledge that it would be used in the felony burglaries, we would not have been able to confiscate the car. So when we traded the car back to him for all the information, we had made a good deal.

This was a hard story to write for some reason. It happened around 1993. At this time I was unable to find anything in print to corroborate the times. The owner's memories were fading as well as those of the police officers I talked to.

However, last evening I was looking through some old newspaper articles I had clipped out and saved from years ago. One article had a reference to Halloween and also to when the clinic was moved to the back of the hospital. Doing some investigating, I found that was in 1993. I headed for the Grand Rapids Herald Review to search in their archives for the book "Oct; Nov; Dec. 1993"; they must have 300 large books. As I walked in the door, there were three books lying on the table; the top book was the exact book I was looking for! I soon had all of my information.

How do you account for that?

References: Harvey Dahline
Grand Rapids Herald Review
Oct. 29, 1993
Police Officer Steve Valley, Ret

~

108
MINNIE MANESS - EARL BASIL CURRIE

As a very young boy, you don't think, "Who is my father." That time is like a dream. Some things slip through your mind; the drafty old cabin, the frozen dead rabbits laying outside the door in the snow that had been snared, that big barrel stove that huffed and puffed, glowing red from the tamarack stuffed into its belly.

In the summer going to the creek just across the railroad tracks that flowed next to the Remer City dump; this is where I learned to swim. There was a pond in the creek perhaps four or five feet deep and sixty feet across. I had gotten a large enamel dishpan from the dump. It had some holes in the bottom of it. Holding it out in front of me, kicking my feet, I started across the pond. The pan filled and sank about half way over. I didn't do real good swimming but I was soon sinking my feet into the squishy black earth at the bottom.

Later that day Harry, Ron and I found a gunnysack floating in the creek. It had four or five little kittens in it; that is how they got rid of their animals in those days. They were too far gone.

It must have been 1936 or 1937 when we moved to a tarpaper shack closer to town. It's in this area of time my mind takes me back to more memories of my grandmother, Minnie Maness, a small frail older woman with long white hair tied back or in a bun.

At this time she was living with us; my brothers Harry and Ron and sisters Margie and Judie along with my mother Hazel Maness Dahline. My brother Don may have been there too.

My Grandmother Minnie tried her best with us. At this time we thought she was a little different but we didn't know what it was. Years later, we would understand.

It's about this time we were starting to wonder where or who our father really was. A few times there would be a man over and we would sneak around to see what he looked like. Then for some time thinking it just might be, Arnold, a man my mother had divorced.

The next thing, we were in a courtroom in Walker. The welfare had us there on a petition. Ron, Harry and I would be spending the winter on a farm just outside of Hackensack, Minnesota.

The next summer we were back with my mother and grandmother.

The strange behavior from my grandmother, we were to learn, was somehow connected to a terrible firestorm she had gone through.

It seemed she had been married to a William Dohr who had left her to go to the goldfields of the Dakotas. He had written saying he was on his way back with the money to buy a farm. She never heard from him again.

He had left her with two small girls and pregnant. They had been living in Hinckley in 1894. This fire was to be known as the Great Hinckley Fire. Over 400 lives had been lost. Three hundred and fifty thousand acres burned in just hours. Two thousand people trapped. It would be many years before we knew Minnie's full story.

In a short time, Harry, Ron and I were again taken from home. Marge and Judie were sent to other homes. It would be many more years before we would see each other again.

While we were in the Gene Martin Brown Home, an orphanage in St.Paul which was close to the Como Park Zoo, my younger brother Ron was adopted out. This was in about 1945. It seemed no one wanted the twins.

Harry and I spent some time in various homes. One was on the Johnson Resort on Coon Lake, then to the Cliff Farber farm close to Staples, Minnesota.

In the summer of 1949 my brother, Don, showed up at the farm one afternoon saying, "Get your things, I'm taking you home." He was now at an age where he could be responsible for us. At this time he was living in an upstairs apartment in Grand Rapids with his wife, Betty. My mother had the three room apartment across the hall. These were known as the Mohaupt Apartments located where the paper mill parking lot is now across from the American Legion.

Minnie and my mother slept in the back bedroom. My grandmother oft times would be talking to herself, words we didn't understand. She could be seen walking from room to room poking the ceiling with the broom handle looking up. She was a small frail woman, a wonderful person but you knew something was wrong.

Along the way we learned more about her having been in the

Hinckley Fire of 1894, had ridden a burning train out of town and had three children. Somewhere along the way she had lost reality ending up in a hospital in Duluth. The two girls had been adopted out as well as the boy she had been carrying.

It was said she must have lost her senses from the horrible ordeal of riding the flaming car with her children.

After arriving home in 1949 I went to work in the Gambles food store. Going into the ninth grade and joining the National Guard, I was then inducted into the Army as the Korean War had started. After a short time while training at Camp Rucker in Alabama I was notified that my grandmother had died. The date, October 16, 1951.

Shortly thereafter I was on a troop ship to Korea.

In the fall of 1952 I was discharged from the armed services. Coming back to Grand Rapids, was soon back in high school for a few months. During these months I met, Doris, the girl I would marry.

Going into debt, I quit school to work in the iron mines. In time Doris and I were dating, she was a bright, beautiful girl with a very inquisitive mind wanting to know all about me; where I came from, who my parents were.

Now to be blunt, I knew who my mother was and the story about my grandmother, Minnie Maness but really had no idea who my father was. Through the years only having scraps of information, nothing factual. At this stage of the game I didn't seem to care, I had made it this far.

One day at the home of my sister, Marjorie Snyder, the subject came up. She told me who my father was. She said his name was Earl Currie.

Doris and I continued to date and were married July 9, 1954. In a short time I was hired onto the Grand Rapids Police Department on June 1, 1955 and was now living in a small apartment behind the courthouse. Our first son had arrived.

One day my aunt and uncle came to visit, Pansy and Bill Joslin. They lived in Remer, Minnesota. Bill said he had some information that he thought I should know, that an Earl Currie, a man he knew and a Civil Engineer for the Mn Dept of Transportation was my father. The man had been around Remer for some time in 1932 building the road from Walker to Grand Rapids and had visited his house. Pansy was my mother's sister.

We should have questioned Bill and gotten more information at that time; the spelling of the last name and so forth, but we didn't.

This was a new time in our lives; working on the police department and other jobs trying to raise a growing family.

Computers were to come much later.

As the years were going by, if we were in the Twin Cities we would oft times look in the area phone books but as we did not know the correct spelling we were lost.

One thing we always had in mind, we did not want to upset some family, not knowing how we would approach them if we found something. We didn't have much to go on. During this time we were made aware of a picture of my year or so old twin, Harry, and I with snowsuits on which we were told had been from Earl Currie. Also, my brother, Don, told us at a much later date he had seen letters with money in them from Earl Currie to my mother.

In about 2002, Doris, called MnDot asking for information about an Earl Currie. The woman said she could not tell her any information about him. Doris then asked if she could just tell her if he ever worked there. Not expecting an answer, the next day the woman called back and told us that he had worked there and the dates.

Then Doris being new to computers entered the correct name, Earl Currie, into Ancestory.com. She got a hit with the name on a site belonging to Earl's ex-son-in-law, Donald Carlson with Earl's name in it. Donald then responded saying he would forward the letter to Carol, Earl's granddaughter.   Carol then contacted us saying that the information on Earl Currie was true and that we would have to talk. Carol Eddelman turned out to be my niece living in Ohio. She also had a sister, Janice Fehn living there.

Through these contacts information started to flow. Along with pictures and a past history of my father, Earl Basil Currie, who it turned out had been in the Hinckley fire of 1894, the same fire that my grandmother, Minnie Dohr Maness had been in.

This was at a later date to raise questions in my mind. Did my grandmother know the Curries? Did they ride the same fire train out? When Earl Currie was going with my mother in 1932 did he know Hazel's mother had been in the Hinckley fire? Earl Currie would have been two years old when he rode the fire train out with his family to Superior.

It was a short time later we drove to Hinckley; we stopped at the Hinckley Fire Museum, touring it and going through all of the exhibits. One exhibit was a movie of the fire. The curator gave us some information that John Currie, my grandfather had many relatives throughout the area, had buildings in the town both before and after the fire, had taken charge with other town leaders in opening the trenches and the burying of over four hundred lost souls and had also been instrumental in the large memorial monument erected at the cemetery.

After visiting the museum we visited my dad's sister-in-law, Selma Currie, a few blocks away. The date, May 16, 2002.

We were welcomed and treated to cookies and a great welcome to the family. Some things we learned along the way; Earl Currie died in 1959 and was buried in Minneapolis, was married two times, had three children with his first wife, Cora, had one child Rose with his second wife, Lilly and had been a school teacher at one time. He had spent many years working for the MnDot as an engineer building roads. He was a brilliant man having a photographic memory which was passed on to some of his children. Earl served in both WW1 and WW2.

I was to learn that I had a ninety year old half sister, Margaret. She also had a photographic mind and could quote full chapters from the Bible and not miss a word. We were able to spend time getting to know each other. She passed on a couple years later.

We learned many answers to our questions by researching information from the Hinckley Museum, a booklet from the Great Hinckley Fire, The Hundred Year Anniversary issued in 1994. I thoroughly read a book Under a Flaming Sky by Daniel Brown and was able to determine that my grandmother Minnie Dohr Maness and the John Currie family had ridden separate trains from the Hinckley fire, my grandmother, the train to Skunk Lake at 4:25, the train engineer, Root.

John Currie, my grandfather and family rode the Best/Berry train with two engines six to seven miles on the eastern Mn, tracks towards Sandstone, picking up survivors, stopping in Sandstone to pick up anyone that would get aboard. Everyone thought they were safe, no one got aboard. The train then ended up at the Duluth Union Station with 476 survivors. They were later to learn, Sandstone had burned with over 60 lives lost.

I never thought I would write a story on a father I never had but don't we all wonder where we came from, our history? No, I never regretted not having a father as I believe I'm a much stronger person because of it. I could have let it lay but I have a wife who wants to know everything about me and we went digging, learning so much about my extended family.

Recently I pulled an envelope from a drawer, opening it. In it was a notarized copy dated November 18, 1997 from my older sister, Marjorie. It relates what was told her by my grandmother, Minnie Maness, starting in the 1930's and through the 1940's.

I started to think, this is a unique story that has to be told not only for me but for my children and grandchildren to follow.

In a couple days, I called my sister, Marjorie Snyder asking her if I could use the notarized copy of Grandmother's story she wrote in a story I was writing.

This is the rest of the story:

Minnie Caroline Smith

Born in Germany, on December 17, 1869
Married William (Willie) Dohr in the 1890s & George W. Maness in 1902
Died on Oct. 16, 1951, in Grand Rapids, Minn.

This is an account of events related to me, Minnie's granddaughter, Marjorie J. Dahline Snyder, in the 1930s and 40s by Minnie Maness:

I remember sitting on the floor by my grandmother's rocking chair, resting my head on the arm of her chair, or laying my head on her knees and forever questioning her about her life. I realize now, that some of my questions must have been very painful to her. She would always answer them with a thoughtful look on her face, or a slight smile, while brushing my hair away from my face with her hand. I was spell-bound as she would tell me about her joys and sorrows. Yet, the Hinckley fire remains one of the most vivid and irreparable events that impacted her life.

Minnie's parents were William Henry and Anna Lillian (Schmidt) Smith. Minnie was the third child of the ten children born into this union. They immigrated to the United States from Germany. They bought an orchard (farm) in Calhoun County, Iowa. William passed away in about 1885, and his family moved to the St. Cloud, Minn., area.

Minnie married William Dohr and they had two girls and were expecting another child (boy). They moved to Hinckley, Minn. William worked on a potato farm and Minnie cooked for the family. The Black Hills gold rush was on and Willie decided to go out there and make enough money to buy a farm for his expanding family. Disaster struck the young mother. William never returned home, even though Minnie had received a letter saying he was on his way home with enough money to purchase their farm. Minnie said she figured he was murdered on his way home for the money.

The summer of 1894, Hinckley was excessively hot and crops simmered as little puffs of smoke would pop up in the fields. The sweltering ground seemed to be sizzling; you could see heat waves rising from the ground. A summer never to be forgotten!

ON the morning of Sept. 1, 1894, the sky was black with ashes, soot and flying cinders. The sky in the distant horizon was fire red and angry orange. The air was suffocatingly hot; the smoke stung their noses and throats. They wet rags and put them over their nose and mouth, and also placed pieces of wet rags on their heads. There was always the danger that the live ashes and cinders flying in the air would ignite their hair. Everyone was coughing and gasping for air.

People were frantic, running around and gathering their family and belongings together. Desperation set in as they tried to save the few possessions that they had. It was a frightening and chaotic time for all. Minnie, with her two little girls, dragged her trunk out into a potato field by the railroad. She was looking for an opportunity to save their lives and their few, but treasured belongings. A man came running across the scorching field, waving his hands and yelling that he would help Minnie and her children. A great twirling gust of fiery heat rolled across the field and engulfed the Good Samaritan. With tears in her eyes, Minnie relayed how the man just disintegrated before them to nothing but bones and ashes.

A train from St. Paul picked up Minnie and the girls. However, they traveled in a humbling style as they shared quarters with steers and a mass of escaping people in the cattle car. Shoulder to shoulder they were packed in the smelly compartment, but they realized how lucky they were to flee with a few of their precious things and more importantly with their lives. Minnie was pregnant and not willing to give up easily. She cuddled her girls and told them that they would make it to safety. The girls shuddered and clung to their mother's side.

Wooden barrels inside the cattle car were filled with water to completely dunk the children in. The children would scream out in fear as they were wholly immersed in water. The railroad car was an inferno, but it was their only chance for escape. The heat was so intense that the slats on the sides of the cattle car would smolder and then like magic, burst into flames. Gunnysacks were dipped in water and slapped against the slats in an attempt to control the fire. Yet, there was no way to control the fear in the folks' hearts as the fire surrounded them.

They stopped the train near a small body of water and all of the frantic passengers jumped in. Many of the survivors broke off chucks of reed and stayed underneath the water by breathing threw those ingenious straws. Yet, they realized that they could not stay in the reservoir for the duration of the fire. Crews of people began filling up the wooden water barrels that were in the railroad cars. Others sought to contain the fire on their cattle car by dousing the walls with whatever water they could carry. The last thing that Minnie remembered was struggling to get her children and herself on the train.

When Minnie awakened, she saw white walls about her and a nurse bending over her. She asked the nurse where her two children were and if they were saved from the fire. The nurse wouldn't reply and said she'd go and get her doctor. Minnie immediately sensed that something was very wrong and she trembled with sadness.

Another tragedy was about to enfold as Minnie was told that her two daughters and the son that she gave birth to in that very hospital had been adopted to other families. The doctor had not expected Minnie to regain consciousness and they knew that the newborn child and sisters needed a home immediately. The year was now 1899 and she had no knowledge of what had happened from Sept. 1, 1894. For over five years she had been in a coma and unable to care for her children or herself.

Once again she had to come to terms with a great loss. First her husband, then her home, and now her dear children. The doctor ushered Minnie over to a dresser with a mirror. Minnie had always had dark, glossy hair that had never been touched by scissors. She gasped as she looked into the mirror and saw snow white hair. Time had taken its toll on her in many ways.

Minnie left the hospital and got a job taking care of the children of Mr. and Mrs. Magner. It was once again a season of new beginnings. For a while, she thought that maybe she would never be happy again. Then she met a widower named George Maness. They fell in love, were married and raised three of his children as well as six of their own children. Yet, she never forgot the two little girls and the infant son that were taken from her.

In the 1930s, she found one of her daughters, Agnes and her son, Leonard. There is no way I can describe the look in Grandma's eyes, or the despair in her voice when she would tell me about the Hinckley fire.

On and off for the rest of her life, she would have nightmares, would yell out or cry. Mother would go in her room and gently shake her. She would comfort her and tell her that everything is all right. It was all over now.

I'm so thankful now, that I would pester my grandmother about her background. She was so very special to me.

~

109
UNDER THE SNOW

In the 1950's it was something to see as you were driving in the downtown at night; only one stop light and no cars, but there he would be, the street sweeper pushing his white cart with two bicycle wheels and a 4x5 x 3foot high box, a push handle on one end and his push brooms sticking out of their holders. A little man taking pride in his work cleaning the streets and gutters of sand and refuse.

In the daytime you could see John in his little truck pulling a two wheeled small white trailer with a box on it. A hose could be attached to the pickup's exhaust and run to the box. This was our humane way of taking care of stray animal problems.

This was the time of the pinball machines, bowling alleys and pool halls as well as bars. Gambling was not to be done in any form but you could drive and enjoy a beer in your car.

There were some rumors that a game of chance may be taking place in the back of the Coast to Coast store in the late night but nothing that could be proved. It was also said that if you ran up a high score on the pinball machines, it may be worth your while. But, of course, that was just a rumor. Playing a game of poker was perfectly legal as long as no money changed hands. So, of course, there were never any winners.

There weren't any TV's to speak of and radios were not the best. Big fun for the weekend was to go dancing or to the weekly card game at a friend's house. Then if that didn't cut it you could head for a bar and a drink and if you were lucky, find some companionship. There were other families who would get together for potluck, jigsaw puzzles or a picnic. A lot of them would mingle in church the next Sunday.

In these days there were more bars and drunks on the streets than now. Giving someone a ride home was not unusual. One of these stands out, as I was called to his home many a time. The name of Cal will have to do. He was about 5 ft. 7 and around 140 pounds, getting up in age but very strong. He worked for a vending machine company and was a top of the line drinker.

Back then he lived with two older sisters in a cabin across the street from the old Gym 400 next to the alley in the north part of town. Oft times I would get a call there. Most of the time it went well, but there were a couple times that stand out in my memory that didn't.

I received a call in the later part of the day in what I would call a blizzard. Wading through a path three feet wide with as much as three feet of fresh snow filling the path, I got to the door. Entering, I found Cal had more than his share of the bottle and had been getting physical with his sisters. Under these conditions he was going to be spending the night in jail.

He at this time agreed to go with me. Things were going quite well until we got to the front outside step. The man then came out in him, and he started to resist. Deciding to put the cuffs on him led to a match I will always remember. I, 180 pounds, young, he, older and 140 pounds. The next thing I can remember is being under a foot of snow trying to get the cuffs on this wiry old guy without hurting him.

After a short time under the snow I managed to get the cuffs on him. Lying there breathing somewhat faster, I looked up at the older sisters. Could you believe they had not come to my aid? In a short time he was tucked away for the night.

There were more contacts with him over the years, nothing serious. However, receiving a call late this night was going to prove quite different.

Arriving at the front steps I was met by the two aging sisters saying that Cal was going to commit suicide with a 12 gauge shotgun. He had said if anyone came close they would be sorry. Asking the sisters where he was, they took me into the little cabin, showing me to the back door and saying he was at the bottom of the outside back steps sitting in a chair.

The house was built on a high level of ground; the back was at a lower level about 8 feet down. There was a small wood porch just outside the back door with steps angling down to the left. Supporting the deck were two large poles out from the house 6-8 feet reaching almost to the eaves.

Taking my time, I came out on the deck. Looking down, I saw Cal sitting on a chair with a double barreled shotgun across his legs seemingly unaware anyone was above him. Not saying anything I grabbed the big pole to the left, going over the stair railing, dropping the 6-8 feet and just as I was landing pulling the shotgun from his lap. He just sat there like he was stunned. He was again taken and put away for the night because he was drunk and for his own safety.

The years have come and gone as well as the sisters and Cal. The little log covered cabin is just a memory. Where it once stood is now a church parking lot. Where Gym 400 and the high school once were is a housing addition.

And though Cal and his sisters are gone, they will always enrich my memories of the past.

Harvey Dahline
3/12/2014
218-326-2497

~

110
THE UNEXPECTED

We go through life, friends slip away, and there are only a few left. Time is counting down.

One day you are taking a shower, you look down and a drop of blood hits the shower floor. You think, "Did I bump or injure myself?" It will go away. A day later and you are standing in the bathroom, more blood, this can't be good.

What to do? I had a physical exam in a few days. At that time I told the doctor about it. He felt it was nothing to be concerned about: "We'll keep an eye on it."

For two and a half weeks I checked consistently and there was blood. On January 25th I went to see the doctor at the clinic and he ordered blood and urine testing. He called me a few days later telling me there was blood in my urine and that he was setting me up for a CT scan.

Up to this point I hadn't told my wife what was going on for the last month or so, thinking she had enough to worry about. Receiving a telephone call from the clinic, she wanted to know what was going on and wasn't very happy with my answer.

On February 1st I had the CT scan. After the weekend the doctor called, stating my prostate was somewhat enlarged. There were two cysts on my kidneys which were nothing to worry about. He now wanted me to have an MRI which was set up for February 11th. An appointment was also set up with an urologist on the 13th at the Duluth Clinic.

Now you sit and wait. The wife seemed to take it very well considering you don't know what you have and that it could be serious. Then I walked into the bathroom, all she said was that she needed a little cry. We looked at each other and hugged.

It's funny what runs through your mind. I knew it could be bad but was mostly thinking about my wife rather than worrying about myself. She is what counts.

I have lived a life many men can only dream of. Whatever comes, good or bad, I will handle. But in trying times we must think of others. So now I think of my wife. What if? But, no, I knew better, you find out if there is a problem and go from there.

Like most men I want to know what is going on in my body, good or bad. Wednesday we went to the appointment at the Duluth Clinic. I was interviewed by a professional caring nurse who asked many pertinent questions on what I thought my problem was plus past history.

In a short time the doctor came in as he had already reviewed the MRI and read through a lot of reports. He then questioned me about what I thought my problem was and when did it start. I then received a thorough examination including watching a video of the MRI and getting an explanation of what we were looking at. They performed a cystoscopy which is looking into the bladder, nothing worrisome there. Even though the prostate was somewhat enlarged it was still normal for someone my age, 80 years old. His conclusion was a probable prostate inflammation; saying between 40 to 60% of all men will have this. He would prescribe an antibiotic. We would keep an eye on it. It should clear up in a couple weeks; it started to clear in about a week and was normal in two weeks. It would appear I am one of the lucky ones.

As we left Duluth we stopped at the Pizza Hut. I was not celebrating but I had to admit I had two large Mountain Dews!!!

When I first saw the blood, as a man I knew this could go in many directions. Hoping I'm level headed, thinking that I was going to journal this to see how I handle whatever comes.

You find there is a lot of waiting for appointments to do the CT scan, MRI, seeing the urologist and waiting for the test results.

I had no idea I would write an article on this as, for most men, this is a very private matter. This is taboo, we're men, this doesn't happen to us---but it can. Even when a problem is very obvious to us, we are reluctant to confide in our own wives. Then, why am I confiding to the world? Why? Because too many men are dying simply because of their pride.

But when all of your excuses fail, go back to where you should have been in the first place, your family. They love you and want you around for years to come. You owe them that.

This is serious. Pride is one thing, death is forever.

If this saves one life it will be worth sharing.

Go in today, you may thank me tomorrow.

~

111
BLUE BOY

Years ago, Jim, the owner of Jim's 76 Station on E. 4th St. came to see me. He was losing money that he was leaving in the office for whoever opened the next morning. It was happening once a week or more. He started hiding the money, but it was still being found and taken. He ruled out employees in different ways. Jim didn't think there were any extra keys out there, but someone was getting in during the night.

We sat a car to keep watch on the place several times until change of shift at 7 a.m. and yet he would come to find the money gone every few days, including some of the nights we had been sitting there.

So, what was going on? Maybe it was after 7 to 8 a.m. when the first person came to work. I thought "paperboy".

Thinking back a year or so, there was a family out toward the bowling alley that had been reporting feminine undergarments being taken from their clothesline. This was happening quite often. In this case, I had a young man in mind, but how could you prove he was taking the garments if you couldn't catch him doing it?

I had a jar of what you would call "invisible ink". I spread it quite liberally into the bottom of the girl's swimsuit then hung it on the line. What happens when this ink comes in contact with moisture on the hands and in this case the face, is that it turns a dark blue, getting in the pores and cracks of the skin. It is almost impossible to remove. Within a day or so, the suit was missing.

I then contacted the young man, a paper carrier. Can you believe he was blue in the face to see me? He had been washing to no avail. He soon "fessed up" to the clothesline thefts.

Back at the 76 Station, Jim had gotten hit again. In this case I got a large peanut butter jar and cut a slot in the top. Jim then put $15 of bills and assorted change in the jar. I then sprinkled it with the invisible powder, put tape around the lid making it hard to get into, and then taped a note to the jar saying, "Hunting money, do not touch," and left it on the counter.

Two days later I was called to Jim's. He was irate and mad at me, because he had been taken again and was now out of his $15 as well. I listened for a few more minutes, and then I was out looking for my very young friend of years past.

He was a very bright boy and having had contact with ink before had done a wonderful job of washing up but again to no avail. It was under his fingernails, in the cracks of his hands and on his clothing.

It didn't take long and he was explaining how with his slight frame was able to remove a pane of glass from a side window, reach up, unlock a swinging window above and enter through the swinging window, leaving the same way and then replacing the pane of glass. He was doing that after 7 a.m. while on his paper route.

He was to appear in juvenile court.

I know the young man to this day. He may have an aversion to anything with ink in or on it.

~

112
I ALMOST KILLED MY FRIEND

I started working for the police department on June 1, 1955. I had a payment on an Olds '98, and lived in a small, two room apartment in an old, two story house across the street from Acheson Tire in downtown Grand Rapids with a wife and baby son.

It didn't take long to figure out we weren't going to get far on $360 a month. At this time there were only six men on the department so we worked a lot of extra hours having to attend funerals and parades, do court time and cover if someone went on vacation. We were expected to fill all these hours, too, without compensation.

I'm not complaining, at least I had a job. I had worked in the mines, expecting to get laid off each winter. At least this was year around.

I ran into a Mr. Acheson from Acheson Trailer Court located on Hwy. 2. He asked me if I would do some work at the trailer court on his sewer system digging with a shovel. He soon had me doing small jobs around the place.

At this time he owned a house, a two story just across 4th St N.E. from where the Subway now stands. I was working installing a TV antenna on the high slanted roof. Looking down there was a young man watching me and then he was asking, "Does height bother you?" When I replied it didn't, he then asked me if I would like to do some work for him.

The man I was talking to was Arnold Burt, owner of Burt's TV in Grand Rapids.

I informed him I had no real knowledge of TV's or their installations. He then told me he would advise me on any help I would need. Taking him at his word, I was soon working taking down, installing and repairing TV antennas. Some of the towers stood 40 feet high, and I installed them by myself.

This is a relationship I treasure to this day. I have often thought that Arnold was perhaps the most honest man I ever met.

As the years went by I had branched out on my own, so a lot of the time I would need supplies. Arnold had his shop two miles out on the River Road. I would show up at his shop unannounced and he would often be gone. I would take whatever I needed: standoffs, a thousand feet of wire, or TV antennas. A value of maybe $200 to $300.

Going back to town we would sometimes pass each other and wave. As soon as I was finished with the job, which may have been a week later, I would show up at his place telling what I had taken and pay him cash. Over the years he never once asked me, did I take this or that? A man has to be honest within himself to trust me the way he did.

It was a trust I never betrayed although I almost killed the man at one time. I am sure he has forgiven me now though he probably still carries some of the scars.

Through the years I had assisted him on some work. On a very cold day in the winter, he and I were climbing the high GBAZ tower located in the S.W. part of town to do some repairs.

We were well bundled due to the extreme cold. I was perhaps a hundred feet off the ground carrying a heavy set of wrenches in a leather belt around my waist when I heard a loud clang. Looking down I could see a large wrench falling. Arnold was 30-40 ft below me. The wrench hit him squarely in the head then bounced off into space.

I know I held my breath as I expected my friend to follow the wrench. Dazed as he was, he was able to hang on. As I was above him, it was impossible for me to help him down. This took some time.

Soon I was driving him to the hospital; he not only had a head-ache but also had to receive some stitches.

I don't think he blamed me as much as I blamed myself. I do know he never climbed below me again.

When I got home I wasn't greeted too warmly either, as my wife had received a call from the operator who broke in as she was talking to someone on the line, telling her I was at the hospital and didn't know why.

I recently saw a familiar looking young man at church. I thought, "That's a Burt". So after church I approached him saying, "You look like an old friend of mine." He replied that he was the son of Arnold

Burt and they had talked about the flying wrench just a couple days ago. I then asked how my old friend was as it had been some time since I had seen him. Would you believe that as I sat down in the waiting room at the hospital the next morning, sitting two seats down from me was my old friend?

He smiled as he rubbed his head and, yes, he still remembered me. We are still the best of friends.

~

113
THE DREADED CALL

I had worked with Arlis Hopkins on many a call and knew he feared little as he was once a boxer, a strong fearless man.

We had gone into many a fray together but this one we knew would be different. The time was drawing near, we could feel it.

It was one where we knew our fellow officers would find a reason to ignore our call for backup as fearless as they were.

This thing I speak of was about to take place again. This was in the late 50's. At this time our police officers had not been properly trained on how to handle this ammonia effect on eyes, nose and throat.

I, having been in the Korean War, had at least been indoctrinated in gas warfare and the use of a gas mask, but we were police officers without proper equipment and yet we knew it was to be our duty. It was a cold lonely night, not a breeze moving a whiff of air. This was the kind of night we most dreaded.

The radio crackled. This was it, our fate was sealed. I took my foot off the foot feed, slowed the car, took a deep breath, getting as much oxygen into my lungs as I could. Hopkins was doing the same.

We could now see the house we were being summoned to. Two occupants, each being 400 pounds or so. The house was a single story, 40 feet long with screened-in porch in the front. You would enter the porch from the side. The door to the house itself was in the middle of the porch.

Parking the car some distance from the house, we started our stealthy approach. As we got closer our fears increased. We knew it was still in the porch waiting.

Deciding our best approach was to rush in with speed; we looked at each other, took in as much air as we could and rushed the screened-in porch. Opening the door, there it stood. Four feet tall as it had been two months ago and getting stronger each day. A pyramid of dirty diapers with the ammonia so strong our eyes were

253

already tearing up.

Now taking a breath because we had good lungs, we rushed the front door and were met by the lady of the house, all four hundred pounds of her wearing a flimsy nightgown.

She began telling how she was being threatened and hollered at, not feeling safe in her own house. Saying the drinking must stop.

The husband was sitting in a small bathroom, all 450 pounds on the pot with just his shorts around his ankles, leaning forward exerting himself and by the aroma you knew what was happening.

It was about this time I took another breath with some regret. After some words with the husband he understood if we got a call back he would be spending a night in jail.

We looked around and unwashed dishes were on the table and in the sink. You might say the place could use a bit of tidying up. The kids were in diapers, crying, probably because of the hollering going on. We told the lady we would be reporting what we were seeing to the proper authorities. She didn't appear overly concerned as this was not the first time she had been told this. She did offer to make us a cup of coffee, not seeming offended when we told her we had other calls to make.

As we left the happy couple, quite hurriedly, I might add, we knew we had gone where other officers feared to tread. In a year or so the couple moved to a farm a few miles from town on a hill where strong winds blow.

This story is true and was not meant to degrade anyone but to show just how deplorable some people lived in these times.

~

114
GIRL IN THE LAKE

Sometimes when I'm sleeping, I see a picture in my mind, a picture of a young boy running in the snow. It's early evening, street lights are on, great fluffy flakes are drifting down carried by a gentle breeze. What a wondrous night to be out.

Then it starts to come back to me. Memories of many years past of the early 60's. I had been called to a part of town that had been called Skunk Hollow in the S.E. part of town close to the river.

The man calling lived along the River Road next to the alley. Watching TV in the early evening, he was startled when a big rock came crashing through his large picture window and ended up in the middle of his living room floor.

Looking out he could see no one. Soon he was on the phone to the police. Arriving and getting an explanation on what had just happened, I was out on the trail, following it down alleys and side roads. The trail would go to the tar and disappear. After twenty minutes of this I stopped and thought, "I could lose the trail because he had so much time on me". Thinking, "Don't be stupid, when does a man try to hide his trail?" The answer was, "After he has done something." The rock was a thing of opportunity, coming upon the rock and throwing it.

The answer was, back trail him. Go back picking up the trail where the rock had been laying, then follow the footprints back through the alleys to a yellow house just past the park on 14th Ave S.E.

A woman answered my knock on the door. Asking to talk to her young son, I was told he had left a short time ago.

I had noted the footprints in the snow which later matched the young man's. He was set to appear in juvenile court. What happened to him there, I have no idea, as I cannot recall ever having been told of the disposition of a juvenile after his court appearance.

Time went by; in the fall there was a report of a missing girl that lived on 7th St. S.E. Her name was Amy Lou Howe, age sixteen.

It seems she liked to take her books down by Lily Lake to study, which is a quarter of a mile south of her home across a field close to the Grand Rapids Airport.

This being a Saturday, the parents were not concerned when she didn't show up when expected. As time wore on, they started to worry. She couldn't be seen as they looked over the fields.

On Saturday, Oct. 5, 1963, Walt Craig, the Chief of Police for the Village of Grand Rapids, was notified of the missing girl.

A search was intensified in the area of the field and the edge of the lake. It was not long and the books were found scattered close to the lake. The grass here is uncut and quite high as well as the tall reeds growing on the edge of the lake. It was obvious a lot of the grass was trampled down. Further searching took them to the edge of the water where her body was found.

Pulled from the water, it was evident that Amy Lou had been attacked, stabbed and slashed many times. The area around the lake showed that a terrible struggle had taken place. She had been pulled into the lake to make sure the body was hidden.

Soon the body was taken to the Rowe Funeral Home where it was examined by the County Coroner, Evan Henderson of Nashwauk, who said the body had received over 60 knife wounds.

Shortly after, Chief Craig had reports of a boy seen in the area and was soon talking to the young man. The boy had just come from his home, appeared to be nervous and to have tried to clean up his clothing and his shoes were wet. In a short time he admitted that he had lost his watch in the struggle and had gone back to find it.

Craig then took the boy to the yellow house on 14th Ave. S.E. and was able to secure a small pocket knife. The boy was taken into custody Saturday afternoon.

Monday, October 7, 1963: Herald Review Volume 61-80.
A boy will appear in juvenile court on Monday for questioning in the death of Amy Lou Howe, 16, who had been stabbed 60 times and killed Saturday.

Authorities said the boy is being held on a delinquency petition. He is a schoolmate and neighbor of the Howe girl.

Thursday, Oct 10, 1963: Herald Review Volume 61-81.
Second degree murder charges have been placed against the boy,

14, suspected in the murder of Amy Lou Howe, 16. Juvenile Court Judge John Benton, entered an order referring the violation to the county attorney for prosecution and said he will be tried as an adult. He had been brought before Benton on a delinquency petition.

Warren Anderson was appointed as legal counsel for the boy.

Ben Grussendorf, who will be handling the prosecution, asked for a 10 day delay to obtain legal counsel before being arraigned.

Thursday, October 31, 1963: Herald Review Volume 61-87. Court grants delay for murder trial. No plea to be made until Nov 10th for the boy. He appeared in dist court on a second degree murder charge. Bail was set at a $100,000.00. An indictment was returned by a grand jury Monday. If found guilty of 2nd Degree the boy could not get more than 40 years.

Thursday, December 26, 1963: Herald Review Volume 61-103. Boy, 14, pleads guilty of 3rd Degree murder Monday before District Court Judge Arnold C. Forbes.

The youth was sentenced to not more than 25 years under the direction of the Youth Conservation Commission. He is to be taken to St Cloud by Sheriff John Muhar for psychiatric evaluation.

Earlier the boy had admitted stabbing the girl to death with a pocket knife but he told the court Monday he had not intended to kill her.

Defense Attorney, Warren Anderson and Paul Shaw requested the reduction from 2nd Degree to 3rd Degree.

County Attorney, Ben Grussendorf reluctantly agreed because there was some doubt he intended her death.

I will never forget the young girl or the yellow house on 14th Ave SE. 50 years later; it still slips into my mind. Soon I will be gone, and then who will remember?

~

115
THE SHOEBOX

In June 1955 I went to work for the village of Grand Rapids as a patrolman, a job I learned to love. The only drawback was the wages, so my wife, with two children, and wanting to help, went to work part time for Kremer's Ben Franklin. It was a type of variety store that sold dry goods, clothing, furniture and also had a lunch counter. It was a large, two story brick building with a basement located on the corner of 1st Ave. N.W. and 4th St., now a parking lot.

It was during this time I became acquainted with the Asst. Manager Leo Voltz. A most capable, understanding person as you would ever want to meet.

Within a few short years we began having a problem at the high school. A note would be found saying there was a bomb in the school or there would be lipstick on a mirror stating that a bomb would be going off.

This was raising havoc with the administration, but I don't ever remember closing down the school although searches were made.

One afternoon the school received a call on the phone stating there was a bomb set to go off in the high school. The person answering the phone said it sounded like a young man but something was odd in the background. It sounded like a parrot talking.

It didn't take us long to make it over to Kremer's as we were all aware of the talking myna bird located close to the phone booth.

Talking to some of the employees they were able to tell us of a young boy seen using the pay phone at about the right time. The young man was picked up, and he admitted making the phone threat to the school as well as the notes left at the school. He was turned over to the juvenile court.

A few years later, to my surprise, Leo Voltz came running into the police station all out of breath. The police station was located a block from the Kremer's building. Leo had run the full distance. It was now getting onto 9:00 p.m., still daylight on a hot summer day.

Leo stated he had gone back to the store after closing to catch up on some work. He had entered the store through the front door and was walking around a clothing rack when he almost bumped into a man in his thirties. He didn't know if the man was armed or not, as he said his feet took over.

We were soon at Kremer's, some of us searching the building, some outside watching to see if someone came out. We never found anyone in the building as it's a safe bet he left as fast as Leo did.

Some months later, Walter Craig the Chief of Police, called Dale Fox and me into his office saying he had good information that Kremer's was to be burglarized and the safe cracked. This was to happen tonight, Christmas Eve.

Walt had a key to the Kremer's building. We were to wait until dark around 6:00 p.m., sneak in and stake out the inside, and wait for the person or persons to show during the night. Not knowing if they had hid in the building before closing, perhaps in the basement.

Dale Fox was supposed to find a place in the back of the building to hide. The building was around 200 feet long, a hundred feet wide with rooms on the second floor, lots of rooms, nooks and crannies in the basement. The main floor had a very high ceiling covered in ornate tin design. In the front of the main floor was a stair case up to a small office that was supposed to be my stake out place. Making my way up the stairway to the office as quietly as possible and locating the safe, I found a place to settle in.

You sit there waiting for any sound but there are so many in an old building: a fan starts somewhere or an air blower turns on, the creaks and strains of the old building, a grain truck goes by rattling the windows, you're straining to hear, how alert can you be? Time goes ticking by; it's 1:00 in the morning. They should be coming soon, then there are sounds that you can't identify. Do you hear something on the stairs? You crawl over and look, nothing.

The chief had said that this was reliable information, it was going to happen. So, you stay alert, you know Fox is in the back of the store. You don't have radios; they would be coming years later. You haven't heard anything from him, he must be all right.

It's getting onto 2 a.m., nothing. But, yes there is. You need to go; it's been some eight hours. Where is the bathroom? Probably downstairs to the back, can you find it? No, you can't leave where you are. The time for them to come must be soon. You just have to hold it. A half hour goes by, this ain't working, you're getting desperate. Looking around for a jar, a can, anything, then I see a shoebox--10 ½, my size shoes.

Taking the box down and opening it, I did what any man would do. There must be a half inch in that box. Putting the lid back on, I sat it in a corner. But I'm a happy man.

The rest of the night goes by slowly. At 6:00 a.m. Walt Craig shows up to relieve us. Its Christmas morning. I did set the shoes on the box before leaving.

My oldest son's favorite story.

~

116
THE KEY - 32 ARRESTED

During the summer of 1970 there seemed to be a rash of crimes in the city of Grand Rapids and throughout Itasca County.

You name it, from car thefts to house break-ins and outboard motors. We were asking the citizens for any information they might have. Our officers were covering the pawn shops but nothing seemed to be paying off. They must be taking the loot to the Cities or somewhere out of town.

The two young boys were getting close to the fence. This was the third or fourth time they had burglarized the downtown creamery located on the corner of 3rd St. N.W. and 2nd Ave. Later the Royal Bar would be built there.

This was big money to them and they were getting good at it. Tonight they would make off with 6 8 glass milk jugs. Tomorrow they would bring them back and collect 25 cents apiece for them. The manager never seemed to catch on. They had a good night. At around 10 a.m. they were at the creamery and collected their $2.

Shortly after 10 a.m. I was called to the creamery by the manager. Quickly he told me how he suspected what the boys were doing. He did know who the two boys were and where they lived, in a yellow house next to the Riverside School. I, too, knew who they were and the fact that they had problems of their own.

The boys were from 13 to 14 years of age and came out to greet me. I told them I was doing some investigation about some burglaries at the creamery where some fingerprints may turn out to be theirs. They soon were telling me all about it and me telling them that I knew about some other things. The older brother admitted the theft of some copper wire which he had sold. Then he seemed to get agitated and mad.

Asked why, he said here he was getting in trouble over some milk jugs and 10 pounds of copper wire while he knew some guys who were getting away with over 1,000 pounds of copper wire and other things.

The key. It seems there is always a key that opens up a case you are working. It may be a word like: milk jug, a look, on the way something may be denied; the real key is listening. The keys to the following cases were: milk jugs and copper wire.

It took some time for me to get all of what the boys knew and it was extensive.

I now had as suspects two young men living in the west end of town. Taking time to validate what I was finding, after a couple days I talked to the boys and broke things wide open. Some of what had been going on happened in Grand Rapids but most was out in the county. I knew I needed help, there was just too much for one person. I contacted the Itasca County Sherriff's office and was soon working with Deputy Lou Hince, a capable young man.

Scores of crimes were getting solved over the next couple weeks. House prowls, burglaries, gas siphoning, auto stripping.

Before we were done, 32 individuals had been involved in the crimes which went back as far as two years. The list was 11 juveniles, 19 minors and 2 adults.

One person was turned over to the FBI on federal charges stemming from the theft of an outboard motor at Federal Dam.

It was found during the investigation that the persons involved had intertwined connections but were not an organized gang.

Their crimes covered a wide range of activity including house prowls, car thefts, boat motor thefts, tire, battery and radiator thefts, a break-in at the Texaco Station, a break-in at the county garage in Cohasset, Cohasset Mill and Lumber Company, cabin break-ins, vandalism, gas siphoning, shop lifting and the theft of copper tubing and fittings from different buildings including the Catholic school.

Many of the thefts reflected the vacation aspect of the Grand Rapids area. Six houseboats near the thoroughfare bridge were entered, fishing tackle and an outboard motor taken. The motor was recovered.

Wild rice was stolen from Hick's Wild Rice Company, commercial fishing nets were stolen from the Mississippi River, and also targeted was Beer's Minnow Station in Cohasset.

Recovery of many of the articles was difficult as some things had been sold or lost, some even stolen from the thieves themselves.

Other cases included car prowls, pinball machines, burglary at Sugar Hills, and a break-in at Rapid's Tackle. Five pistols were recovered. Copper wiring had been stripped out of several houses. Tires were taken from the Sunset, Rapids Body and Riverside auto. Credit cards were stolen and used along with forged checks in the area and throughout the state. Gas stealing was going on all over the place.

Vehicles were a favorite target. The theft of bucket seats from Maki's Auto Body, two cars stolen and recovered, a stolen pickup recovered in Duluth with charges pending as the thieves were in custody. Car washes and Laundromats were not overlooked for their coins.

It is impossible to cover every part of a massive investigation in a short story such as this. Next the courts had their work to do with the 32.

The key: listening.

The milk jug boys made restitution to the creamery and pretty much stayed out of trouble. We were still friends.

Grand Rapids Herald Review   Monday, October 12, 1970
Volume 76 Number 82

~

117
ONIONS

It was just a short time into our marriage that I could see something was not right.

It had been agreed that if we could not come to a mutual decision that I, being the man of the house, would make it.

But if I made this decision I knew it could tear us apart so I held off.

The years were going fast and this thing was eating me up, tearing me apart. I was a man, the head of the house, and could not seem to look her in the eye and say it. So, I held off.

50 years of marriage and I knew what was coming. Thanksgiving was in a few days, I could feel the pressure inside of me. This could go no further. This was it if I was ever to be a man.

The day before Thanksgiving I slowly walked into the kitchen and I knew it. She came right out and said, "Harv, I need you to run down to the store and get me some onions."

I never batted an eye, turning, I thought, "I can get what I want." She stopped me cold saying, "Make sure they are yellow onions."

The dam burst, my courage was there, I turned and defiantly said, "I don't like yellow onions, I like white onions."

I knew it was coming, she looked me right in the eye, not exploding, saying, "Honey," with a sweet smile, "if you want white onions, you get white onions."

All these years and that's all she had to say?

I came home with a big bag of white onions, the man of the house.

Well, that was a real rift of my own making and we had our laughs over it.

But somehow these things have a way of leaking out. Looking under the Christmas tree there was some strange packaging, two wrapped in tinfoil from my older brother, Don; one to myself and one to my wife, Doris.

We open our gifts on Christmas Eve. Doris opened her tinfoil gift first. It was a beautiful yellow onion. I opened mine next and it was even a more gorgeous white onion. We did get our laughs. How word gets around.

Christmas was not over with. I have a son, Ron, a sculptor who works with clay, and I consider him one of the best in his profession. We had more gifts to open and Ron's were next.

I opened mine first and there stood a white onion, 6 inches tall with feet and a nose. It was a caricature of me. Mother's was next and no surprise, a yellow onion, a caricature of herself, lipstick and all, with feet fashioned and molded in clay.

I guess a man can change after 50 years; this is one yellow onion I can go for.

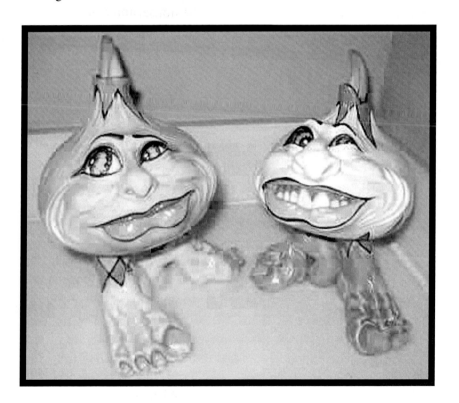

~

118
SOMEONE'S LAST MOMENTS

Arlis Hopkins, my partner for the night, and I were patrolling in the early springtime many years ago with Arlis driving. We had taken a few minor calls just after starting our shift at 11 p.m. Since that time it looked like we would have an uneventful night.

It being a warm night we had our car windows down. Having just come from coffee, it must have been close to 2 a.m.

Deciding to leave the downtown area, we were going to sweep the southwest part of town. Heading up Powers Hill we made a right on 4th St. S.W. (this would be where the new stoplights are now). Continuing west on 4th St., we made a right turn onto 10th Ave. Heading north toward the river, as we were going down the hill, we were approaching the old Schirber house on the left hand side of the 200 block. This was a very large white house well known to us as they had 15 children.

The night was warm with some snow banks on the side of the road. The pavement was melted in some areas but some ice and snow remained in others. There was some lighting but visibility was poor. As we were coming down the hill, I suddenly said to Arlis, "There is a man walking in the road toward us", he said, "Where?" I answered, "In front of the Schirbers." He was almost impossible to see as the light was bad and he was wearing a long gray coat that was blending into the road, ice and fog. There was a car coming up behind the man from the area of the river. The man was in his lane of traffic.

You could see what was about to happen and if you had not seen it you would have thought the car was going faster than it was. The driver apparently hit his brakes, but still the man was struck in the back by the airplane hood ornament. His body and head came back, denting the hood. His legs snapped back under the bumper. Then, the man was flying for 20 feet. Legs broken, landing 40 feet in front of our police car on his back. Getting out as fast as we could, it was obvious there was nothing we could do for the man as the damage from the car and contact with the pavement had done its job. The car that struck the man was a fairly new Dodge, red and black, now with a lot of hood damage.

The young man getting out of the Dodge said that due to the fog and the color of the man's coat (a gray herringbone), he had not seen the man in the middle of the road until he was almost on him.

An ambulance was called but nothing could be done. It was our opinion he had died immediately upon striking the hood and the road.

If we had not seen this happen, there may have been an arrest made. However, because the car was not speeding and the poor road conditions and the gray herringbone coat and the fog, we could not hold the driver of the car responsible.

The driver was quite distraught, having known the man for some time.

We later heard the young driver had received his first bicycle from the deceased.

My recollection of what happened, uh, so many years ago

You do wonder sometimes if someone is watching over you. You were there at the precise time to see someone's last moment on this earth.

~

119
DESTINY

There I sat waiting. It's been some time now, but I know she will be back. The pain, the frustration. I cringe but that won't do any good. It's happened to me before. The woman has no sense of decency. It may be a mental block when she gets me in her hand and squeezes me; anything that may have been human seems to disappear.

Does anyone out there really care? So I sit and wait.

If I were much bigger would she treat me this way? No, I think not. Her arms would tire much faster; I would be able to rest.

Meanwhile, I hide in the closet hoping she won't find me, but she will. Then it's going to go on for weeks. She calls it therapy and good for her but what about me?

She walks by the closet, is she looking for me? Her husband, a gentle soul, God bless him, tries to tell her it is not right but does she listen? I think not.

I know he has tried to help her but she brushes him aside, saying she knows what she is doing.

The last time this spring she took me into her bedroom. Before she was done she had me in every room upstairs. This went on for three months. Her husband tried to intervene, just how much is a 1 1/4 inch brush supposed to take? No, she says I'm at least 1 ½ inches wide. We have had several experts in trying to get true measurements using tape measures, lasers and other scientific equipment but this flies out the window when she puts her foot down.

I know my time is coming to an end. I'm seriously thinking of suicide. I did get into the turpentine, she pulled me out. The smell was pretty bad but she used some of her husband's deodorant.

Now she has me out in the sun most days painting the outside of the house. I'm starting to fade away. Sunstroke, I hope!

~

120
DESTINY II - A HUSBAND'S PLEA

Today I sit in my lonely nest; the little guy was not the only victim. He at least lies in a lonely graveyard set free by the sun. What am I to do?

I had told my brother of my dilemma, but he just laughed, said it couldn't be that bad. He brushed me aside.

He hired her to paint his upstairs at $2.00 an hour. She is now on her third month with a bigger brush, 1 ¾ inches.

There is something wrong with the paint as it dries on the brush before it gets to the wall. With some tact, I told her she might be a little slow.

I might have used the wrong words. Having been to war, I was very brave, doing my duty with a gun and bayonet, but now I sit and tremble. I went to the VA for help; they told me it was PTSD. The looks, the tight lips, the silence.

My brother called me today saying he may be moving. He is being sued by the US Government. He could get a couple years; he had not been paying into Withholding, SS and Workers Comp. He asked me as a brother, "What should I do?" I told him the cheapest thing to do is change his name. Take nothing with him and leave the state.

Today I tried calling him, his phone had been disconnected. I thought I might go with him but it appears I'm too late.

She's acquired quite a reputation. The paint and brush manufacturing company showed up at our house this morning saying their company and its stocks are at an all time low. They were willing to offer her a hefty sum if she would sign an agreement saying she had never used any of their paint brushes or products in the past.

She refused them, asking them to leave as she would be in the basement painting.

~

121
OLD TIME CHARACTERS

They sat in majestic brick splendor; one and two story houses nestled on the shores of Hale and Crystal Lake in the northern part of town and perhaps Pokegama Ave. If you were of the elite this was the place to live.

At that time ice boxes were serviced by the large barnlike icehouse that sat on the shore of Crystal Lake, now the fairgrounds parking lot. Coal was delivered to the coal chute door to your basement. Most of the older houses were wired with the old two strand electrical wire.

Now we were getting into the modern age, the fifties were here. Almost everyone had the up-to-date oil furnace, washer and dryer, running water and a black and white TV.

Back in the forties and early fifties Skunk Hollow was considered one of the poorer sections of town and it could be heard that a lot of "riff raff" lived there. This was located on the outskirts of town on the S.E. River Road.

On the south side of the river where the Horn Bridge now stands, a garbage dump sat back into the bank of the river. Across the road was the Hamm's Beer warehouse which is now the River Road Market. A few of the houses had dirt floors and outside "biffys". It is true they did have some interesting characters living there.

One was an older man, well-known, possibly in his seventies who oft times could be seen walking the streets at night on his wooden peg leg. It would be a good bet that he had too much of the bottle. He also had a son, Junior, who lived with him. Junior was very easy to recognize as he was also a drinker. The more he drank, the further his arms came out from his sides. So pretty soon his arms would be straight out like wings and he would be bending over at night on his way home.

On this night we were coming north across Pokegama Bridge at about 1:00 a.m. It was raining, a downpour, and hard to see through the windshield. Approaching 2nd St. N. with the Riverside Hotel on our right, we could see a car stopped on Pokegama Ave. with its lights on. A man was standing in the street; there was also a man lying on the street unconscious.

The driver told us the unconscious man had been cutting across the intersection kitty corner in the hard rain and due to his dark clothing had not been seen until he was almost on him.

Checking the unconscious man, we knew who he was. An ambulance was called and arrived shortly. The man was loaded into a station-wagon ambulance which soon had Junior in the hospital. He was still unconscious but alive with his right leg broken. While lying on the hospital bed, he would groan then lift the broken leg, dangling it in the air. The doctor didn't think he would need much painkiller. Not knowing the full extent of his injuries, he thought we should notify his father.

We drove to Skunk Hollow to the tar paper shack. Knocking on the door but getting no response, we continued pounding on the door still with no results. Finally, we just walked in. As we stepped over the threshold, we stepped into a two inch pool of water from the rain. The floor was dirt.

Going further, we entered a small room, the father lying on the bed. After some shaking we were able to wake him. He was not happy. We told him his son had been hit by a car, had a broken leg and other injuries. He may want to go to the hospital to see him.

He said, "Do I have to go see him tonight?" not in happy terms. Telling him it was up to him, we left, we had done our best.

Junior did live but I can never remember seeing either of them walking the night streets again.

~

122
BLOWING A CLUE

Recently I was driving in the west end of town. Looking over I could see a large building, cream with green trim. It was located at 1707 N.W. 4th St. A new business, J.M.B Automotive, was going in there. It took me back many years into the early 80's when it was a big, green cement block building, two stories high with seven apartments upstairs and a thriving furniture store on the east side of the downstairs called Kel-Dee's Furniture. It was owned by Brad and Bobbie Frisk, my son's In-laws.

Back then it so happened a storm had passed through that weekend with strong winds and a heavy accumulation of snow. Many roads had yet to be plowed.

Early Monday morning I received a call from Kel-Dee's saying they had been burglarized some time over the weekend. On the scene I was told they had installed a unique, expensive lighting system outside that was now missing.

There was snow up to two feet outside of the building, some from the storm and some blowing off the roof. You could see someone had walked in the snowdrifts. The tracks in some areas were totally drifted in. Working my way around the building, I found a couple of them that had only 8-10 inches in them. Taking my time, getting down on my knees, I huffed and puffed, blowing as hard as I could into the loose snow in the print. Soon my face was red and wet with snow in my hair. After some time I had two nice boot prints. They appeared to be some kind of "pac" boot prints with heavy tread.

Walking to the north side of the building, I noted that the bottom stair had been stepped on and that the snow on the edge of the roof at the top of the stairs had been disturbed. I'm always looking for some evidence or a key that will open up a case. It looked like the boot print was all I would have, that and the disturbed snow on the edge of roof.

Going up the stairs, I entered a short hallway. At the end I made a left. There was a long hallway with numbers on the doors showing there were as many as seven apartments. Most of them gave me a feeling that they were empty. Standing in the middle of the hallway about half way, I just stood and listened for about five minutes, nothing. Then I thought I heard a sound in Apt. 2. I went knocking on the door. Robin, my son, was close behind me. A young man answered looking like he had just gotten out of bed but mostly dressed.

As he opened the door I could see a pair of "pac" boots sitting just inside the door. Entering and pretending I had not seen the boots, I "stumbled" over them, knocking them over and almost falling. I reached down to set them back up seeing what I had expected; they had the same prints on the bottom as the ones outside in the snow.

We were in for another surprise. Looking up and across the room at the head of the bed, we saw the stolen lights hung in their brilliant red array.

It was soon learned the young man had just gotten out of jail a few days earlier.

The lights were turned over to their owner and the man was charged with theft, not burglary, as he had not entered the building.

~

123
DRIVE-BY-SHOOTING

During the summer of the late 80's we were receiving reports of some windows in the downtown being shot with BB guns. Now and then some young kid would be picked up and charged with shooting BB guns in town. Now, this can be a serious matter as large window replacement can be very costly.

We thought we were pretty lucky--at least we were not having drive-by shootings of people and houses as was being reported in the Cities. But, we do get surprises in our small town.

One summer day I received a call that a home on 9th St. N.W. was reporting that a daughter's bedroom window had a bullet hole in it. Arriving and being taken to the bedroom you could see that both a storm window and the inside window on the west side had holes in them.

Looking closely, following what would be the trajectory, a .22 caliber bullet was found lodged in the side of a dresser. The owner had no idea of the time this happened. It had to be within the last day or so.

Looking at the holes in the window, I concluded they could not have come from the road or a car.

I asked the owner if he had a small, long piece of wood. He brought me an arrow. I then stuck the arrow into the dresser, lined it up with the holes in the window and sighted along the arrow. It pointed directly to an upstairs porch about two blocks away.

I then drove to the house and rang the doorbell; a very nice lady answered the door. I asked her if she had any sons and if they had been doing any shooting. She said she had two boys; they did own a .22 rifle but hadn't been doing any shooting. I asked her if I might look on the back porch and she gave me permission. It didn't take long until I found several spent .22 casings, both on the porch and on the ground.

The boys were talked to and admitted shooting the .22 from the porch, not knowing it had gone through a neighbors' window. They paid for the window replacement. We never had any further trouble with the boys.

A year later I came to work one day and heard there had been a drive-by shooting at 516 10th Ave. N.E. Having had a lot of luck some time ago, I drove over to have a look. It turned out to be a house just across the street from where I used to live. Arriving at the house, I was shown a couch with what looked like a shotgun slug in it.

I then lined the hole in the couch with the hole through both doors and made the determination that the trajectory of the bullet was too high and could not have come from a car. It did line up with a house on a hill across the street. I then went to the old Fox house which had new people living there.

As I knocked on the back door, it was answered by a lady saying, "I have been expecting you. Is it about the bullet holes?" I replied that it was and asked what had happened. She said her son of about 14 had been handling a 12 gauge shotgun a couple days ago when it went off.

Taking me into a back bedroom, she showed me where it had happened. She then showed me the path of the slug. When it went off, it went through the wood on the back of a rocking chair, through the wall, across the living room, through both doors--one wood and one glass, across the street where it went through both doors--again one glass and one wood and 15 feet into a couch.

This again is one of those things; if you hadn't seen it, you would not have believed it.

These two examples are as close to being drive-by "shootings" as I can recall over the years.

~

124
MONEY IN THE SOCK

As I recall, it was a Saturday morning in the late 80's when I was called to a break-in at the Riverside Car Wash located three blocks down on 3rd St. N.E. at the top side of the river bank.

It so happened we had a rather hard snow storm the past few days with two foot snow banks around the building. The manager proceeded to show me a side door that had been forced. After gaining entry the thieves had entered the offices. Missing at this time was a cloth sack full of quarters.

There was little chance of picking up any usable finger prints due to the fact so many people are in and out of the building and offices. Then I concentrated on what could be found in the snow drifts. The only thing I could discern was snow-filled footprints that led in the direction of the Horn Bridge.

After talking to the manager as to who may have been around that would be out of place the last day or so, we came up with a few names. Knowing where some of them lived, I ruled them out for now because of the direction the prints seemed to lead. Then zeroing in on the ones who lived across the bridge, I went to the River South Apartments. I knocked on the door of one of my suspects.

James answered the door and I asked if I could come in and talk to him for a few minutes. He very graciously invited me in as we had known each other for some time. We sat and chit-chatted for a little while, then I asked him if he had been in the area of the Riverside Car Wash the last couple of days. He said he had not. A few more questions were asked. I didn't seem to be getting anywhere.

This was a small apartment with nothing suspicious or out of place.

Now I don't know why I looked down at an air vent and said, "Do you mind if I look around a little?" James said, "No, I have nothing to hide." I picked up a butter knife and asked if I could use it and he said, "Go ahead."

Going over to the air vent, unscrewing two screws, removing the vent plate, looking inside, I could see nothing. Lying down on my side, reaching in as far as I could, I touched something soft and pulled it out, a sock full of quarters!

It didn't take him long to fess up, as he must have thought one of his friends had given him up.

Seeing that the quarters were only a small part of the loot he would have to pay back, he agreed to show me where the rest of the money was.

We went back across the bridge. On the N.E. side of the bridge is a small area next to the park that had been dug into for dirt fill. There was a large snow bank 20-30 ft from the sidewalk. He had taken some of the quarters out of the sack, then swung it to get momentum, throwing it into the snow bank. After a short time we were able to locate the sack which felt like it weighed 15 pounds or more!

The young man was then arrested for burglary and theft.

To the end of his days, he thought one of his friends had given him up, but I would never tell him who. To the end of my days, I will never know why I looked into that hot air vent.

~

125
DROWNING DOG RESCUED

Years ago, possibly the 1980's, I was called to the bank of the Mississippi River along 11th Ave. S.W. The time was early spring and quite cold. Upon arriving a man pointed out what appeared to be a black Lab floundering in the water perhaps 200 feet from shore. He was in a six foot hole in the ice.

As hard as he tried, he couldn't get up on the ice. As you watched you could see he was losing the battle. He was starting to go under the water, then back up.

I noted that if the dog had broken through the ice it would not hold a man. What to do? As the dog kept going under, there was not much time.

I asked the man if he had a long wooden ladder and he soon had one down to the river bank.

Pushing the ladder on my hands and knees, in a short time I was out to the dog that by this time was motionless and floating close to the surface. While lying on the ladder, I reached out and getting the dog by the collar and hair, I tried to pull him up on the ice. It was difficult as the dog must have weighed 60 to 70 pounds and the water was so cold.

After getting the dog on the ladder, pulling it back to where the ice seemed safe, and rolling him off the ladder, I started to do some sort of artificial respiration both by pushing on his chest with both hands and working his chest with my foot.

After a few minutes, the dog seemed to cough and started to breathe on its own. A short time later he was able to walk. He had a license on his collar so the pound master was able to return him to his owner, Alf Madsen, who lived over across the river in the northwest part of town.

I later heard the dog had been doing very well over night but died some time the next day.

All you can do is try your best.

Sometimes?

~

126
THE IGUANA

Some times you go to write a story and you get a little lost as some may go back almost 60 years. What were the facts? What officers were with you? And not wanting to be self-serving, you try to remember. Some officers were with you a short time, some many years.

This story starts with a little history on the building itself. Somewhere in the 1950's a building was moved to 1313 7th St. N.E. by Jake Makedonsky, an old, Russian man. Industrious and a hard worker, he made it into what was then called the Keoki Reef, a bar and a dance hall. It was well known for fights but not any worse than other establishments of its kind. In the early 60's it burned down.

In 1963 IJC (Itasca Junior College) moved from Greenway of Coleraine to the North Central Experiment Station on the east edge of Grand Rapids. There was now a need for housing for its students. Lee Hall, a small dormitory, was built where Keoki Reef once stood.

My partner Gene Bennett and I were called to Lee Hall one summer weekend. There had been an entry made on a downstairs apartment. Missing was a small amount of jewelry, one piece being a necklace. Also missing was a live two foot long iguana which had been kept in a long glass case.

As we left there we had little to work with. Iguanas are not stolen every day, so I recall we were asking a lot of questions over the next few days.

One day a young man told us he had heard a rumor that a tow truck driver from Jim's 76 Station had pulled a stalled car that had an iguana in it into Grand Rapids from the Hill City area.

Checking with the driver at the 76 Station, he told us this was true. Asking if he had a slip with the car license plate number on it, he said he also had the name of the driver as well as his address, which turned out to be in Bemidji.

Bennett and I were soon on our way to Bemidji. Arriving we talked to the police department about the young men. They told us they were aware the boys were doing some break-ins. They were watching, not having any luck.

We then went to the apartment where the two boys lived. Knocking on the door, we were met by three or four young men. We had conversations over the next hour. They told us that the two men we were looking for had left some time ago.

As we were about to leave, we asked for some identification to show we weren't getting a snow job. They, possibly being the men we were looking for. They produced some identification, but as they did so some ID's came out that were not theirs.

Looking at the assorted licenses and other ID's in their possession, we knew there was something wrong. They proved not to be the persons we were looking for. We then called the Bemidji police to check out the false ID's in their possession. It didn't take long for them to put it together; they came from several house burglaries that recently had been reported. As a result, several of their cases were solved.

By this time it was getting quite late at night. One of their officers listening to his radio scanner said, "This might be of interest to you." There was a motorcycle being pursued over in the Park Rapids area ridden by one of our suspects.

Shortly, Bennett and I were speeding in that direction. Soon we heard that the cycle had crashed, the rider was taken to a Wadena hospital and that he might be released. We arrived there about 3:00 a.m.

We met the suspect who agreed to talk to us. He admitted that he and his friends did the break-in at Lee Hall, with his friend getting jewelry--and the iguana.

After talking to both suspects the iguana was recovered from a pet shop close to Cass Lake. Their car had been abandoned in a lot by the tall pines east of Cass Lake with some of the items being recovered from it. The necklace was hanging from a rearview mirror.

The boys were to appear in Itasca District Court.

~

127
THE TIME BOMB

How would you feel if you were driving around town knowing there was a middle-aged man out there sharing the road with you that has sudden black-outs and that might lose control of his pickup at any time, a time bomb?

This matter first came to my attention in the 1980's. To the best of my recollection, Gildemeister Motors had a business almost across the street from the courthouse on 4th St. N.E. where there had been a head-on collision.

One of the drivers, Devon Holmstrom, had blacked out, crossing the center line and hitting the oncoming car head on. The driver of the other car, Dan, was almost killed. He received massive head injuries. He was taken to the hospital by ambulance and spent quite some time there to recover. From the reports and rumors I later received, he never fully recovered from his head injuries. He died some years later, in all probability from those head injuries.

Devon Holmstrom was a well known business man that had to take medication for a seizure disorder, we knew this.

Over the next few years we had at least nine accident reports on him. He had been having his driver's license revoked and surrendered to the state, the first time in 1985 for failure to supply a proper medical statement. A print- out of his driver's license shows his license had been reinstated seven times.

On May 11, 1992, at 11 a.m. the office manager and a co-worker were sitting behind the counter in Dr. Singsank's dental office located at 303 S.E. 1st St. in Grand Rapids, in a solid brick building.

Described by those at the scene, "It was like a bomb went off." Bricks and dust were flying and a large hole appeared in the corner of the office. Most of the equipment was damaged in some way with a lot of structural damage to the building. A pickup was lodged in the hole. The office manager and co-worker had both gone over the four foot counter. The manager's shoes were still on the floor where she had been sitting. A brick had also struck her chair.

~

Holmstrom, who had blacked out, was still sitting in the pickup. He was treated by Meds1 Ambulance personnel and taken to Itasca Medical Center where he was treated and released with minor injuries.

At this time he had facial cuts and bruises along with injuries to his thumbs and legs. He also told the police officers he had just passed out before the accident, saying that he takes meds for the disorder but described
the last few times he had passed out as just happening suddenly, saying, "I'm going to get this checked out."

I was interviewed by a reporter and reiterated the facts that Holmstrom had a history with our department with at least nine different driving and accident reports. That, in fact, his Minnesota driving records show he had been reinstated seven times. The police department had been helpless in the face of these continual reinstatements by the Minn. Driver's License Bureau that I would be talking to.

Dr. Singsank could only guess about the damages, possibly $10,000, saying, "My whole business was trashed and I am amazed there were not more injuries to my office staff than minor injuries and bruises."

After clearing the accident scene, I went back and called the driver's license bureau. After talking to a person from the bureau and giving them all the information on Holmstrom, she came back with his record saying there was nothing they could do as he was coming in with a doctor's certificate saying he could drive, they would have to reinstate him.

Needless to say it didn't take long to see we were getting back to the old story. I then asked to talk to a supervisor and started to get the same story about the doctors signing to get his license back. I decided to use a different approach.

I said, "What in the hell is wrong with you people down there? If you look, you will see he is jumping doctors. Make him go back to his first doctor. In all probabilities, he has killed one person and come close to killing others." The supervisor said he would do what he could. We left on friendlier terms. This conversation took place in 1992.

Just about the time I was to retire in 1995, I was served with papers from Holmstrom, who was suing for a sum of at least $50,000 because of the loss of his driving privileges. As I was working for the city at the time, this was handled by the city attorney. The lawsuit was dismissed by the courts with prejudice.

Devon left this world of ours a few years ago still waiting for reinstatement.

The facts in this story are all true but the names have been changed on advice of counsel.

Reference   Harvey Dahline
Herald Review, May 13, 1992

~

128
A MOST RESPECTED LETTER

In 1955 I joined the Grand Rapids Police Dept. Shortly thereafter I met John Spellacy, a much respected lawyer with an impeccable reputation. It was said if you wanted the best lawyer, it would be John Spellacy. I knew him for many years both as a lawyer and also as a friend who gave me some good advice to help someone else out. Also, through many years as a judge, he was always there day or night when needed for warrants or advice.

There is no one that I had more respect for over the 40 years I was a police officer than Judge John J. Spellacy.

As I was about to retire in 1995, I received an unexpected letter from Judge Spellacy telling me he had sent a letter to the Grand Rapids Herald Review. Enclosed was a copy of that letter.

Editor:
If I were to nominate anyone as the outstanding citizen of this city and county during the 20th Century, it would be Harvey Dahline. The recent articles in the papers have brought back many memories and made me reflect on your outstanding accomplishments and unique personality traits.

I knew and represented your mother when I was a lawyer. In spite of her problems, you always accorded her complete love and respect. That says a lot about the character of a man.

I vividly recall an occasion when my wife and I had been in the Twin Cities, arrived home and found our baby sitter in tears. She said that our oldest son, then 15, had been "put in jail." I was to call you. You were, indeed, holding Kevin, but not in jail, because he had been caught at a beer party. Kevin is now a successful attorney in St. Cloud. He often mentions your kind and gentle words of admonishment. Kevin was a classmate of David Black and we have often discussed your courageous act of placing your life on the line in order to save others on that fateful day in 1966.

I also recall when you came into my chambers and announced that Ted Flannigan was innocent and had to be retrieved from prison. Ted's attorney had removed me from the case, so it was tried by Judge Warren Saetre. I immediately called Judge Saetre, you talked to him, and you were well on your way to righting a horrible wrong.

I never heard you say anything bad about anyone or lose your temper. If you ever made an enemy, I never heard of it.

For years I've thought of you and present Sheriff Pat Medure, as a team because you acted together in so many drug busts and solving other crimes. I playfully chided you both about coming to my home for search warrants long after hours. On Monday, Aug. 21, when a jail prisoner escaped while in route from the jail to the courtroom, you and Pat apprehended him within a few minutes. What a continuing example of law enforcement cooperation.

You are irreplaceable, Harvey! There is no crime crisis in Grand Rapids nor would there be one anyplace if we had more Harvey Dahlines wearing police uniforms. We'll miss your cheery smile and your friendly, humble attitude. May God bless you and your lovely wife, Doris, many happy and healthy years of retirement.

Sincerely,
Judge John Spellacy, retired

A postscript he added to his letter, handwritten and sent to our home that wasn't entered into the article in the Herald Review: Harvey---I'm sending this to the editor of the Herald Review. As I told you today I can't be there on August 31, but no one will keep us from being present on Oct. 14. God love you.

J.S.

~

129
TWENTY DOLLARS ($20.00)

In early 1952 I ended up in the Korean War. At this time I was assigned to the 16th Infantry Regiment, Co. D, 3rd Division, as a Tech Sergeant in a machine gun platoon. We arrived in Inchon Harbor, Korea, shipped over from Seattle, Washington, on a large troop ship, the General Howe. We sat in the harbor a day or two, then with full packs on our backs and carrying our weapons, we descended from the ship, climbing down rope cargo nets to small landing crafts that took us to shore.

By this time the fighting had moved out of this area to the north, more along the 38th Parallel which separated North and South Korea. Loaded onto trucks, we were driven a few hundred miles inland somewhere close to where our units would be.

We marched over rugged terrain and after some time were climbing a large hill to the top of a ridge overlooking a large valley. Within a short time we were introduced to our squadrons and then shown the location of other machine gun emplacements where our interlocking field of fire would be.

In the distance over a valley were two mountainous hills, one called 317 or Baldy, the other one, Breadloaf. They were out in what was called "no man's land". The hills were very high and so were used as observation posts in the daytime. They could not be held at night so they would be abandoned each evening and the process of conquering it would be repeated the next morning. There were nights you could hear grenades down the side of the hill, someone thinking they heard the enemy.

It was a wondrous thing to see at night when several half-tracks with four .50 caliber machine guns would open up shooting down the valley. The valley would light up as one of the tracers burned a light green. Each one of the four guns could fire up to 600 rounds a minute, every fifth one being a tracer.

War is not fun. We didn't have the proper footwear and a lot of the time was spent building emplacements: carrying logs up steep hills, filling sandbags, digging in the earth. The cold, always the cold.

When I first arrived there was some resentment as I was an eighteen-year-old Tech Sergeant; some of the men were privates with much more war time experience, having served in World War II. We seemed to work through it as you do your share of the work and lead by example, never asking them to do things you would not do yourself.

These can be lonely times for a soldier. Sometimes you have someone writing to you, perhaps a young lady. Then you wait, the letters stop coming, you wait and then you know.

Time has been passing. One day you hear that an airplane will be taking some of the men to Japan for R&R (Rest and Recuperation). You could be one of them but you had to have at least $20 cash. I didn't have any money; I can never remember getting paid while there. My checks were being sent home to help out, hoping some would be set aside for me when I left the service. But, $94 a month doesn't go far.

A young soldier, knowing I would not be going otherwise, came up to me and gave me $20. I knew I would be paying him back.

We were in Japan for a week on R&R. I don't drink and yet I have little memory of that week so long ago.

It seems we had just gotten back to our unit in Korea when we were told we would be going home. I still had not paid Frank back the $20 as I had vowed I would.

Getting back to the States was a hectic time: discharged out of Camp Carson, Colorado, riding home on a Greyhound bus back to Grand Rapids,
looking forward to getting home, arriving in late September of '52, moving in with my mother into that little apartment, getting back together with my twin brother, Harry, who had also been in the army but had been state-side.

There was no money saved for me. It was gone, but that's life. I knew my mother was working in what I call "sweat shops", doing laundry in hotels where the temperature would get up to 125 degrees without air-conditioning for 30 cents an hour. Soon I was back in high school playing football on a great team. After football season I joined the wrestling team, my first year at this.

In the early part of February I learned I owed a lot of money at

Johnson's Food Mart--my family had been charging to my name. The store was located next to the 1st National Bank and is now part of that building.

At that time in the back of my mind and even now is the $20 that Frank had given me.

I must admit I am not good at names and after some time I forgot Frank's Italian last name, never knowing where he was from. I was not good at forgetting the $20.

Before leaving school I met the girl I was to marry, I just didn't know it. She was a wonderful person but I had nothing.

Standing, waiting for the evening to come, as I would be wrestling for the 165 pound championship in the Regional Tournament, a young girl came up to me saying she had a friend, Doris. They would like to make supper for me and her boyfriend after the matches, would I come? With some hesitation, I said yes. Now, I had no car, no money or good clothes; furthermore, I had no idea where they lived. I won the championship but afterwards felt lost inside and went back to my small apartment instead of to the dinner invitation. I didn't think I would ever see the girl again.

Soon I had to quit school and get a job in the iron mines to catch up on bills.

It was some time before I saw Doris again. I was at the roller rink one evening and there she was, quite unsteady on her feet and required much attention as it was her first time on rollerblades. She was there with her youth group from church. We seemed to hit it off. I asked her brother if I could take her home; I don't think he was too bright as he said "Yes."

We started dating; I don't think they make them like her any more. Doris and I were married in a little over a year.

Several months later I started working for the police department but with a growing family I had to take several part time jobs: school bus driver, TV installation and repair, digging graves and other odd jobs.

One of our first Christmases we decided we wanted to help someone. We chose a young woman who was having a hard time making it. Putting a $20 bill in an envelope, walking to her door, knocking. When she answered, I handed her the envelope, said "Merry Christmas" and walked away. Doris was waiting in the car.

The lady didn't know who we were. That was the first of many $20 bills donated over the coming years. We have done well. Do unto others.

A few years back I was at the County Market. Coming around the aisle I was face to face with our first Christmas lady from over 50 years ago. I recognized her, said "Hi' and started to move on. Stopping me, she said, "I know you from that Christmas long ago. You'll never know how much that helped me. Thank you." We still talk.

Last week I needed some advice from a friend who owns a business; he gave it to me but wouldn't take any money. I asked how his wife was doing, knowing she had been struggling the last time I had talked to him. He said she wasn't doing well. I also knew his business was doing poorly.

As I left, I put a $20 bill in his hand and said, "Take your wife out for dinner." I could see it in his eyes as he got choked up, saying, "I was hoping I would make enough today to take her to the show tonight."

Through the years, my wife and I have made several mission trips to foreign countries, one to Honduras to work with an eye doctor in a poorer section of that country and more trips to Bogota, Columbia, to work at an orphanage and also to help in the construction there. These trips were with our church friends.

Frank gave me a gift that day in Korea, not the $20, but a gift of the heart. I know I'll keep on trying; some day my debt will be paid. Thank you, Frank.

A Merry Christmas to all---Harvey and Doris Dahline

~

130
THE LEWIS AND CLARK EXPEDITION

A few days ago a man who I considered a friend of mine asked me if I would like to go with him and another friend blueberry picking up past Orr, about a hundred miles from here.

Now to be honest, I had gone blueberry picking a few years ago, spending several hours going to the northern part of the state. Then after a fierce battle with deer flies and mosquitoes, we had escaped. I with a whole quarter bucket of blueberries, him with a half bucket. We still had our long drive home. I still have a taste for wild blueberries but not as much as I used to.

Now this. I have considered this person a wonderful close friend. What to do? How could I turn him down? A man always has his one resource he can turn to. Turning to my wife, I said, "Harold wants me to go blueberry picking with him on Monday up north. We would be gone all day." (I emphasized all day). She said, "What a wonderful idea! You'll have so much fun." That took care of that!

So, I told Harold, "Great, what time will we leave?" The answer was 6:00 a.m., so I proceeded to get things ready, my clothes and setting my alarm clock which I didn't need to do as I always wake on time. And I always have my backup, my wife, for an alarm clock as she thinks it's a reflection on her if I'm late or not dressed well.

It was no surprise to me when she started to shake me not too gently at 5:45. My alarm had not gone off, bad batteries. I did manage to dress and eat breakfast and was ready at 6:00, not thinking anyone would notice my not shaving as we were headed for the wild.

We were on the road by 6:10. Harold introduced his friend who was quite likeable. It turned out he was a lumberjack, a very spry young man at 71.

We had a nice drive on a beautiful morning and seemed to get along quite well. I did notice a few barbs from Harold that I might miss my donuts this morning (this really hurt as I used to be a police officer).

Along the way the subject turned to politics which didn't last too long as we found that everyone doesn't think the way we do. But it was easy to understand as he was only 71 and still in his formative years.

Eventually we did enter the forest about seven miles past Orr, and both men seemed confident in knowing the area. Our next turn-off onto a road should have been around eight miles farther.

At this time we were heading down a dirt logging road and after 10 to 12 miles figured we might have missed our turn-off, so we started back- tracking. Do you know how many turn-offs there can be in 12 miles? There were a lot of them. Each one we came to, Harold would say he was quite confident that this was it.

After about an hour I started to think about the Lewis and Clark expedition and the fact that I had not brought my compass with me. Many times Harold said that there maybe a cross road up ahead. Harold must have a GPS in his head because he always got us back to the main road.

I might say I'm a 'naysayer" because after some time, I was having some doubts.

On the way back out we did come to a clearing. We were always looking for an area that had been logged or burned a few years ago. These areas are the best for blueberry picking.

Thinking we would get out and look the area over, the friend went to the far side, Harold and I to the near side. We did find some low bush berries but not a great number. On the friend's side it was somewhat better. After about an hour we drove down the main road. We talked to a road grader operator; he did not know the road we were looking for.

So we continued our exploration. Soon we came to a grown over side road. Harold once again said with confidence, "This is it!" He was right again. We drove the road for two miles through many over hanging tree limbs and pot holes, up and down steep hills, then a big rock, our destination. Getting out of the pick-up, we talked to a man by the road with his dog. He pointed to a tall pine a quarter of a mile away atop of a steep hill. This was to be our rendezvous point.

In a short time we were close to the big, tall pine. There were many blueberry plants throughout the area but it soon became apparent the area had been picked recently. But if you looked real good there were berries to be had. I spent the next several hours either on my knees or lying down going from plant to plant, crawling on my hands and knees, never walking. I could see Harold was on his knees much of the time.

The friend, younger and maybe a little smarter, had brought with him a home-made scoop about six inches wide with prongs on it, and as we would reach for a few berries at a time, he would scoop through several plants.

I must admit after several hours of crawling on my hands and knees, over logs, plants and bushes I was starting to tire somewhat, but as you know, I could say nothing. The last half hour I was on my back a few times admiring the blue sky.

At 5:15 the words were spoken. The friend said, "I think it's time to go." We had to find our other buckets. The friend was showing the way, I was close behind. I had no idea where we were and the brush was thick. It was about this time I stepped on a rock that wasn't there, falling to my left with the bucket in my right hand. Grabbing a small sapling with my left hand, I kept control, landing on my face in the brush, bucket of berries upright. I never lost one berry. Harold and the friend looked amazed that I had such control every time I fell down.

15 minutes later we came out where the truck was parked. It didn't take much to see who had the most berries. I had close to a gallon and a half, Harold had two gallons or more, the friend had at least six gallons. His family was going to be very happy.

Harold drove the bad part of the road going out to the highway; I then drove the rest of the way home. Along the way we stopped in Orr to get an ice cream cone. We had to buy six to a pack so we each had two.

I got home about 8:30 then spent almost an hour cleaning berries. You know the old saying, "You catch 'em, you clean 'em!" I had spent a good day with good friends.

Now, this should be the end to the story. Going to bed, I slept very well but when I woke in the morning, there was this 90-year-old guy in bed. I tried to turn over and get my feet to the floor, but nothing wanted to move, and if it did, it was not pleasant. After some time, I had my feet on the floor but my rear was still on the bed. Reaching over to the bureau I helped myself stand, taking a few three inch steps. Then someone laughed behind me. Then she said, "I'm sorry!"

Making it to the living room, I started walking it off. After a time, I headed to the biff. The only thing saving me there was that I had a new toilet which is three or four inches higher than the older ones. Also the vanity is next to it which would help me get up. For the next day and a half, every time I would sit down for a while, I would have to walk it off.

I write this not to tell you of my pain or the wonderful pie my wife made.

Just to say that I had two friends out there that I hoped were sharing my pain!

It's been almost a year now. The other day I ran into my 71 year old friend. He said it looked like the blueberries are going to be plentiful this year.

I haven't been sleeping well.

~

131
SUGAR IN THE GAS TANK

If you've ever lived in town, you know you always want to get along with your neighbors. But, there is always one that stands out from the rest. Little things like parking on your side of the street or being out at six in the morning mowing his lawn. You worked nights. He has a large dog that is certified to have the best vocal chords in the state that is let out late in the evening and barks the rest of the night.

The amazing thing is, the owner's family is all deaf, not hearing a thing.

Being a good neighbor you can't walk over and complain nor call the police, but we all have our limits.

Eventually the police are called; the dog has been barking loudly the past two hours. They respond to a small house up in a field on 9th St. N.W. across the road from Neumann's old sawmill close to Blandin Beach.

We arrive and are told about the barking dog. We stand and listen, nothing. The complaining couple didn't want their name used.

So we sit nearby and listen for a half hour or so. We do hear a dog several blocks away, nothing from the house pointed out to us. We drive off. This goes on for a week. A couple more calls but nothing we can hear.

As police officers we can understand someone not wanting their name used so we sit and listen. The dog starts barking. We go to the owners telling them we have been getting complaints. The dog must be taken inside or a citation will be issued.

Although the neighbor with the dog may act deaf, he is not blind and may see where the police have been talking to a neighbor.

This is what happened one summer night many years ago. Having been called on the same barking dog several times over the last couple weeks, it was made very clear to the dog's owner they would be cited. The dog was taken inside.

Nothing was heard over the next couple days, but then I was called to the little house in the field. It happened that my brother,

Don, lived there. As I recall it was a Sunday morning.

He was quite irate. Coming out to his car, he noticed the door to the gas cap was open. Getting close, there was sugar on the ground and in the filler cap. Stating he had not gotten close to the car, he called.

My investigation showed a good amount of sugar on the ground and around the filler cap, also some shoe prints on the ground. Looking closely you could see where someone had been on his knee in the sand. It had stripes in the knee imprints. I then took pictures of the evidence.

I asked Don if there was anyone he knew or suspected of doing this. He then brought up the neighbor with the barking dog. Leaving Don, I went to the neighbor. I knocked on the door and a young man I knew answered. Asking him to step out and talk to me, we went to the side of the house. I explained why I was there. He denied putting the sugar in the gas tank.

One thing I noted when he came to the door, he had on corduroy pants with some damp sand on his right knee. Looking at his shoe prints they were the same prints noted in the sand.

I told him I had pictures of the prints in the sand matching his shoe and pants print as well as a possible fingerprint. I would have to have his pants and shoes for comparison.

I said he had been mad and gone too far but if he would work with me, I'm sure we could work this out. He listened, he could hear after all.

My proposition was this: admit what he had done, agree to pay for the full cost to professionally have the sugar removed from the tank, apologize, and I would talk to my brother to make sure there would be no charges filed.

After a moment, he agreed that he had gone too far, he would pay for the gas tank cleaning. They did work it out.

I don't ever remember getting any more complaints on the dog. Good neighbors.

~

132
A FATAL MISTAKE

In the early evening hours of Feb. 3, 1985, a Monday, a young man of 23 was walking the streets of Grand Rapids looking to steal a car. This was to be a fatal mistake, one he would regret the rest of his life.

It was getting dark, getting on to 5:30 p.m. The evening was warm for this time of year. At about 6 p.m. the Grand Rapids police were answering a report of a car just stolen from a parking lot of the Itasca Memorial Hospital. The owner, a Bovey resident, had seen his 1978 Buick Skylark driven away from the hospital parking lot by a single person. The location of the hospital is on S.E. 1st St. next to the river.

A few minutes later reports were coming in of a head-on accident two miles south of town on Hwy. 169 just past the Harris Township road. The description of one of the vehicles was the same as the car just stolen in town. One man was reportedly dead at the scene, and a witness reported seeing a man run from the accident.

At the scene of the accident were the Minnesota Hwy. Patrol, Itasca County Sheriff's Deputies and the Grand Rapids Police. An ambulance had been called.

Each of the departments was doing its part in controlling the traffic and talking to witnesses, one of whom had seen a man run from the scene some time ago. As there were some tracks in the snow, I was elected to see if I could follow them as the other men were busy at the scene. I started to follow a trail in the snow which in some areas was 10 to 15 inches deep.

Keep in mind that at this writing, it was some 27 years ago. Buildings have gone up, brush and trees have grown, and the road has changed.

My recollection is that I ran up a steep bank somewhere this side of the Black Cherry Bar, following the trail behind a barn-like structure; we were going in a southerly direction. Judging by the tracks in the snow, it appeared he was running.

At this time, I was trying to set a good, even pace, one I thought

I could do for an hour or two. The terrain now led over into an open field, still heading south. If we kept in the same direction, we would come to the edge of Pokegama Lake a quarter mile east of the bridge. The trail was now going through the woods, not hard to follow as there was some light and I had a large flashlight. A few times, I thought I may have seen something far ahead of me. We were now heading down some roads, getting close to the lake. Going between some houses, the trail went out onto the lake ice and headed for the south shore. According to his tracks, this guy was in good shape, long strides, still running. He had had a good head start; I didn't think I was gaining. The lake had some snow on it, but I couldn't see anyone. I continued to run, pacing myself. After some time I was following the tracks up the bank and through the trees and brush. We came out onto the Southwood Rd. There was just too much blacktop, the trail disappeared. After some time, I made my way back to the accident scene.

The next morning I was contacted by the sheriff's office. They had received two telephone calls from a person claiming to have information on the fatal accident south of town the previous night but who would not give his name.

After listening to both tapes a couple times, I believed it was the voice of a man, Randy M. We had had contact with him on several occasions. Randy was contacted and interviewed a short time later Tuesday at the Sheriff's office. He said he was hitchhiking on S. 169 by the KMart Monday evening when he was picked up by two men. He said they pulled a knife, demanded money and accosted him when he wouldn't comply. His leg injury had happened when the car left the roadway and he had jumped and ran. But after a short interview it was determined that Randy had stolen the car and then ran from the scene of the accident. He thought someone may have recognized him; he then made up a story to clear himself.

At this time he was out on bail on a complaint filed in 1984. His next court appearance had been set for Monday, February 11th.

On February 13th, Randy was charged with second degree murder in the February 3rd traffic death.

The charge of murder is derived from a Minnesota statute which holds that such a charge can be imposed if a death results while an individual is committing a crime.

Randy was arraigned in Itasca County Court the day after the accident on the murder charge as well as being responsible for the hit-and-run accident resulting in death and for unauthorized use of a motor vehicle. Bail was set at $100,000.00.

Randy M. pled guilty and has now served his time.

Herald Review   February 6, 1985 Vol 90, No. 11
Herald Review   February 13, 1985 Vol 90, No13

~

133
KOREAN WAR VETERANS: ATTENTION

While reading through my monthly copy of the Minnesota Legionnaire, December 2013, a small article caught my eye. The headline was "Korean War Book".

The book highlighted: Korea Reborn: A Grateful Nation Honors War Veterans for 60 Years of Growth. Further text explained how the book was now available to Korean War vets and their families as a gift from the Korean government. The books had been shipped to each state for distribution to the veterans.

In Minnesota, the books were shipped to Ed Valle, president of the Korean War Veterans. His contact information is 651-210-1816 or edwardo322003k@yahoo.com. His mailing address is: Ed Valle, 1410 Foster St., River Falls, Wisconsin 54022.

Having spent time in a machine gun platoon in Korea in 1952, this was of great interest to me.

I called Ed Valle asking for more information and was told all I had to do was enclose a $6.00 check for postage and a return address; there was no charge for the book. I did as he said and within 10 days received the book and was more than surprised at the quality. It has 165 pages bound in a hard cover with an attractive jacket. The book is 9x11 inches with glossy pages. I couldn't begin to guess what its value would be bought outright.

The first half tells the history of the Republic of Korea, and goes into the details of the war itself. Its pictures and descriptions take you back to another era, reminders of a time past.

The second part paints a picture of what a free nation can do for itself, changing from a nation in poverty to one of the leading industrial nations of the world. Throughout the book it makes it very clear who they give credit to. It is you, the Korean War Veterans.

Reading the book, I knew I was going to share the word. Korean Veterans, you can all be proud of yourselves.

This is not the end; the grateful nation of South Korea is also offering more.

There was a chapter in the book, "Revisiting Korea--Making the

'Forgotten War' Unforgotten".

In 1975 the Republic of Korea established the Korean War Veteran's Revisit Program, a program to honor and show appreciation to all UN forces who fought to liberate the country from aggression during the Korean War. Korea, through its Ministry of Patriots and Veterans Affairs, pays all expenses and half of the transportation cost for veterans to visit Korea for five days.

During this visit, participants tour war memorials and battle sites around Inchon and Seoul, the demilitarized zone, and old Korean villages. Also, they visit the site where the armistice was signed in 1953. At the end of their visit the MPVA holds a banquet in their honor and presents each veteran with an Ambassador Peace Medal and several other gifts.

Since 1975, over 26,000 veterans have returned to the Republic of Korea to experience for themselves the transformation they helped create in the country they served. In honor of the 60th Anniversary, the government has expanded the program to include the grandchildren of veterans, including a Peace Camps for Youth program, which furthers education about Korea and the profound impact of the Korean War veterans in South Korea.

"I think it's probably unique, the way South Korea has attempted to thank and help people with their revisit program," says veteran William McCulloch. "I've been to France, Germany and Italy and so on and they're all appreciative of U.S. help, but the way South Korea has set up this revisit program is unique. It's called a forgotten war, but I think the revisit program has done a great deal to keep the United States informed on what went on then and what is going on now. The South Koreans ought to be complimented for rebuilding their country and for their program of revisit. It does a lot to make the so-called Forgotten War unforgotten."

For information on the Revisit Korea Program call 703-590-1091 and ask for Jamie.

In January 1951 Company D, 136 Infantry Reg., 47th Division, from Grand Rapids, Minn was activated into the regular Army. Some 80 to 100 men left to go to war. Are they now forgotten?

We were driven to Duluth by bus then on to Camp Rucker, Alabama, by train for further training. Many were then sent to serve in Korea.

Company D, I would like to say I am proud to have served with each and every one of you. Harvey Dahline

You are eligible if you served between 1950-1955 or if you served in Korea at any time.

I have contacted the VFW and the American Legion with this information.

If you would like to contact me, you can reach me at 218-326-2497.

~

134
THE YELLOW DIRT BIKE

Some time in the late '80s, as I remember, between 1:00 and 2:00 a.m., while driving a Ford Interceptor squad car in a westerly direction in the area of the 66 Station on 4th St. N.W., I could hear a motorcycle in the distance that seemed to be coming from the Forest Lake area. It sounded like it was moving fast, definitely not muffled.

Making a right turn on 13th Ave., I approached 5th St. which is the road that goes by Forest Lake. Driving by to my left on 5th St. was a bright yellow dirt bike exceeding the speed limit by at least 20 mph. As it went by no license plate was visible. The rider had on a yellow helmet with the face plate down. He was looking my way as he went by. From what I could make out, he appeared to be young, about 6 feet tall, 170 pounds or so. Going by, he cracked the throttle and was soon up to 60 mph.

I fell in behind him; he had the jump on me. We were driving in an easterly direction, Forest Lake on our left. He came to the 10th Ave. stop sign, and going through it he barely made the left hand corner. He was now going by Blandin Beach heading north. As he came to 9th St. he made another left onto a dirt road.

This was an area that I knew quite well. As a boy I had lived in the big house on the corner for a short time, the Harry Lesseuer house, and knew that this was a dead end road. All that was back there perhaps only a quarter mile was two old buildings from what had been a mink ranch. One of the buildings was a large barn structure on the right next to the lake. On this side of the building was a dump perhaps 60 feet wide with all sorts of discarded junk and cans.

As we proceeded down the dirt road, the yellow bike made a right turn behind the white building, so I stopped my squad on this side of the building and jumped out, thinking he may be coming around from the other side. I heard him coming, and I met him in the middle of the dump at perhaps 15 mph. I came in from the side; the bike went down, me on top of him and the bike. After a short tussle, the helmet was off. Surprise! A close neighbor, not a bad kid and one who has done well since that time.

All the same, he appeared in court on a careless driving charge.

HLD 2/11/2014

~

135
FOOTPRINT ON GLASS

The key to good police work is sometimes doing the simplest of things, such as photographing a pry mark on a door or a piece of glass with a footprint on it.

On a Saturday in 1978, an older car bearing Wisconsin plates and two men were entering Grand Rapids on 169 from the south. They were here for one purpose only, the burglary of Con's Sales and Service, a business on the east end of town that was known for having a large inventory of chain saws on hand.

Their job for the rest of the afternoon would be to drive occasionally throughout the area, locate the building, and find the best place to park where their car wouldn't be seen.

It was finally decided to park some distance away, steal the chain saws, chains and bars, take them out back a couple hundred feet, hide them by a dumpster, get the car and pick up the stolen items.

They had found in the past, that Saturday nights were the best time to burglarize a place, as a forced entry might not be discovered until Monday morning.

It was well after midnight when walking through the snow they approached Con's Service from the back of the building. Somehow, they were able to get to the roof with their tools. There was snow on the roof, and it could be seen they had done some roof damage. Then deciding this could be too much work and getting down and going to the front of the building, they kicked the glass on the door in.

After entering the building, they took their pick of several chain saws and corresponding parts and bars off the wall that would only fit the saws they were stealing as well as some large rolls of chains.

At a later time, Con, the owner, was to say these persons would have to have a great knowledge of chainsaws to be able to pick parts off the wall that only fit the machines they were taking.

Getting what they wanted, they made several trips through the snow out back behind some buildings, stacking the saws and other items by the dumpster. Getting the car and loading the items into the trunk and back seat, they were on their way.

Sunday morning the police were notified of a broken glass door at Con's Sales, and Con was notified. The officers doing the investigation first took pictures of the building and prints in the snow. They noted a foot print on a piece of glass where the door had been kicked in. They took a picture of the footprint on the glass and took the glass as evidence.

At this time it was noted that an attempt had been made to get in through the roof. Also, the tracks out back were followed to where the items had been loaded into the car. Con said it appeared that several chain saws had been taken; he would be getting us an itemized list and the value of the items. It was expected to be over $2,000. The officers were told this was the third time Con's had been broken into. The other two times were several years ago, one of them at another location where he had lost several outboard motors.

Some days after this Con received a call from a police officer in Wisconsin asking if he had lost any chain saws. The officer said he had stopped a car and became suspicious at the number of chain saws in the back of the car. He had traced one of the serial numbers back to Con's Sales and Service. Con, upon checking, found it was one of his stolen chain saws.

The investigating officers were notified; they then sent a picture of the footprint on the glass to the Wisconsin officer. The print proved to match the shoe of the driver of the stopped car. Further investigation led investigators to a warehouse in St. Cloud with a large amount of stolen goods.

One man was subsequently charged with burglary and possession of stolen goods and brought back to Grand Rapids.

Footprint on glass

HLD 2/16/2014

~

136
THE ZIPPO LIGHTER

This morning, October 6, 2014, I was sitting reading the newspaper when the wife brought in the mail. Saying, "You have a box in the mail from Ron."

Ron, our second son now 58, lives in Florida. He has lived away from home many years, making his living as an artist, molding clay and selling his wares on eBay. As a father, I think at what he does, he may be the best in the world.

She handed me a 5x6 inch box wrapped as though it had something very valuable in it. After going through layers of bubble wrap I came to a small draw string silk bag with a very oriental design; bright flowers and butterflies adorning it. On both ends of the drawstrings were copper beads.

Looking into the bag could be seen something vaguely familiar. Something that had been put in a drawer some sixty years ago after coming home from the Korean War and then forgotten until now.

Taking it out, a silver Zippo cigarette lighter. In Korea it had been worth its weight in gold. Every foot soldier in that frozen land had one; it was small to carry in ones pocket. To stay warm, it was the only thing you had to start a fire with.

Looking at the Zippo lighter you could see it had been around the world. With different names scratched into its sides. Some of the names: Korea, Eddy, Ronny, Osage, Ken, Aratex, Wash, Calf, Manatewish, Wis, Hawaii, Minnesota, Harvey, Colorado, Japan. There wasn't a note in the box.

Looking on, my wife told me she knew Ron was sending me something. He acted like it was to be a surprise so she had not asked what it was.

Somehow I knew he had the lighter over those many years. I then called him to thank him for his thoughtfulness.

Ron said, "Dad, I am so proud of what you have done, serving in the Army in Korea so many years ago but I had something of yours and I thought it should go back to the one who deserves it."

Now I do treasure that Zippo lighter but I treasure the words of my son even more.

~

137
THE LITTLE WATCH MAKER

In March of 1953 I left school to work in the mines. Having no close friends, you may say I was a loner. I would go to the movie theaters, the bowling alley, and one night to the roller rink; this was to be my saving grace. A young girl was there with her brother taking part in a church youth group outing. I had met her in school. We were soon talking and to my surprise, I drove Doris home that night. From that time on, we were inseparable.

The girl, although shy, seemed to see something in me. Remembering back, it wasn't her beauty that attracted me so much as her caring and thoughtfulness. We'd been dating for a year and talked of marriage. Deciding to look for an engagement ring, we went shopping at a little jewelry shop, Salmela's Jewelry.

We approached apprehensively, not having much money. The "little watch maker" met us at the door, making us feel welcome. Listening, he seemed to know our situation, showing us what he thought we could afford, always helpful and accommodating.

After some time we picked out an engagement ring, gold with a diamond in the middle and silver leaf design on both sides. As the "little watch maker" helped put the ring on Doris's finger, he bowed a little and kissed the back of her hand. Doris was glowing; the ring was only $80. We left the shop knowing when it came time for a wedding ring for both of us we would be back. Within a few months we had set our wedding date for July 9, 1954.

Returning to the little shop, the "little watch maker" again welcomed us. We were looking for a match to the engagement ring, nothing close. He seemed disappointed, thought for a moment, and then went to the back of the shop, bringing a small box, and saying, "Look through these, perhaps you will find something."

Looking into all of those many rings, it seemed impossible but there it was, the perfect match. A gold band with silver leaves on it and a perfect fit, the cost, $20. We also purchased my wedding band, $20.

This story has been told many times, our 60th anniversary will be on July 9th.

Within a year, I was working for the GR Police department. Overall I would be there for over 40 years working at many positions. The one I always enjoyed most was investigations.

One type of crime was most interesting, burglaries. All of them somewhat follow a pattern. Some break a glass in a window or pry the door in, not much planning or sophistication. Most of the time, you will think someone local. Almost always, you would be proved right when arrests are made.

Starting in the early 1970's and over the next fifteen years we were having burglaries showing a sophistication in MO's (modus operandi which means mode of operation), unfamiliar to this area. We had locks pulled at drug stores and some cases holes cut through roofs just large enough for a small man to go through and drop into the drug store where drugs were taken. The Royal Bar, Country Kitchen, Miner's Grocery, and others; it seemed most of them stuck in my mind. I was to find out many years later I had forgotten one.

On Thursday, August 7, 1975, we were called to Salmela's Jewelry which was now on 4th St. West across the street from the old Kremer building. Some time during the night he had been burglarized and an estimated $20,000 in watches and rings taken, discovered by Art Salmela when he opened for business.

An investigation showed the hasp had been broken off the door in the alley to enter a boiler room behind Scott's Television Repair Shop. Then a hole had been made to gain entrance into the TV shop. Proceeding to the bathroom another hole was made through the bathroom wall gaining entrance to Salmela's bathroom. No hole was larger than 12 by 14 inches; it had to be a small man going through.

Nothing in our investigation gave us a clue as to who had done this except the MO. This was not common to this area. The years went by, the case almost forgotten except for one person.

In the second week of March (2014), I went to see Len Salmela, of Salmela's Jewelery in south Grand Rapids to get some information. As we were talking, I brought up that my wife and I had bought our wedding rings from Art Salmela, his father, the "little watch maker" some 60 years ago.

Len then said, "Harvey, do you remember my father being burglarized many years ago in his little shop, when he lost $20,000 worth of rings and watches?" He also said his father had told him this might be the best thing that could have happened to him, because then everyone knew where his little shop was!

I must admit my mind went blank, there seemed to be something there. Len then brought out a clipping from the newspaper, the date, August 7, 1975. As I read the clipping, it started to come back. I thought, "The perfect match." I told Len I knew who had robbed the "little watch maker" so many years ago.

I had arrested a man in November of 1981 for the Reed's Drug Store burglary, a unique job, cutting a hole in the roof, dropping through with a rope. He had already spent 17 years in prison and had just been sentenced to four more years in St. Cloud.

I was aware he belonged to a well known gang called the "Walleye Gang" operating out of the northern part of this state but also going into Nebraska and North Dakota burglarizing mainly jewelry and drug stores.

I questioned this man on many of these burglaries I had on my mind that happened over the last 15 years in Grand Rapids. He admitted they had done all of them, giving me many details no one else would know. He knew full well the statutes of limitations had run on each case and he could not be prosecuted on them.

This was a case I messed up on, I simply forgot the Salmela case while questioning the man, and this case could have been closed many years ago. It was a match to the others that had taken place over the 15 years.

A little reminiscence.

Herald Review August 7, 1975
Len Salmela
Harvey Dahline 3/17/2014

~

138
THE JACKET AND THE HEADDRESS

I first came to Grand Rapids in 1949, having spent the last few years in foster homes, farms and orphanages, our family broken up, two sisters and a brother adopted out.

A man had once told me some years back that what you think of yourself at the end of the day is so important. I never had trouble getting a job. Some times manually working as a carryout and stock boy at the Gambles Skogmo grocery store located where the Blandin parking lot is now across the street from the American Legion. The money I earned there helped out at home.

My mother did the laundry all by herself for the Pokegama Hotel getting paid somewhere around 40 cents an hour. One day she wasn't feeling well so I went with her to work thinking I was in good shape. I learned what real work was. The laundry room on this summer day had a constant temperature of about 125 degrees. The washer was made of wood. The door when wet weighed 75 lbs. To get the 30 sheets out of the washer you had to pull and untangle all of these wet sheets from each other.

The sheets, pillowcases, towels and wash cloths all had to be dried then the sheets and pillow cases had to be put through a mangle which was a 10 foot roller that was super hot to press them. All of this heat was in the basement with no air conditioning. It was stifling hot down there. By noon I had had it. How anyone could work in these conditions day after day and not miss work.

In the fall, I went out for the football team. As I said before, I was in good shape, fudging my age I had worked for the Great Northern railroad that summer in Staples throwing a 10 pound mall all day building railroad tracks, then running home six miles to do the chores.

Now going out for the football team was something I never expected to do. I was told if you weren't someone you could not get on the team. My thinking was that the coach wanted to win; he would pick the players that would do it. After three days of practice, learning to hit, picking them up and driving them into the ground, Noble Hall came up to me and said, "You're on the team, but you have to back off. I only have so many players and some are getting hurt."

Something happened to me here, for the first time I was being accepted as a team player and as a person. I was playing for the Grand Rapids Indians.

We went on and won the conference. Players were soon wearing their conference Indian letter jackets. I couldn't afford one.

I had joined the National Guard and was soon inducted into the service so again became a team player. Only this time, it was in the Korean War.

Getting out of the service and getting home, I was soon on the football team again, this time helping to win the 1952 conference championship. The team was proudly wearing their Grand Rapids Indian letter jackets. I too had one, as the Lasker and Upin clothing store had bought it for me. Although I had to work it off, rules are rules. I had earned the right to wear my jacket.

Soon I was on the wrestling team and was fortunate enough to win the 165 lb Regional Championship on our Indian's team. My girlfriend proudly shared wearing the jacket.

Some years later my daughter was a Grand Rapids Indian wrestling cheerleader and with great pride she wore the Indian headdress.

Now the beautiful Indian headdress and the 1952 Indian football jacket are in the Historical Museum artifacts in downtown Grand Rapids.

Never again to be worn with the dignity and respect they so richly deserve.

I came to Grand Rapids with nothing but ended up with a Grand Rapids Indian jacket and my self respect.

~

139
A BRUSH WITH THE LAW

It's been many years now, time has flown by. I've been retired some 20 years but some times I awake in a sweat. My wife seems to understand, I don't think she does. She calls it Post Traumatic Stress Disorder (PTSD). I don't think it is, as that is something a soldier comes home with and this started a long time after my discharge. I had met this person on many occasions. Tough, I thought but forgiving. He could look you in the eye and stare you down, not blink an eye. There was something about him, you could feel he was above average intelligence but these are the ones that can be dangerous. They almost always bide their time, strike at an opportune time, and then fade into the night.

I had always kept my eye out for him. His dad was a well known local politician so I knew if I ever had the chance to make an arrest he would have some pull with the judges so I bided my time. It was a hot summer day; I was patrolling in my unmarked police car and was on the Golf Course Road looking for criminal activity. Knowing I was getting close.

There he was standing by his cycle on the side of the road looking like he didn't have a care in the world. Just standing there looking down, not breaking any laws. I was still apprehensive. As I was driving by at about 25 mph he straightened, took aim and fired. My front windows were both down. A 2 1/2 inch rock came through the passenger side window, missed my nose and out the driver's side window. Realizing what had just happened, I was a couple hundred feet down the road. Hitting my brakes and making a U-turn.

At this time the boy must have realized he had thrown a rock at a police car. He had gotten on his small bike and for a boy of about six; those knees were pumping up and down at a furious rate. Looking back as he was heading down his black topped driveway a couple hundred yards from the house with a police car some thirty feet behind him in hot pursuit.

I know the parents have always done the best with the boy but I like to think Kevin's brush with the law at such a young age is what made him turn into such a fine young man.

~

140
I MET MYSELF

Recently I went to the Middle School to talk to a class taught by Sigri Dorholt. The 5th and 6th graders are so eager to learn. Since I had been a police officer for many years and am now retired, I do some writings and we were talking about them and some of my past cases in Grand Rapids. The class size is about twelve. As we talked someone was always raising their hand, questions, always questions.

There was a young girl in the class from Remer. She and her mother drive from there to the Grand Rapids Middle school five days a week. It so happens that I lived there when I was a little boy. Some in the class want to be police officers and they soak up information like sponges. This was the second time I was privileged to talk to this class. They all want to know how to write a story. How do you start and where does the story come from? This question was from a young boy whose middle name was Xander. I thought as an author that name would stand out.
Seeing myself in him at this young age wanting to write knowing your spelling is not good, telling him go ahead and write, they can be corrected later.

I told Xander some times you don't know what you are going to write. Sit down and write a first line. Let your imagination carry you. It's your story; take it a step at a time.

As I said, this was my second time in Sigri's class, she is so enthused. As I was ending my session with the class, Xander presented me with a story he had written for me. As in my own writing there were some misspelled words. In the story, he wrote of a weekend with his family, how they had gone to a water park sliding on the slides and enjoying the hot tub, having pizza together and not wanting to go home.

Coming home, they had stopped at McDonalds and of course, he had his happy meal and his sister had her 20 pieces of chicken nuggets.

Arriving home he had gone upstairs. Mother called and had him come down to say "goodnight." He then went upstairs to bed.

That night he had a dream, he was living at the water park.
I was pleased and honored to receive Xander's first story he had ever written. I will treasure it.

Someday perhaps I will read a book written by the author, Xander.

~

141
A BODY BEHIND THE HOSPITAL

Very early one summer morning in the late 1970's we received a report that the Itasca Memorial Hospital had found a young boy's body close to the rear emergency entrance.

Upon answering the call we were told the bell at the emergency entrance had been rung. At first no one had been seen. Then a young boy's body had been found. It was obvious to them the boy had been in some sort of an accident.

There wasn't much we could do at this time as we had no idea what had happened or who the person was.

By midmorning I was working with Beefy Lawson of the Itasca County Sheriffs Department. He had a report of a burglary of the Great River Energy building located just across the LaPrairie Bridge three miles out of town on Hwy 2.

During the night one or more people had forcibly entered the large building. They had stolen one of the trucks in the garage apparently not knowing how to operate the garage doors, had backed the truck through the garage door. The truck is now missing. In a short time another report came in to the Itasca County dispatcher. A truck had rolled on a comer in the Trout Lake area and was in a field. It may have caught fire. No one was in the truck or the area at this time.

Further investigation was to show that Tim the dead boy at the hospital had been with some friends the day before. One of the boys, Don, had a relative who lived north of Bovey. His name was Louie who had a 1976 station wagon for sale. Don had taken the car to try out to see if he wanted to buy it (so the story goes). Don is under the age of 18 years.

The boys had been driving around for some time and drove through the gate at the drive-in theater in Grand Rapids doing some damage to the car. Then Don drove the station wagon out to the Great Energy Building on Hwy 2; they had decided to burglarize it. Upon forcibly entering the building, they drove the tmck backwards through the garage door.

Don along with the other boys then drove the truck and car out into the Trout Lake area where they had fun driving the truck in a careless manner around corners and then control had been lost with the truck rolling into a field. The door to the truck had come open. Tim, the boy at the hospital had been pinned between the truck and a door.

Don and the other boys had been able to get Tim out but to no avail, he was gone. Not knowing what else to do since the truck was stolen and not wanting to leave him, the only thing they could think of was to drop him at the hospital emergency entrance. Their evening of fun was now a nightmare.

I have recently interviewed Louie, a relative and owner of the station wagon used that night. He was to tell me the station wagon was held by the sheriffs office for over a year before he got it back. He vaguely remembers giving the station wagon to Don to try out. It was not returned to him by Don.

Much of the investigation was handled by Beefy Lawson as the burglary and death happened in Itasca County. The boys did appear in court. Some received jail time.

Trying to put vague memories together of something that happened over thirty five years ago is not easy. Some people don't remember but some people are protective.

I have chosen to change some of the names.

~

142
A TRIBUTE TO MIKE

As I sit at my desk tonight wondering what to write, a file stands out from all the rest, a file on one of my best friends and one of the finest police officers I had the pleasure of working with in my 40 years on the police force. Mike (Harold) Sande, lost to all of us January 10, 2014.

All too often we lose someone, a few words are said, and in a short time they are forgotten. But, sometimes a word is written that may carry their memory through the ages.

When Mike left us, I was privileged to give the eulogy at his gathering: Who Was Mike?

I first met Mike over 30 years ago when he first came to work for the Grand Rapids Police Department, soon finding out he was a unique individual. Mike had a talent, maybe it was his smile that was always there. He was a good cop and he could make friends of anyone.

Remembering one fall day in particular, it was fair time. We were picking up information that there was a school bus parked on the midway that was selling marijuana to the public. Wondering how to approach the drug dealers, Mike volunteered to go in and make the buy.

Mike was not known for wearing high priced suits; he put on his everyday attire, walked up and made the buy. The arrest was made and we ended up confiscating this large orange school bus.

Mike was not without his little jokes, even on the brass. One week he went pheasant hunting in North Dakota with some friends promising to bring me back a pheasant. After getting back he took me to the back room saying, "I have a pheasant for you." I should have known, some of the guys were standing around. He had this great big brown paper bag with something in it. Just as he was handing it to me and opening the top, it happened so fast, I think he hit the bottom of the bag. There was a live hen pheasant in my face.

I never forgave him, he never stopped laughing.

We got along with the sheriffs office but as soon as we had some new talent, they were soon working for the sheriffs office. This is what happened to Mike. He was with us a few short years, the next thing I knew he was a gate-keeper for the jail.

Even as a gate-keeper or jailer, his talent came through. Mike had a good heart. Sometimes someone, a prisoner, would be having a bad time and about ready to lose it. Often times in the evening he would have them out of their cell, counseling them and cheering them up.

At times, he would call me saying, "Harvey, I have a young man here who wants to meet you. He wants to get some things off his chest." Mike never wanted the credit for all the information he passed along.

It is said he once made up a poster, posting it where it could be seen in the jail. The sign read, "Get out of jail sooner, come and see me." A few of them did!

It also seemed Mike was quite frugal, liking to save money. While Mike and Wally Herschbach were on patrol on the Scenic Highway one afternoon they came upon a deer. The doe was in the ditch stunned. Wally thought the best thing to do was shoot it. Mike said, "Save your bullet, Wally." Taking his buck knife he straddled the deer's neck, grabbing it by the ear and pulling the head up. Just then the deer stood up with Mike astraddle it, taking off with him hanging on for dear life! It went over a hundred feet before dropping over and dying.

Who was Mike? He was a good husband, father, cop and a true friend. He was also a proud US Navy veteran. While serving on the aircraft carrier, the USS Yorktown he was privileged to take part in the recovery of some US astronauts from the sea.

I expect to see Mike again. I'm not kidding myself. I'm 81 years old. I'm not perfect, I'm just hoping when I approach those gates, that Mike the gatekeeper will be there to say, "Welcome, Harvey, come right in."

Mike, in our hearts we will always remember you—we salute you.

~

143
NO BRAKES

A car was traveling through town at between 60 to 70 mph through all of the red lights and heading east past Central School. I thought he must really be in a hurry. Taking my time behind him to get through the stop lights safely with the red lights on my car, I started to catch up to him by the bowling alley, but he did not pull over even with the siren on.

He was not stopped until under the bridge going to Coleraine. The man driving had been drinking but he was not under the influence.

I recognized Mr. Bright right away as he got out and came hurrying back saying, "Harvey, I have got a good excuse for speeding. I was in a hurry to get home as I don't have any brakes on my car." And he did not. I got a wrecker, I ticketed him, I got him home, I said, "Good night."

~

144
HOT CARS

At one time the Marlon block was the hot spot in town. Looking for something to do in the later 1950s, it seemed if you had a hot car this was the place to show it off mostly on Friday and Saturday nights.

This block, like it was back then, had center parking but when there weren't any cars parked in the center and a few on the sides, this was the time to "smoke 'em" to show off by doing "donuts" by making circles while spinning your back wheels. Some could peel rubber a hundred feet or more.

More than once as a young police officer, I would stand inside the glass doors of the 1st National Bank and step out as they spun their wheels. Then coming to the stop sign on First Ave and 3rd Street they were given a ticket for unlawful acceleration.

We had a Ford Interceptor v8 that could really move. As I remember the teenagers didn't seem to care if there were any police officers in the area. But, now things were changing, they were putting points on their driver's license for infractions. It was also a time if you were old enough you could drive with an open bottle or a can of beer!

One night about 10:30 I was by the Marlon Cafe when I heard a crash by the old Gambles Store which is now the New China. Looking over I could see a small yellow King Lumber delivery truck with a stake bed in the back speeding north toward the 1st National Bank.

I ran across the avenue and jumped into a car just like you see in the movies, telling the guy to follow the yellow truck as he had just hit a parked car. My driver then took off. We got the truck stopped on the far side of the block on the Pokegama comer, two men were in it. The driver of the truck pointed south to a car making a right turn on Corcoran's comer, saying, "I'm chasing the car that hit the car. Not arguing, I jumped onto the running board on the passenger side of the truck and we were now chasing the car that hit the car by the Gamble's Store. Coming around the comer by the old State Bank we could see the car we were chasing stopped as the car he had hit was blocking the driving lane and he could go no further.

Jumping off the yellow truck and running up to the stopped car, the driver seemed to be in a dazed condition. I recognized the man as a local business man that had a drinking problem. He was arrested for leaving the scene of an accident and driving under the influence.

The next weekend after dark I was approaching the comer of the 1st National Bank in my squad. Looking to my left toward the Marlon block a black car was laying rubber for a half block, then running the stop sign in front of me at better than 30mph. The chase was on, going to Fourth St.

West and up Hwy 38 North exceeding 80mph, then around the comers by McKinney Lake. This kid could drive. I had my red lights and siren on. Hwy 38 was much narrower then and without shoulders. We were going over 100 mph at times.

My right foot was getting jumpy from extending the toe down on the gas pedal pushing it to the floor. I just hung in behind him thinking he would have to stop some time. As we got to the Marcell area on 38, the car pulled over. The driver got out walking back to my patrol car, looking at me saying, "Not you again!"

The name Fred will have to do.

Fred said, "The only reason I pulled over was the kids in the car were screaming and crying so much!" Over the years I must have stopped Fred seven or eight times. He had the heaviest foot I ever knew of. Along the way he got some breaks, I appreciated his driving skills and he mine. We always parted as friends.

Where Fred is now I know they don't have any stop signs but I bet once in a while he is looking in his rearview mirror to see if I'm there.

~

145
A LETTER TO MARGARET

This morning while going through some papers from years past we came upon a letter I had written to a ninety year old sister that up until a few years ago I was not aware of.

When I was in my early twenties I was told what my father's real name was. His name was Earl Currie from the Hinckley area. We searched for him off and on for years. Then in 2001 with the help of the internet we found him but he had passed away in 1959. In the process we found two of my nieces and that I had a sister.

After communicating with the nieces and the people she was now living with were hesitant saying they didn't know me. All of them were very protective of her and didn't want to see her hurt. I didn't want to hurt her either and said I could say anything I wanted to on the phone but I did have a large scrapbook that I could send her to read.

The scrapbook covered my forty years on the police department. A short time later, now knowing her birthday, I sent her a dozen yellow roses.

She was reluctant to meet me in the first place just finding out about a brother from many years ago but after reading the scrapbook and getting the roses, she decided she wanted to meet me. Saying, she knew she had a scallywag for a father.

I received word that she wanted to meet me so arrangements were made for us to meet. We had a wonderful afternoon. And yes, there was a resemblance in us. She was an older, vibrant, bright person able to quote full chapters of the Bible.

But, life had taken its toll; her health was not the best.

After getting acquainted with her in the Cities, she visited us for a few days getting to know some of the rest of our family. We found out she never had much in material possessions so we enjoyed spoiling her and buying things for her. We visited her as much as we could over the next few years enjoying every minute of it until her passing.

The Letter:

Dear Margaret,

I received a most welcome letter—one I had been hoping and praying for!

I have talked to Janice and Jeb and have made arrangements with them to come in November for an afternoon and spend time with you.

Since finding out about you, I have wanted to meet you but did not want to hurt you in any way. At the time we started seriously looking for Earl, we thought any one who would have been hurt by it would be long gone! Much to my surprise, we found he had a daughter living in California and due to the distance made me wonder if I would ever get to see her. However, God works in mysterious way and shortly after finding out about you, Margaret, you moved back to Minnesota only around 10 miles from my sister-in-law.

I can't say I am the best at expressing myself on paper—I hope you will take that into account as you read this.

I, like you was raised without a father in the home. It seems that I have so much inside me and that I may never be able to express to you.

First, a few notes on myself. We were raised as ragamuffins. We would run in the snow barefooted to the outhouse. We didn't have enough to eat and at times would steal canned goods from our neighbor's cellar. We fund out much later that he knew that but also knew we needed it. We missed a lot of schooling and instead of keeping us in a grade, they would just pass us on so we never got a lot of the basics. One year I got 9 BIG red F's on my report card! We were in several different places—a children's home in Little Falls, a foster home in Hackensack, an orphanage in St Paul and a foster home on a resort in Forest Lake were among them. I went to work on the railroad at 15 and threw a 10 pound sledge hammer all day which was good for me! In the latter part of 1949 we (my twin brother Harry) came home to live with my mother. She was working in a hotel laundry washing and mangling the linens. Her health wasn't the best and she was also drinking. Even though she had a drinking problem, she was a beautiful woman in a way. I remember when we lived in Remer around 1940 and there was a house burning with 2 children in it. Everyone was standing around and she was the one who went in and pulled them out. I will always remember the pain she suffered from the burns she received. I got a part time job in a grocery store in 1949 and lied about my age to join the National Guard to make some money. The guard was brought into the regular Army and shortly after that I ended up in the Korean War as a sergeant in an infantry machine gun platoon. After coming home from there I tried going back to school. I played football and wrestled but had to quit to help support the family. It wasn't too long after that I met a girl (Doris) who would become my wife who turned out to be my saving grace. I was a pretty rough person when she brought me home to meet her parents. Later her mom told her that my language made the hair stand up on the back of her neck! We married in 1954. I was working for the mines for a while but got laid off due to lack of work. I held some short term jobs but in 1955 I took the test for the police department and got a job. The pay was very poor at the time so I worked other jobs to support our growing family. Among them was driving school bus, shoveling roofs, digging graves, putting up TV antennas and etc. Doris didn't work out of the home as taking care of 4 boys and one girl was enough. We did have quite a scare in 1977 when we found she had a large hole in her heart and had to have open heart surgery to repair it. Open heart surgery was just getting off the ground—we did a lot of praying and she turned out real well.

I spent a little over 40 years on the police department and loved every minute of it. I was Chief for the last 8 years but spent a lot of the time working the streets on investigations. I believe I was a good policeman trying to treat people right and to do a good job. Through life I have made mistakes but have always thought that through them you learn and become a better person. I look back over the years and try to think how I would change any part of it—I don't think I would change any part of what happened to me now because the past is what makes us what we are today. I may not have had the wife I have nor had *the same children. No, I did not have a father there and there was always a little empty place in the back of my mind but now we are getting to know your family and that takes care of that. Margaret, I don't want you to worry about meeting me—I have admired sunsets, wondered at birds swooping and flying in the air, I too have seen the beauty of a dozen roses, but for some reason God saved you for the last!!!*

Not only your brother but your brother in Christ,
Harvey

~

146
LASKER & UPIN BURGLARY

Early Sunday morning what appeared to be a beautiful fall day on October 7, 1963, we at the Grand Rapids Police Department were alerted that something may be amiss at the Lasker and Upin men's clothing store located on the corner of 1st Ave. N.W. and 3rd St., it was just across the street from the 1st National Bank.

We were to meet Orren Upin, the owner, and Wayne Bishop an employee in front of the store as they believed the store may have been burglarized and there could be someone inside. Wayne Bishop had been there to lower the awning at 5:30 a.m. The lock to the front door had been in good condition at that time.

Mr. Upin had come to the store at 9:30 a.m. He could see when he was attempting to use his key the round cylinder lock had been forcibly pulled and then put back.

Harold Snyder, my partner for the day, had also notified the chief, Walter Craig and we were soon on the scene.

Upon examining the round key cylinder lock it was obvious that a clamping lock puller had been used to remove the lock. This is a type of lock puller we would become all too familiar with over the coming years.

We then entered the building doing a thorough search. It became obvious our burglars had been long gone.

In the back office stood a large steel safe. Generally there are a few different ways to enter a safe; work the dial, knock the dial off, peel the front door or the side of the safe, use a torch or go through the bottom which is generally much thinner or as many a thief has found out after all of his hard work just turn the handle, it wasn't locked in the first place.

A lot of hard work had been done on this safe, the dial had been knocked off, then the front door of the one quarter inch steel had been pried out, starting in the upper corner and peeled down so the inner workings could be reached.

Whoever had peeled the safe was well versed in how to go about it. Also they had to bring some heavy sledge hammers, chisels and pry bars with them.

There were various papers and things strewn about but other

than the safe the rest of the store didn't seem to have been touched. After examine the safe, looking for finger prints and tool marks, Mr. Upin was allowed to go through the safe to see if he could account for what might be missing.

In a short time he came to us with something that raised your eyebrows, there was $400 in cash missing and thousands of dollars worth of stocks and bonds. The total amount could not be accounted for. It would be some time before we would be able to get all of this information.

What information we were able to gather was passed on to the Itasca County Sheriffs Office and anyone in the state that we thought might be able to help us.

A few weeks went by. Then in what you may call a stroke of good luck, a police officer stopped a car for an infraction in the Twin Cities area. In a custodial search of the car, in the trunk of the car was to be found the thousands of dollars worth of stocks and bonds matching the description of those taken in the burglary with the name of Orren Upin on them.

The driver, Dale Orten, was subsequently brought back to Itasca County and charged with burglary and the possession of stolen goods. Having pleaded guilty, he was sentenced to Stillwater Prison to serve his time.

~

147
HOW I GOT MY PILOT'S LICENSE

One afternoon in 1953 my girlfriend Doris and I were driving into Grand Rapids on Hwy 2 East. At that time Itasca Street angled in next to the railroad tracks. On the left starting almost where the Horn Bridge is now.

The Horn Bridge was built much later.

Driving west on Itasca Street for a short distance a car could be seen off the road on a slant with what appeared to be a man slumped over the steering wheel. Driving past the car, we became concerned maybe he needed help. Making a U-turn and driving back we parked next to the car.

Opening the door, the man at first was unresponsive, your first thought is that he may have been drinking, but there are other reasons one can act this way, a heart attack or even a diabetic. He then started mumbling the words airport and Ned Powers.

It may be noted this was prior to the days of instant communication.

We at the time were driving a 1949 Oldsmobile 98 which had a large single bench seat in the front. The man was not large and seemed quite fragile. Picking him up, I carried him to the car. Doris had the door open. I was able to slide him in next to her. She cradled his head on her shoulder to keep him upright.

Arriving at the airport asking some questions, we were soon talking to Ned Powers who told us this was his brother, Robert. That he was a diabetic and this wasn't the first time this had happened. He knew what he needed, giving him some orange juice and soon he was doing much better.

Later, talking to Ned, he was telling us how grateful he was that we stopped to assist his brother and he would like to give us a plane ride to show his appreciation. We soon learned he was a flying instructor at the airport. He also introduced us to Jim Frizzle also an instructor.

I was to learn later that both of these men had trained pilots for the air force during World War II.

Within a few days we were headed for the airport. This was to be our first ride in a small plane, Doris in any airplane. She said she was looking forward to the flight but she was nervous. I was proud of her as she was not the type to take chances.

Ned soon had us high above the earth in a Cessna showing us Grand Rapids and the surrounding area far below. Doris seemed to be enjoying herself then we hit an air pocket and dropped a short distance. She was thinking we were going to earth faster than she had expected. Overall she took the flight quite well. Ned was a good pilot; it had been a terrific experience for both of us.

Later I was to learn that Ned at that time was licensed and checked out on almost everything there is to fly including multiengines and helicopters. He was also an airplane mechanic.

After the ride he asked me if I would like to learn to fly and if I had used up my G.I. eligibility. Telling him I had attempted to use it to finish high school and not knowing how to go about it had been turned down.

We decided to see if I could get the G.I. Bill to put me through flight training.

One of the first things you learn to do is a pre flight check on your plane before getting into it. It was not long and I was up with Jim Frizzle, we were to spend many hours together.

An exciting moment was when I was attempting to land the plane for the first time. I must have bounced the plane 20 to 25 feet in the air. My instructor pushed the throttle forward; we went around and came in, this time it settled in nicely.

After 20 hours with the instructor I made my first solo flight with a perfect landing. Then over the next year it was many hours of practice on my own circling pylons and practicing stalls. Then it was on to cross country flights.

On my first cross country flight to Bemidji it was in the winter. Something they try to instill in you is to always be aware of your surroundings so if you get into trouble is there a spot to make a landing. As I was crossing the west end of Pokegama Lake my engine started to sputter. The prop would spin and then come almost to a dead stop. Instantly I reached over and turned on the carburetor heat. In a few seconds it started to run smoothly.

I always enjoyed the long flights. Sometimes I would have to land on a lake with skis and refuel from a gas can.

In 1956 I received my single engine land pilot's license. I was proud of what I had accomplished. However, after some time I had to discontinue flying due to the high cost of $25 an hour.

Indescribably high above the earth all alone, you can see forever. The silence, just you and the engine, your thoughts can wander. Recently I was privileged to talk to Ron Powers, the son of Ned Powers. He was able to give me some information on this incident that happened some 60 years ago. As we talked, the pride in his father came through.

~

148
THE PHANTOM KLEPTOMANIAC

In the late 50's and early 60's we were struggling along. We had 5 children but police wages were pretty low so I took other work to make it; driving school bus once a day, digging graves, setting head stones, shoveling off roofs in the winter and had a small business installing, repairing and taking down tv antennas. Not getting much sleep and not complaining, it's just the way it was.

But this is just leading into something else.

I had a very good friend that I looked up to. One day my wife and 1 got to discussing him and his wife. It seemed they had all the bells and whistles, buying things we could never consider being able to afford to buy. My friend was not in a high paying job. His wife was very well liked in the job she was in but it wasn't high paying either.

During this time my wife was having some health problems and the medical bills were adding up. As we were discussing this she said she wondered how they could afford everything they were buying. And just to show how insensitive a man can be, I said he probably does not have to pay all those medical bills.

Now I knew right away what I had said and how it made her feel. She will never forget it and neither will T.

In the early 70's we learned that part of her problems was a defective heart and she would have to have surgery to repair it if she w as to live. In 1977 she had the surgery which was in the infancy of this type of surgery. How she had lived taking care of 5 children and a husband was a good question. After 58 years of marriage she is still with me.

Over the next 15 years or so there were many rumors going around about my friend's wife. You hear them but you don't really believe them.

I started hearing them more often with a few women coming to see me saying Gina had been at their party and had gone in the bedroom to get her purse and that several of the women swore that money had been taken from their purses.

How do you handle this? I started to document every rumor and complaint.

Gina had been in a clothing store, something was missing. She had been to a party, someone had money missing. Nothing you could prove, she was gone. Over a period of time I was building quite a list but no evidence.

There was just too much and only one thing I could do. I called my trusted friend, Del, asking him to come and see me that I had something to discuss with him. He came to me right away. We shook hands and went into a private room.

How do you tell a friend like this that his wife is a kleptomaniac and has been for years. You don't. I took out my long list of documentation and started to read it. Where she had been, time and articles missing or money out of purses. After about 10 items, Del said, "I cannot believe this. As far as I know she was at all of these places but I just can't believe she would do this/* I then continued reading at least another 20 items of the many left. Del then stopped me saying that I had convinced him and what do you want me to do.

After a little more talking I suggested he look over the list very carefully, go home and think about it. Then, do what you think is right. We shook hands and he left, not happy.

Early the next morning he was in to see me and to be blunt, he looked like hell. All drug out like he hadn't slept and he hadn't. We went back to the room and there he told me, she is really good. For everything I said she had an answer. But there was just too much. He had kept after her all night and it wasn't until early morning she broke down and told him everything. She had problems and that this had been going on for years but she just couldn't seem to help herself.

Now we had a new problem. What to do and how to handle it. I had no evidence. Not one person who would step forward and say they had seen her take something.

I told Del I wouldn't try to prosecute her if she would agree to go through the list and put a value on each item and agree to make restitution. Also adding to what was not on the list. This he agreed to. It came to several thousand dollars.

This was how it was handled up to this time.

Things went well in his household for many years. Then one day I received a call from a local bank wanting to talk to a police officer. I responded and a teller proceeded to tell me that she had been counting money on her counter amounting to around $5,000. A lady had come to her counter and made some small talk then asked to see something that required her to leave her desk and go to another room. When the clerk returned, the woman was gone and so was the money. Asking her if she knew the woman she replied, "Somewhat." Her name was Gina and worked somewhere she knew. The bank in those days had no security cameras nor did anyone see Gina take the money.

One thing to do. I called my friend again telling him what had happened and the amount of money.

He said, "Harvey, I will take care of it." Within an hour the money was returned. No questions asked.

We are still friends. He mourns the love of his life as she passed some years ago.

We all have our crosses to bear.

~

149
BURGLARY OF GILDEMEISTER MOTORS

On the morning of July 25, 1975, at 8:15 a.m., Dave Gildemeister, owner of Gildemeister Motors located at 120 N.E. 4th St. in Grand Rapids, reported that the side shack of the car lot had been broken into. Sixty-six pair of keys are stolen and at least four cars missing from the car lot over night.

Officer Hansen of the police department handled the initial report, gathering information, passing this on to Greg Lease and myself.

On this same day, Joe Burt from the sheriffs office called me at about 6 p.m. stating he wanted me to take a ride with him six miles out on Hwy 38. He had received a report of a car parked in a field and there could be a connection to our car thefts at Gildemeister.

Joe then drove us out to the Jensen place on Hwy 38. Meeting Mr. Jensen, he reported that a red Charger had been left in a field about a half mile from their house. Mr. Jensen then drove us to the car, which had a 1968 license EU1920, which proved to be one of our stolen cars.

As we were looking the car over, I glanced down to the end of the field about three hundred yards and could see a break in the trees indicating there could be a road through. Walking down, there was a narrow road back to a small clearing. Hidden in the brush were five more stolen cars.

After talking it over with Joe, it was decided a stake-out would be the way to handle the situation.

Driving back to Grand Rapids, I contacted Chief Arnie Witherill and, after telling him what was going on, asked if we could get some shifts changed around. It was decided that Dave Bennett would come in at 7 p.m. and Al Brooks at 8 p.m... Officer Greg Lease and I would go stake out the stolen cars at 8 p.m. just before dark in hopes that some one would come for them.

We drove to the Jensen's in Lease's car, leaving it there, and made our way to the Charger parked in the field. We spent some uncomfortable time in the brush, eventually making our way over and into the Charger.

It wasn't until 2:15 a.m. that a light could be seen coming across the field with two parties. As they came to the Charger, we stepped out telling them to freeze. After taking one or two steps, they stopped.

Getting the two young men against the car and cuffing them, we found the keys to the Charger in the pocket of one of the boys. Both boys were well known to us, living only a short distance away. They stated they had driven by on the main road earlier that morning, and after seeing the car in the field, had walked over and removed the keys.

Having been read their rights, the boys were separated and questioned, both telling different stories.

As we got out of the police car at Gildemeister's car lot, one of the boys started talking, saying he had done it. Supposedly he had broken into the shed, got the keys, then started stealing the cars about 11 p.m. that night, taking them out to the field then hitchhiked back to town to get more. Later he had told the other boy what he had done.

Eventually both boys admitted they were going out to the field to get all of the cars farther into the back of the field to hide them. Their intentions were to come back later and to strip them for parts to make money. The stolen cars were worth several thousand dollars in 1975.

At this time we had another problem; there were at least 66 keys for other cars missing. The value to get a locksmith to come and put new locks in was estimated to be $2,000.

When told this, the boys directed us out to the bridge crossing Pokegama Lake a few miles south of town. They had thrown them in the water on the east side of the bridge.

Greg Lease contacted Bob Rabey, a scuba diver who would be in charge of recovering the keys from the water. Sheriffs boats would be in control of boat traffic while the divers were in the water which took about two hours. Most of the keys were recovered.

The boys also went with us to one of their homes on Hwy 38 where four more sets of keys were recovered from a hole cut in the mattress on a bunk bed.

One of the pickups recovered from back in the woods had been stolen from Casper Construction the week before.

Most of the cars were pulled from the marshy area by Dale Hirt of Rapids Body Shop and were to be released to Gildemeister Motors.

The two boys were placed in Itasca County Jail to go through the juvenile court system.

Amazingly one of the boys had three other members of his family in jail the same weekend.

~

150
DEER HUNTING

I went to the store to get some things for the wife and ran into an old friend; he was picking up some things before heading out to fix up his deer stand.

Sun shining, 32 degrees out, a slight wind. What wonderful thoughts come to my mind just remembering how it was so many years ago. Indian summer, walking through the trees, stopping, listening, squirrels running through the leaves.

We had our little gang that used to hunt down in the Jacobson area; my brother Harry, Ray Barton and his brother, and sometimes Harold Snyder, who was a partner on the police force.

To get there, I drove down the River Road from Grand Rapids, crossing Hwy 200 just this side of Jacobson, then following the River Road perhaps another 10 miles. At one time, there was an old two story building sitting next to the Mississippi River, a boarding house for people plying the river on river boats now owned by a man from Forest Lake, Minn.

We would leave our cars there and go across the main road into some very rough country; swamps, pines and poplar trees. We split up most of the time on the way to our stand.

Much of this land was worked over many years ago by the government. Since it was low land, they had to dredged it so it would drain the water. Every half mile there would be a 15 foot high bank of dirt and a creek next to it. This went back as far as you could see. Through the years trees and brush had covered almost everything. It was a rugged country with a few beaver ponds.

When starting to hunt, I never had much luck since the area was covered in a swamp grass that came to the middle of your chest. This never really bothered me as I would just enjoy being by myself, in the solitude.

One day I decided to climb a tree. I was 40 feet off the ground with a rope tied around me, and had been there perhaps 20 minutes when I saw the blaze red coats coming through the woods, making a drive. I just looked in admiration as a big buck in the drive darted to and fro in the bush to stay hidden. Staying low, he was sometimes within 40 feet of a driver working back through. The man on the drive never saw him. It was worth watching. From that day on, I hunted from a tree perch.

I know that hunting sounds like it's all fun, but you got up at four in the morning, it may be below zero and two feet of snow, but you have to get going.

Most deer hunters you meet in the woods are pretty friendly. Now at this time I was carrying a 30-30 Marlin rifle with a magazine that was spring loaded with a release in the front of the magazine. At times I would bump the release while going through the brush and spent forever looking for it.

I met a hunter from Grand Rapids that owned a small business; he was carrying a .32 Winchester Special. As we talked, he said he always liked the gun I was carrying, the 30-30 Marlin. I said I always admired his 32 with the buck sights. He then said, "Let's trade and I will throw in a box of shells." I walked away a happy man. I treasured that rifle, many years later my grandsons would be using it.

Then there was the morning of November 19, 1962. One I'll never forget. I had shot a doe from my perch high in an oak tree between two large pine trees. I had gotten down and walked over to where the deer lay. There was a small oak tree with a crotch about six feet off the ground.

Harold helped me lift the deer up so its head was stuck in the crotch, the body hanging off the ground.

We both went back to our stands. There was a beaten path going almost under my stand. After being back in my stand perhaps a half hour, a hunter came striding down the path carrying a rifle with scope and sling. Everything a hunter could want. I thought, he's from the Cities. Not seeing me in the tree, and after getting down the trail a 100 feet further, he saw the deer hanging. The sling came off his shoulder and he was taking aim at the deer hanging there 70 feet away.

He must have stood there 10 minutes looking at the deer. Then he started to look all around him, and walked back under my tree. Then he started to call, not very loudly, "Hey, who owns this deer?" He did this for perhaps five minutes. Getting no answer, he was soon over to the deer. The next thing I knew, he was lifting the deer's body, trying to dislodge the head from the tree. But as he would lift, the neck would bend and the head would stay put.

He spent a good 15 minutes before the deer came down. He then spent time tying a rope onto the legs and head making a pulling harness that went over both of his shoulders. He must have pulled it around 15 feet when he heard a voice from the heavens saying, "You'd better put it back." He stopped dead in his tracks. Looking around, he started pulling the deer again. This time much louder, "You had better put it back." Looking all around, he couldn't see me high in between the pine trees. He then pulled the deer back to the tree. There was no way one man could lift that deer and get it back into the crotch of that tree.

Then a voice could be heard saying, "Hey, gang, there's a guy over here trying to steal our deer."

The man picked up his rifle and was gone running down the rough trail. He must have been well over 200 pounds. The last I saw of him a quarter of a mile away, he was still going strong.

The next year, I was back to my deer stand. How can anyone spend two days in the top of a tree enjoying the cold crisp air and the warm sun, watching the squirrels chase each other and the birds all around you. "Was it the solitude, a time to think, to let your mind wander. Would I ever know the answer?"

Then I hear the rustle, something coming through the brush and leaves; it's a yearling deer. I aim and fire and it goes down, but its back up running, dragging its rear legs. Soon I'm down following its trail. Suddenly I see it there on its front legs. It can go no further. It's looking at me.

I'm thinking I know what has to be done but this is not who I am. It is one thing to kill or be killed. I've done what I've had to in the past -- this will be the last time.

Do I condemn those who hunt? No, the answer to that must come from within each of us.

~

151
TO INTIMIDATE

I was talking to a friend of mine of many years one day. Of course, the subject came up, "How is your family doing?" He began telling me one of his boys would be leaving, moving to California.

This really surprised me because the boy was very young, easy to get along with, and didn't seem to be the type to strike out on his own at such a young age.

Something seemed to be wrong, not being said. Intuition perhaps, tone of voice?

Looking at my friend, I asked, "Is there something wrong, something I can help with?"

He looked almost relieved, then started telling me his mild mannered son had been bullied and harassed by three boys over an extended period of time. They would show up unexpectedly where ever he would be. He didn't know how but they would be there. Not only was he starting to fear for his life; he wasn't getting any sleep. Upset and confused, he told his father he wanted to leave town. He had no other choice.

I asked the father if he knew the names of the boys and where they lived. He had the information. This was in the early afternoon. The boys were from 17 to 18 years old.

I told my friend to go home and see his son, tell him I would be handling this personally, and if these boys so much as blinked at him from now on I was to be called.

So I called two of my officers in and told them what I wanted done. They were to pick up the three boys, bring them to the back office, and sit them down by themselves, not telling them what this was about.

They were brought into the back office and sat down. I was setting at a desk in the front. After they had sat there for a few minutes, they were starting to get nervous.

Then I told the boys how it was going to be. I had looked into what they had been doing, the bullying and harassment of Danny over the last couple years. I was not asking them, I knew it was true. The boy was making arrangements to leave town. I had asked him not to; I would personally handle the matter. "Now you may think there is nothing I can do, but you drive cars, we know what kind, color, and license plate numbers. If Danny leaves town because of you or if he doesn't, if his car shows up with a scratch on it, if he gets a strange phone call in the night, as far as I'm concerned it's you guys. You'd be surprised at how many tickets you could end up getting; turning without signaling, speeding, loosing your license, and the cost of your insurance going up." It didn't take the boys long to speak up, saying that they knew it was wrong what they had been doing to Danny and would be avoiding him from now on.

Danny and his parents were told what had taken place in my office and were relieved. There were no further contacts or problems from then on.

Danny, a mild mannered boy some years later became a well respected police officer in a city far from here.

Someone may say it was not right to intimidate these young men and I would say I was giving them a choice and they made the right one.

~

152
OUR FIRST HOUSE - THE CASTLE

I had gone back to high school after returning from Korea in 1953, becoming active in sports. There was a very attractive young lady that I was bumping into and saying "Hi" to in the halls. She and a friend had invited me to dinner one night but I must confess I didn't show up. I didn't have a car or money.

It was a short time afterward that I finally had to quit school and go to work in the mines. A few months later, I was at the Playmore Roller Rink and I ran into Doris, who was anything but steady on her feet. I enjoyed roller skating and talking to her. I asked to take her home, and she consented. I had borrowed a small two door coup from a friend, so we drove around a short while. I then told her I knew of a high hillside where the moon would be shining on the water below, and asked would she like to see it. She agreed.

Doris was a lovely, shy girl who didn't have a lot to say. We then drove out to the Golf Course Road. Driving perhaps a half mile, we turned left on to the Horseshoe Lake Road going another quarter mile. I told her to close her eyes and I would tell her when to open them. In a short time, turning left, I parked the car on a high hillside. I was looking at a beautiful moon telling her to open her eyes. She did and was looking down below at the city dump. And this is how it started.

This girl was shy but intelligent. We must have talked a couple hours.

She at first, seeing me and my twin brother Harry at school, had thought we were probably from a well-to-do family in town. Talk about a surprise learning about our broken home.

I don't think I had ever met anyone quite like her, always thoughtful and caring. When we first met I was staying in a small apartment downtown with my mother, and shortly after moved in with my sister and her family.

I had been working in the mines but got laid off, then going to work at the Red Owl as a meat cutter. We had been talking of marriage for some time, so we asked my mother and her friend if they would like to get married at the same time, which is what happened.

Like all couples, you want a place of your own. My brother-in-law had a garage just down the road from my in-laws on the Southwood Road on Pokegama Lake about a mile east of 169. He told us if we wanted to fix it up we could live there—rent free.

The garage was on the lake side back in the trees, 22 feet long and 22 feet wide. It was covered in heavy tarpaper with a side door, cement floor and two windows in the front. Two by fours inside and a small hand water pump in the corner.

This was to be our castle. We purchased black covered insulation and installed it between the two by fours. There was a ceiling already in it at least.

We purchased an oil burner for heat, a gas cook stove, and an old belt driven refrigerator that constantly squeaked. We had a green top table and a couple chairs.

As I came home from work each night, I would try to bring some large cardboard boxes with me to cover the insulation on the walls.

To make it so we had some privacy for our bedroom, I got a long heavy wire to stretch high across the room next to the ceiling. We bought some yard goods and hung it on the wire. We now had a bedroom and a living room/kitchen.

Our bathroom was a little drafty as it consisted of a small shed, with two holes some 50 feet behind the cabin.

For some reason, that winter was very cold with lots of snow, but most of the time it was comfortable in the little cabin. One night we woke up and it was very cold. We were shivering, and after checking, discovered we had run out of fuel oil.

Somehow and I don't remember how I got a hold of Hank Roy at H&R Oil. I told him of our plight while it was well below zero outside. As soon as he was able, he was there filling our tank.

There was a short time that winter when I was without work. My mother and her husband, who also had little, would show up smiling with care packages. A couple bags of groceries. At Doris's parents, we were always welcome there at meal time.

We often time had a visitor, a big shaggy old dog that didn't seem to belong to anyone. When he would show up at our door we would give him a good portion of uncooked elbow macaroni right out of the box. His tail would wag like he was eating a steak. Then sadly he was there no more. Coming home from work one evening, there he was lying in the ditch; he had been killed by a car crossing 169.

344

In the later part of winter, our son was born, which turned out quite exciting. One day I was having a lot of pain in my side and I ended up in the hospital to get my appendix removed. That evening, in the same hospital, my son, Alan, was born.

I had been working at Warren and Arfman Motors a short time when my wife saw a short advertisement in the paper. The Grand Rapids Police Department was looking for applicants. She showed it to me and told me she thought I could do it. Now to be honest, there was no way I could qualify to be a police officer. I was 21 years old. Most policemen in Grand Rapids and on the Range were 40 to 50 years old, with many town marshals and watchmen who were 70 or older.

But I took the test. Thirteen men showed up for it, some college grads dressed in suits, while I was in my grease-monkey clothes as I had to take off work to make it. I finished the writing just in time, and then went to the interview. I had no idea how I had done when I went back to work.

A few weeks later I was notified I had gotten the job and would be starting June 1, 1955. I was immediately put on the street with no formal training.

We then had to leave our little castle as one of the requirements of the job at that time was you had to reside in the city limits.

Some time later our little castle was built onto and turned into a home.

~

153
BANDITS ROB BANK

When first getting onto the Grand Rapids Police Department in 1955, the other officers were much older than me and would give me a little history of the town, its buildings and people, as we rode around.

One of them I already knew about was Mickey's Café. As a young man, the National Guard had been activated and while waiting to be shipped out, we spent many a late night hanging out there. Mickey Jetland always treated the young men with much respect. And, there was the Gilbert house with Bob Gilbert always ready to sing and entertain.

One time one of the officers pointed out a brick house, told me what the persons name was that lived there, and said that he could have been one of the men who had been involved in a bank robbery in Grand Rapids many years ago. He didn't say what year or which bank.

It may have been four years or more when I pulled a car over close to the same house, thinking I may have a DWI on my hands. At first the man was quite cooperative. I asked him to exit his car. Looking at his driver's license, I recognized the name as the potential robber of the past, his age the late 60s. I sized the man up; he was very large, quite tall, weighing close to 300 lbs. And he wasn't fat. After talking to the man, I made the determination he was under the influence. I then told him I was arresting him for being under the influence; he was to get into my police car as he would be spending the night in jail. At that he became combative, saying he would not get in. Who would put him in?

Now looking at this guy, I knew that I would have my hands full so I simply told him I would be attempting it myself but if I couldn't there was help on the way. He looked at me, said, "OK" and climbed into the car.

Many years later while doing some research, an article that had been in an old Herald-Review caught my eye. It was dated July 12, 1933. This was the year I was born.

The headline read, "Just Like Big City: Bandits Rob Bank, Slug Man, Escape With $5,000." My mind flashed back to what the police officer had told me many years ago and the man I had arrested for DWI. Going on to read the article, it told of the afternoon of July 12, 1933, how four men had robbed the 1st National Bank in the Village of Grand Rapids of between $5,000 and $7,000, and that so far no trace of them has ever been found.

Before escaping they had slugged one employee in the head. Another employee had not moved quickly enough and was shot in the leg, and a woman had been abducted as a hostage to help in their escape.

The article then went on to give a sequence of the events. Just before 3 p.m., three men entered the bank while a fourth man drove a car into the alley. A lady was making a deposit at the teller's window; she was directed to pull down the shade to indicate the bank was closed.

The robbers in the meantime, covering the others with their pistols, ordered them to lie on the floor. One man then entered the bank's offices. Another man scooped the cash out of the till and with a companion ran to the vault where they seized all of the currency inside.

Mr. Bastien did not lie down quickly enough and was struck in the head with a pistol. Mr. Bauer did not move rapidly and was shot in the leg, a flesh wound. This only took a few minutes and they were making their escape through a window in a lobby, forcing Mrs. McDonald to accompany them through the window. Several other persons had come into the bank; three boys, Joe Olson, Billy Betz, and Johnny Morse. Cursing them, the bandits told them to sit on the floor. Olson had a sack with a hundred dollars in it, and quickly sat on it. Billy Betz seized the opportunity and dashed out the door spreading the alarm that the bank was being robbed. One man sounded the fire alarm. The police and sheriff's office were notified.

Driving south out of the alley, the bandits turned west past Power's store then north to the city lumber company corner. They stopped to let Mrs. McDonald from the car then sped west.

Officers started in pursuit within a few minutes but were unable to find any trace of the robbers. The highway patrol, driving south, also did not succeed in locating them.

Now $5,000 to $7,000 doesn't sound like much, but back when Central School was built, I understand it was done for $47,000.

This is some past history of our little village where nothing exciting ever happens.

154
THE GOLDEN TOILET BOWL AWARD

Monday, the 21st of September, 1970 was to be a day to remember as fellow officer Itasca County Deputy Sheriff Lou Hince and I had been working toward this end for a couple of weeks.

We had been receiving reports that a house on Strader Drive, close to the Old Soldier's Cemetery, was becoming a nest for drug users and that drugs were being sold there.

Reports of a constant string of cars coming and going both day and night; a bus driver had reported he could not get his bus through the parked cars.

We were aware that three young men had rented the house a little over a month ago. All three were known as drug users. One had been arrested for burglary.

We had been given a list of car license plates; also driving through obtaining some of the plate numbers ourselves. Running the plates, many were coming back to persons known to be using drugs.

On Monday morning, when the time was right we made some legal stops on cars that had just left the house on Strader Drive. We were able to find both marijuana and mescaline in one of the cars. The driver seemed eager to cooperate in our investigation giving us a lot of information on who was selling and what.

A team of Grand Rapids police officers with men from the Itasca County Sheriff's Office raided the house later that afternoon, also checking out two more cars.

As we approached the house, people were running everywhere. I saw a couple guys carrying bags into the toilet. As I entered they were stuffing marijuana into the toilet and trying to flush it down. There was just too much. I reached down and pulled much of it out.

Seized, were large quantities of the drug. The sheriff was in possession of at least two pillow cases filled with a home grown variety which he called Minnesota Green and two satchels containing mescaline, a hallucinogenic drug which Sheriff Muhar termed a "kissing cousin" of LSD.

Nine young people, seven of them from the Grand Rapids area, were arrested on drug charges that afternoon. Two older men from out of the area were held on $1,000 bond. Sheriff Muhar commended his men and the Grand Rapids police for their rapid action in seeing that the evidence was not destroyed.

155
MY YOUNGER YEARS

It seems funny, as I'm out jogging around Ice Lake, how my mind will wander, sometimes taking me back in time to my earliest memories, like to that drafty log cabin in Remer in the 1930's, then to some of the welfare homes.

A journey in time goes through my mind. How fortunate I was to experience what I went through at each of these homes. And not just the bad, like a razor strap across the legs (Yes, I had it coming).

I'm going to try to relate a few happenings in my journey.

The third place we were taken to, that being me, my twin Harry, and little brother Ron, was the Gene Martin Brown Home, an orphanage on Como Avenue close to the Como Park Zoo in St. Paul. We were to spend two to three years there. Little Ron would be leaving us from there for several years, adopted out.

This was a large brick building, three stories high with both boys and girls of different ages with a wing for a nursery. One could see almost anything happen underneath these conditions, but one little story stands out. There was a boy, Delbert, who was older than us and was probably there for a good reason. He came to our group saying he had found a bush up the alley behind the post office, and money was growing on the bush.

We were taken up the alley to the bush, and you can imagine Delbert had a lot of help harvesting the money from the bush and the coins on the ground.

This was near a drug store and all the money was spent on ice cream and candy.

But alas, it seems Delbert had been a bad boy, and was soon in Mr. Dahl's office. There was a closet with glass jars with the name of each of the boys and girls on it. The jars held the money of each person's allowance. Delbert had somehow found the keys to the closet, emptying each jar. His sentence would be forth coming.

That ice cream and candy had sure tasted good, but at someone else's expense. Later, finding we had spent our own money, left a bitter taste.

Some good things happened to me there. When it snowed, I would go and shovel sidewalks, making $5 in an evening. In the summer, raking leaves or mowing lawns made a little more.

There were a few weekends Mr. Dahl would take me out on the St. Croix River in his 18 ft. sailboat. There is nothing like a sailboat to feel the wind, the waves, and the elements.

It must have been in early 1946 that Harry and I ended up on the Emil Johnson resort on Coon Lake. They were elderly and needed help to run the place. This was located a few miles from Wyoming, Minn. We were expected to work here. Now I didn't have a problem with that, but old man Johnson was partial to letting my brother off the hook much of the time because I would do the work. One day he told me to do something, and I said, "No, make Harry do some of it." He got really mad and I still refused. The next thing I knew I was dodging the hammer he threw at me.

It was nothing to spend a day washing clothes, pushing a handle up and down on a clothes washer that operated by hand or turning a crank on a wringer to squeeze the water out of the clothes. But all in all, this may be one of the places we had the most fun.

We would take a boat out fishing, rowing to the end of the lake by a creek. We would go over land perhaps a quarter of a mile to a slough hole an acre or two in size but very deep. There was an old flat bottom scow that we had to constantly bail water from as we fished. It was nothing to catch three or four large northern pike. Back at the boat landing at the resort, the "resorters" would pay a dollar to tell where we had caught them. We may have misled them a little as we pointed to a spot across the lake.

In the winter we would help cut blocks of ice from the lake, each weighing some 300 pounds. We then helped load them onto a sleigh and pulled them off with a tractor to a wooden ice house. The ice would then be covered with sawdust and sold in the summer. There weren't any electric refrigerators here.

One winter the lake froze over like glass. We made cloth sails and, in a strong wind, would glide across the lake on skates.

The thing I got the most thrill from was someone had a small black car. Taking it out onto the ice, we would pull two people at a time on skates at the end of 100 foot ropes. We would get going quite fast, then start to circle, getting into a whip at the end of the rope. And you just could not hang on. Once you let go, you would fall down and slide a quarter of a mile on the glass lake.

One day, Harry and a Taylor boy were on the edge of the lake. They saw a skunk on the ice and gave chase almost all the way across to the far side. They had heard that it could not squirt you if you picked it up by the tail. Alas, something went drastically wrong. Back to the Taylor house, Mrs. Taylor met them on the back porch and made the boys strip naked in the cold and then into the bath tub.

In the spring when the ice was going out, perhaps 40 feet from shore, Harry and I would run off the long dock onto the rubbery ice. We did fall in a few times into three to four feet of water. Going out further, the ice was a few inches thicker; you could look through it and see piles of frogs, a hundred or so to a pile.

Something else I enjoyed doing was working on a small steamboat for 25 cents an hour feeding the engine wood.

Coon Lake was shaped like an hourglass with a narrow body of water between the two lakes. The boat was perhaps 25 feet long with a canvas top. Being docked in the narrows between the bodies of water, it would take passengers on steamboat rides.

There was a creek that ran out of the end of the lake, and in the spring the game warden would build a fish trap across the creek with willow poles two and a half inches apart. At times this would be full of northerns and bullheads going upstream to spawn. One day on a Sunday, when we were supposed to be in church, we had a spear and half a gunnysack full of bullheads when we spotted a game warden coming through the brush. I threw the spear across the creek and then, making a little error in judgment, threw the gunnysack with the bullheads in it across my back. You may say I got the points very quickly. Dropping the sack, we made our way into the woods. When we came back later, we couldn't find the spear we had thrown.

It was later that summer, coming home from church on a Sunday morning, I found Mr. Johnson laying in the yard; he had had a heart attack. It was a short time after that we were placed on the Cliff Farber farm a short distance from Staples, Minn.

Harry was to work in the house; I was to be a helper to Cliff on the farm. They had milk cows and a team of horses. While there, I would learn to milk the cows, separate the cream with a hand operated machine, feed cattle, horses, and chicken, clean the barn, and harness a team to operate a plow, side rake, and mowing machine.

When it got real cold, there was more than one way to start the car; but first you had to fill the radiator with warm water as they didn't have any anti-freeze in those days. Sometimes when it would be really cold, you would put a pan of oil under the motor and then start it on fire. Then you had to hand crank the motor, being very careful as the crank could kick back and you could break an arm. At times you would pull the car with a team of horses to start it.

The house was off the road a couple hundred feet so we had a wooden snowplow pulled by a team of horses to clear the road.

We often times went squirrel hunting. One time I saw one go in a hole in a tree about 10 feet off the ground. Climbing the tree, I reached into the hole and the squirrel had me. As I reached around him, he came out of the hole. I was squeezing him and couldn't let go. He went home with us headed for the fry pan. At times we hunted rabbits and squirrels with a 22 single shot rifle.

When first starting school in a one-room, all-class building about a mile from Farbers, we had to earn our right of passage. It seemed the whole school was picking on the two of us. In early winter they would pelt us with snowballs.

Now this was their mistake as my brother had an arm on him and we were getting a little tired of it. One night Harry watered down some snowballs, freezing them. The next day when they started pecking us with snowballs during recess, soon as they stuck their heads around the corner to throw... well, it wasn't long before at least two of them had eyes that would soon be black.

One day, Tony Lansky, a tall boy about a year or two older than us who thought he could run, had walked up and blind-sided me in the side of my face. Then, with me in pursuit, had run out onto the main road. I must admit he was a good runner; but after about a mile, I could see him looking back more often. Shortly he was off the road, over a fence, and into a pasture. After climbing an oak tree, I caught him up there at least 10 feet, and he came tumbling down. He had the wind knocked out of him; we walked back to the school together and became good friends.

It so happened that the one-room school had a cable around the front yard held about two feet off the ground by white posts about every 10 feet. This separated the school yard from the main road. Just beyond the fence was a drop off or ditch five feet deep. The ditch had three feet of water in it.

One of the Johnson boys, who outweighed Harry by 30 pounds and was a couple years older, stood with his back to the cable challenging Harry to a fight. Now I could see what was coming as I had fought Harry a few times. He was a believer of striking first, always to the lower belly, and that was what happened. Johnson went over the cable backwards and into that cold ditch water. If we hadn't gone down and pulled him out, I don't think with the wind knocked out of him he would have made it. It seems we had earned our right of passage. We oddly did not have any further problems.

Come spring it was soon time to work the fields. I was walking behind a single-bladed plow pulled by one horse with the reins behind my neck. This was for a small garden close to the house. Later I would be riding a sulky, a two-bladed plow pulled by a team of horses.

Later in the summer we were in for an unexpected surprise. Harry and I had taken our rod and reels and gone fishing in the Crow Wing River. This was when our brother, Don, had gotten a release from the welfare, so he showed up at the Farber's to take us home to Grand Rapids. Not finding us there, he came down to the river. Surprised to see him, we were also surprised that he was really mad and verbal when he found us. But then we came out of the river with our rod and reels and, looking down, we noticed that we still had our good leather shoes on.

This was the summer of 1949. My younger years had slipped by, never to be forgotten.

~

156
THE SHINY BAYONET

This story took place in the late 1960's or early '70's in the fall of the year.

One of those nights you felt nothing would be happening. Two of our patrol cars were on the street. Arlis, my partner for the night and I had just had coffee at Mickey's Cafe. Back in our cars as it was getting onto 1:30 a.m. and the bars would soon be closing. If something was going to happen be it drunk drivers or a domestic dispute, this seemed to be the time.

I had on a light jacket and a new pair of ankle high boots with smooth leather soles. Now you ask, why would you even mention this? It will be later clarified. Up to this time it had been an uneventful night.

At 1:30 a.m. a stolen car report was being broadcast by the MN Highway Patrol based in Virginia, MN. A white 1964 Chevy had just been reported stolen in the city of Virginia and all cars were to be on the lookout. The car's license plate was also given.

At this time I was in the west part of Grand Rapids and started to think of the time it would normally take to drive here. A fair time would be just over an hour. I thought, "Why not take a chance." In a short time I was parked in the Rendezvous Bar lot.

At the time the bar was located across the street from the 7-Up plant on 4th St NE.

I had been sitting with my lights off for about 20 minutes when the stolen car went by heading west on 4th St. With my lights on, I fell in behind the white Chevy and then onto my radio telling our dispatcher and the local cars what was happening.

Getting close to the stolen car, turning on my red lights and siren, the chase was on! The Chevy picked up speed, hurdling down 4th St, just making the comer onto 3rd Ave E, heading toward the fairgrounds a few blocks. He turned west on 8 St. not stopping for any stop signs, trying to lose the police car behind him. Totally going around a few blocks, always at a high rate of speed. Finally crossing Hwy 38 on Fifth St. going west. On 10th Ave he made a fast left, spinning out, ending up in a field across the street from the Floor to Ceiling Store.

At one time what is now Clusiau's car lot was an open field, a young man got out of the stolen car, perhaps 5 feet 10 inches, 160 pounds and was running south, up and over 4th street toward the railroad tracks, then he was going over the tracks to 3rd street and the Mississippi River.

Out of my car 100 ft or so behind him, it was cold and frosty. Running hard, stepping on the first rail with my slick leather soles, I was on my hands and face, sliding in the cinders. Getting up I stepped on the next rail and was down again. Then we were running across Third Street toward the river.

At this time there were houses all along here, now it is just Blandin's log piles.

There were some street lights along the road. As we were getting closer to the river, it was darker. As we ran, he was looking back and did not see a depression in the ground. He went down hard. He was starting to turn over as I threw myself on him. I had seen a flash of something shiny. After a short tussle I had the handcuffs on the young man.

Then walking back a couple blocks to our cars where the other police car was waiting.

The young man was jailed and Virginia was notified that the stolen car had been recovered and a man was in custody.

The next day I retraced the steps of our run the night before to see if he had dropped or thrown anything. This is something I normally did.

As I approached the area where he had been turning over and I had thrown myself on him, there lay shining in the sun an army bayonet about a foot long.

Never again would I wear leather soled shoes while working, just too slippery.

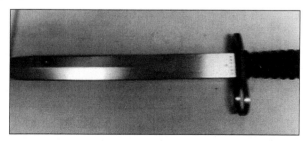

~

157
DRUNK DRIVERS

In 40 years as a police officer you will see some strange drunk driver cases. These were all kinds - some born to be caught.

I must say in the 1950's, it was not uncommon to drive a person home that had been drinking unless he was out right drunk behind the wheel.

This was the days before breathalyzers or blood testing. Then, as the years were going by, the state began to pass laws more stringent on driving under the influence as it was to be called; not drunk driving but driving under the influence.

A few of the many come to mind:

One of these was on Third Street NW, about a block west of where the paper mill now stands and before the Old Dutch Room Bar that was soon razzed or torn down to make room for the paper mill.

Some repair work was being done on Third Street. It had been excavated eight feet deep for at least four blocks. Barricades and lights were blocking all roads leading to this area.

We received a call of a car going through the barricades. It had been traveling east on Third Street.

Upon arriving, there was a light-colored Buick that had dropped front end down into the dugout road so its rear end was still hung up high in the air. The motor was still running and the driver was still in the car not seeming to understand what had just happened to him. He was arrested for DWI and jailed for the night.

•

Another night, I was driving my Hudson police car up Highway 38. It was pouring rain and I had just gone over the hill near Seventh Street when I had to swerve to miss a car parked on the center line in the middle of the road. Parking my police car behind the car with my one red light on, I exited the car.

It was a new dark car with Illinois license plates, a four-door. Walking to the car, looking through its windows, I could see two men either sleeping or passed out.

After opening the driver's door, I soon had them both awake and both had had their share of the bottle.

As it turned out, they were brothers who owned a manufacturing plant for mobile homes in Chicago, Ill. They were very pleasant and even offered to share with me if I was to be so nice as to let them go. Now, how he got that roll of bills out of his pocket I will never know. I told him I would have to decline their generous offer; they were soon tucked away for the night in the county jail.

·

One late morning driving west on Fourth Street, I observed a dark-colored pickup driving east. Looking at the driver I thought - drunk - a gut feeling. Now, the courts may say there is no such thing. I disagree as I say it is a learned response or reaction to a situation you may have seen or been through many times before.

I turned on the pick-up, falling in behind it, my red lights on. There seemed to be no reaction from the driver for some time. Finally he pulled to the side of the road.

Walking to the driver door, he was staring straight ahead - both hands on the wheel. I opened the driver door and he fell sideways all the way to the ground. He had been driving while passed out. He probably never knew a thing until waking in a jail cell the next morning.

·

Coming into town on Fourth Street East, passing the road to Duluth, I noticed a car's lights going back and forth across my back window. Swinging around, falling in behind, I soon had the car pulled over.

The driver was a large man, obviously under the influence. In a short time we were soon walking down the hall to the booking area of the jail.

As we walked in to the booking counter, Bill the jailer was there along with a highway patrol man and Mitchal the sheriff. Everyone had left but us and the jailer.

The man I had just come in with looked around and said "I guess I can't blame them." He was then booked in for the night. Some two hours later, I received a call from the Chief of Police stating he had just been in contact with the Justice of the Peace and the man I had just jailed was now sober enough to go home. I was to make this happen.

Shortly, he was in the booking area. He said, "Give me my car keys and I will drive home."

I then said to him he could either go with me or back to the jail cell.

•

As a bear of a man was getting out of the car at his home, he leaned back into the car and said, "I really respect a man that does his job."

I was later told the man had been back and pled guilty to driving under the influence.

Although checking with the state a couple of times, nothing ever showed up on his driving record.

I had done my job.

•

One of the most unique cases was the flying car and the boxed in driver.

Many years ago, before the road leaving town going to Coleraine had been rebuilt in the area of the Playmor Roller Rink, the road was much narrower with deep ditches.

We received a call that a man had an unwanted driver in his living room. I arrived at the Playmor Roller Rink and was met by the man who made the complaint in the lot.

It was one of those "if you had not seen it you would not believe it."

A car coming into town from the Coleraine area had driven into the right hand ditch, came back across the road into the ditch, catapulting up over the high ditch bank going over the large tongue of the trailer. The car was now sitting in his living room, having gone through the front of the trailer. The driver was still sitting behind the wheel, uninjured and very relaxed.

He was arrested and lodged for the night. I might say he was a distant friend of mine.

Just lately, I ran into his wife. She told me he is no longer with us. He is flying to a better place.

~

158
HER STORY

Editor's note: The following story was written by Doris Dahline.

I was born in a tarpaper shack outside of Warba--not in a hospital.

I was quiet--tired all the time--mother would say, "get up and get your blood circulating and you won't be cold." My mom never knew why I was always so tired and cold.

We went to the Presbyterian Church sometimes--if we had a working car or if we had the proper clothes. We were very poor. I had an awareness of God and always tried to be good.

When I was around my late teens early 20's, I started having mild panic attacks feeling like passing out and a pounding heart.

By the time I was 23 I had four little boys. My energy was waning. I lost my dad when our fourth son was born. I loved my dad so much and it deeply affected me.

Without a good solid faith I didn't do well. Two years later I remember when Christmas was done, I was sitting, talking to Harv, he was getting ready for work, saying it felt good to get my work caught up some. Harv worked mostly afternoons and nights. Plus, he worked side jobs to help with the police wages. He supported me although he was gone a lot.

Later that night my life turned upside down, I had my first major panic attack with a pain in my side. I called Harv at work--he came home and didn't know what to do so he called the doctor.

During the last few years I've been plagued with many urinary infections. The doctor thought it might be one of those coming on but it wasn't. I continued to go downhill with less energy, I couldn't eat, and I just felt totally depressed. We had just gotten a clinical psychiatrist in down and he recommended I go to the U of M and have a full psychiatric evaluation. I ended up being there two and a half months and I started up years of tranquilizers, sleeping pills, and anti-depressants. When I was in my early thirties, there was a situation in my life that led me to seek a closer walk with God. I was 35 years old when I had a born again experience in my life and committed my life to the Lord.

When I was 40 years old I started to have the sweats real bad. I went to the doctor and they had a new instrument to see in my heart. One side of my heart had become very enlarged. He asked me to go to Abbott-Northwestern in the cities for more testing. I was told I had a hole in my heart that needed to be repaired – atrial septal defect. I waited for a couple weeks; Tom was on the wrestling team and was going to state. So, in 1977 I had my heart repaired, also finding out I had another birth defect in my heart - a defective valve. The blood loss from it wasn't enough to need a new valve. They were in the ground floor doing this kind of heart surgery. The surgeon told me my heart was beating like I was running to get the blood out into my system. This was the first reason I knew why I was so tired all my life. Since I was never in shape it took me a long time to feel better. I continued to have a rapid and irregular heart-beat. I eventually went to the Mayo Clinic, where I was told I could take beta-blockers to regulate it, or I could deal with it. I tried the medication, but it made me feel slow and not good. So, I went with just dealing with it. They told me it was coming from an area in my heart that I wasn't going to die from it. So, I thought if I'm not going to die, I'm going to run. My younger sister had been running for a while, and she said she would train me in. On my 61st birth-day, we went to the track by the high school and started to use the program she had started me with where you would run and walk so long and keep increasing your running time. I did well enough that I ran for seven years, even running in 5Ks. My knees and feet eventually made me give it up. Instead of walking on streets of gold, I want to run on them when I go to Heaven.

My home, my safe place.

~

159
HARDLY WORTH MENTIONING

It's How You Say It

One night, I had just taken a man to jail and was getting ready to leave when a couple of officers not from our department were bringing a bull-like man, short but looking very powerful, into the jail.

The man did not appear to be resisting, however I thought they were being pushier than they had to be. He had been booked and they were getting ready to take him back to a cell.

Then he had backed into a corner by a bench. It looked like there was going to be trouble. He was facing four or five officers. They were eight to ten feet in front of him. The officers seemed a little bit unsure of themselves.

At this, hoping I was reading it right, I walked over saying, "back off, I'll take this guy all by myself."

Getting close, I looked him right in the eye and I grinned. He knew I couldn't take him. He knew I knew I couldn't take him.

He grinned and said, "Awe hell, I'll go with," and we walked off down the hall together.

Good cops, bad cops.

The Pit

It sometimes seems as though everything goes our way. Let me tell you, the unexpected can happen to us too.

It was perhaps one in the morning. I had pulled into the Holiday Inn driveway, driving around to the right. Not many parking places were open. As I was looking to my left, in between two cars was a red five-gallon gas can with a hose coming from the rear fender of a car.

I continued driving as though I had seen nothing. Swinging around the back of the inn, then out to the main road, I turned left and headed back toward town. After a few blocks, I turned left off the road and found a place to park.

At this time, between me and the hotel was nothing but big trees, mostly pines for a block or so. I was making good time, running hard on a path in the dark.

Then, everything went black. The breath was knocked out of me. I didn't know what had just happened.

I found I was hanging out of a hole four feet deep, at least two feet across. Public utilities or someone had dug and left it open and I had hit my chest on the side going in. I was out of breath and hurting.

I lay there hanging half out of the hole. And I have to admit I was feeling sorry for myself. Then, I started to think of my friends waiting for me.

Getting out, taking a deep breath, I was running again. Just as I was coming to the edge of the woods, a car pulled next to the gas can. A passenger got out, lifted the over-flowing gas can and set it into the back seat of their car.

The boy was just getting in with the hose when I arrived. The driver wouldn't stop at first, but when the side view mirror came off he did.

He appeared in court and found it was cheaper to buy gas at a filling station.

Attractive Caps

In the mid-1970s, I was at a state wrestling tournament as we had several entered and a very good team then.

As I was walking down a hallway, a man some ten feet in front of me went down. His heart had stopped.

At this time, I was wearing a new, very attractive black and orange Grand Rapids wrestling cap.

I was soon at his side, doing artificial respiration. The cap, being in the way, was set aside. Some others were coming to assist me. Then, a young man came over bending like he wanted to help all at once. He grabbed my new wrestling cap and was running away with it at full speed.

Soon, we had some professionals taking over. Someone had gotten my name, I was contacted and told the man did not make it.

Look as I might, I never again saw my prized cap.

Do unto others.

Red

Driving by the old Dutch Room on Third Street one morning, there was quite a fight going on. I jumped out of my squad car. As I ran over, the combatants saw me coming. One of them, a red head I knew well, laughed and ran over and sat on the steps. The other, took off running at a good clip.

If they run, you have to run after them - so it is written. He must have been 40 feet in front of me and running around to the back of the Dutch Room.

As I came to the back side, my fleet-footed friend could not be seen. Now, I thought, I can't be that slow. Standing there looking, I could see a four-inch metal clothes line pole. He was down. My friend and the pole had met. To this day, I think he thinks I had nailed him from behind.

We were to meet many years later, him aiming a shotgun at me in the dark - another story.

Memory

History to almost everyone, but just a long ago memory to me: The Armistice Day blizzard of Nov. 11-12, 1940.

It was the type of snow story that are legends.

The days leading up to the 11th were cool, then it struck without warning - winds of 32 to 65 miles per hour; temperatures fell 40 degrees in 24 hours.

Telephone and power poles were coated heavily with ice, many braking and coming down. All roads were impassible. People who were stranded where they were without proper clothes died. The snow was as much as four to five feet deep with some drifts well over eight feet.

One of the things I remember most was the day after the blizzard. Us boys were out walking on top of four feet of hard-packed snow while watching a crew of about 10 men with shovels accompanying a snow plow trying to move snow almost as high as the plow. It was constantly getting stuck, then the crew would have to dig it out.

All schools were closed for some time as well as businesses. And many a farm animal froze in the fields.

Even though I was only seven years old at the time, I will always remember those howling winds and sticking close to that wood-burning barrel stove.

~

160
CROSSING THE BORDER

In the summer of 1995, I was preparing to retire after 40 years on the police department and was on my way home from the Blueberry Golf Course in Deer River when I saw a Class 3 motor home for sale on the side of the road. A for sale sign had a price that looked very affordable. Another sign on it read 'Honey.'

At this time, two of my brother-in-laws had motor homes and had been making trips to different states really enjoying their leisure time. Getting home, I explained to my wife what I had seen. After talking it over, we decided to buy it and see if we could stand each other on the road. One thing you had better understand, if you buy an older model motor home, you had better be half mechanic.

Soon we were in a caravan with two other much newer motor homes heading for Utah, the home place of my sister-in-law. The Honey was quite old and, not having fuel injection, we were having a hard time keeping up with the others. As we were getting into much higher elevation, the air was much thinner. Sometimes we were chugging down to 10-13 miles an hour.

We did learn to slingshot the high hills. Topping a hill starting down, we would put the pedal to the floor trying to reach top speed going down the hills hoping the speed would help us top the next hill.

One of the first nights, it was getting late, close to 12 a.m. We decided to hole up where we were which was a deep box canyon - pitch black. The women thought it scary and spooky. The walls around us were so high where we were going there was no phone reception. We found a small clearing and corralled the three RVs close together for the night.

Thinking I had seen a small creek and a picnic table a distance away, after closing up I took a walk in the dark. In a short time, coming to a creek and a dead road, soon an old pick up truck pulled up and stopped. In it were three unkept men - beards and the works - hillbillies might be the best way to describe them. All three had rifles, none were in the gun racks.

Talking to them, they seemed harmless but you did wonder what they were doing back in the hills at that time of night. This did not give my companions a good feeling the rest of the night.

The next morning, up the creek a short distance stood a grinding mill with a 40-foot water wheel abandoned a few years ago. A picturesque relic of days gone by.

My sister-in-law then directed us to the town of Green River with its namesake, the Green River, flowing nearby. She told us this was the area from which most watermelons are shipped throughout the United States.

Before leaving this area, we had visited all the natural parks, arches Zion and Bryce. My favorite was Bryce. There are no words to describe what Mother Nature has done for us with water and time. She had sculptured a land of indescribable beauty - a sight that swims through your mind.

We did make more trips with these same companions and always had a wonderful time through the years, covering many of the states. But with time comes change; along the way we lost two brothers.

It seems there are some small things that stand out in each and every trip. It must have been in about 2002, we were making a trip with my sister-in-law Lorraine and her husband Miles. We were driving through South Carolina on our way to meet some of his relatives. At this time, we were in the deep south and had gone many a day without the opportunity to have our clothes washed. Coming into a small town, a laundry mat could be seen so our two RVs pulled up into a parking place.

Gathering up all our laundry, we were soon entering the doors. As we went in, there was a lot of noise with children running, laughing and playing and with several adults talking. As we entered, all sound stopped and you could hear a pin drop. Looking around, you could see they were all black.

This trip was to prove of great interest.

We went over to some washing machines and proceeded to load them. No one was moving, no children playing, no one talking.

Wondering, "how do you break the ice?"

I knew the answer.

Walking out to the RV, I picked her up, and walked back into the laundry mat. I sat our small black dachshund on the floor. Just like that, the kids were all wanting to see or touch her. And everything was back to normal with everyone talking to each other, it's the simplest things that bring people together.

In a year or so, we were invited to travel with the Craiglows as they had been to Mazatlan, Mexico, many times and thought we could enjoy each other. Karen said she had become fluent in Spanish as she had been studying it.

This was to have a few of those things to remember.

The trip from Grand Rapids to Las Cruces, New Mexico, was quite uneventful. But as we traveled, Doris, my wife, seemed to be having some second thoughts about crossing into Mexico and the long drive to Mazatlan. But Karen was assuring us that every thing would go well as they had driven this way before. Also she knew how to approach the border inspectors as they were always looking for a little extra cash.

We had parked in a large lot next to a chain store for the night before crossing into Mexico the next day. The next morning, I was inspecting the tires on our RV, which was parked on a slight rise. The motor home started to move forward, picking up some speed. No one was behind the wheel. I tried to open the door to get in. I had trouble with this door before. Looking ahead the Craiglows' RV was some 50 feet in front of us.

The only thing I could do was stay off to the side and push against the left side trying to stop 7,000 pounds. The two RVs came together; the only problem, my hand was in there.

There was very little damage to the RVs but I was too tired out. I had broken at least five bones in my left wrist and hand.

I may have left it out of gear when setting the parking break. I might say with the knowledge I had gained came a lot of pain. In a short time, my left arm from hand to elbow was in a cast.

As I have said, my wife had become more reluctant to cross the Mexico border, suggesting now it might be a good time to hole up, recuperate and head home. It didn't quite work out that way, as soon we were at the border crossing into Mexico.

As we approached the border crossing, our friends just in front of us, we were in a long line of RVs. Looking, you could see perhaps 10 other gates that were not being used.

Off to the left, perhaps 150 feet away, were a group of very intimidating soldiers all in black and all carrying what appeared to be machine guns. One of the men had a cup of coffee in hand, saying something to the other soldiers, then starting toward me. Now I had been told how they sometimes singled out a car or RV, emptying the vehicle out and often times receiving some cash before releasing them.

So as he was waving me over, I started to wave back at him in the mean time, closing up tight to the RV in front of me so there was no room to get out of the line.

He started to wave much faster and I continued to wave back like we were friends. At this, you could see all his buddies laughing at him and he threw down his coffee as I was entering the gate.

After entering the gate, I was met by a very polite young man who checked me out and told me I was free to go. Just after being told to go, I saw a young lady passing some money to one of the inspectors who then approached me.

He then told me to park my RV off to the side. As I was standing there, I told him no. I then called to the polite young man who had told me I was free to go, saying you told me I was free to go. The other inspector was left standing there.

The next 700 miles were spent driving with my left arm up in the air through a strap because of the broken hand. We arrived in Mazatlan late at night.

The next day it was setting up our RV in a park for our stay. Then we were off exploring. We found a pool and all the others were soon in. Not to be out done, I found a plastic bag (a big mistake) and some tape. Wrapping the tape around the top of my cast to keep the water out, it did not work too well as the water got into the bag and into the cast on my arm.

The next day we were at the beach. People were going up in parachutes that were pulled by a boat. They were going up as high as 2,000 feet; the cost was only $20. After asking myself if I was perhaps a little chicken, I decided to go for it. But I did have a little problem. I had two metal hips and a broken left wrist and hand.

Now they wanted their $20 first but I said no. If I landed safely, they would get their money.

Soon I was 200 feet off the ground, only able to stabilize myself with one hand. All at once, I jerked down in the harness about six inches, and for a minute it felt like the bottom had fallen out. After that it was a beautiful thing. The boat looked to be five feet long with the waves coming off the bow.

I was in the air perhaps 25 minutes. It was one of the most exhilarating things I have ever done. Coming down to the sand beach, four or five guys were there to catch me. My wife was offered the chance to go up but some how declined.

We were sitting in church a few days later with many other members when someone detected a foul smell in our part of the church. I didn't think it was me. Now my wife, being a helpful sort, picked my left arm up and smelled the cast that had gotten all wet with salt water a few days ago. Needless to say, our worshiping was short lived.

We also were in a 22-foot catamaran sail boat with a couple. The boat drove to a large rock two miles off shore that had seals on it. The boat was made of plastic so if it hit the rocks hard, it could have sank everyone. We were able to push it away.

Now I liked Mazatlan and had a wonderful time there but it did lack in tasty food. So at the border crossing coming back into the states, food was always on my mind. Soon after crossing the border, we were into Country Fried Chicken.

Doris, my wife, said I was acting like I hadn't had anything to eat for a month. It was good to be on our way home.

~

161
OLD WOUNDS

On March 7, 2015 at 7 p.m, we were just settling in to watch Duluth East at the Minnesota State Hockey Tournament when I received a phone call from Dick Westby of Glendale, Ariz.

The Ivar Westby family lived in the Grand Rapids area in the 1950s. Ivar Westby worked for Wayne Mills upstairs at the Mills Lumber Company located just north of the railroad tracks on Pokegama Ave. N. They were later to move to the Bigfork area as Mr. Westby would be managing the King Lumber Company there.

The purpose of Dick Westby's call was to let me know that he had been receiving the Grand Rapids Herald-Review for well over 25 years all over the world, as he had been in the service. At age 67, he was now retired. He had been reading my columns in the paper and was enjoying them as they brought back so many memories saying they would have to take the place of the irreplaceable Ken Hickman.

We sat and reminisced for some time, bringing back those old times. Did I remember where the old courthouse and jail used to be on the banks just north of the river before they were torn down and rebuilt along Fourth Street NE? Where had Janicke Bakery moved to? It had been next to Mickey's Café.

He was soon telling me about his brother, Bob, who was just finishing high school in 1958 and starting at Bemidji State. Bob, at the time, was courting Sharon Green whose father Doug owned the Camp Folly Floral and Greenhouse just south of what is now the Walgreens Drug Store.

At the time Bob was courting Sharon, he was working part time delivering flowers for Dave Shaw, the owner of Shaw Floral located in front of the Pokegama Hotel. Bob did marry Sharon Green and they have been married many years, but this is just leading up to another part of the story.

Dick had recently sent Bob the article, "The Jacket and the Headdress," published Sunday, Oct. 19, 2014.

Bob had called him back saying he had enjoyed the stories in the Herald Review but they were opening old wounds. That he had contact many years ago with the author, a police officer.

It seems while Bob was courting Sharon, whose father owned the floral shop, he was delivering orders for Dave Shaw.

Now Dave owned a nice floral delivery truck which on this day had broke down but he had several delivery orders in the Nashwauk area that had to go out so Dave handed Bob the keys to his car saying his car was parked outside. He was to take the car and make the Nashwauk deliveries.

Bob, taking the floral sprays to the car, loading them in, turning the keys in the ignition was soon on his way to a few hours of relaxation making his deliveries.

Some time later, a call was made to the Grand Rapids Police Department, a car had been reported stolen.

Dahline was soon talking to a lady bartender, stating she had just gotten off work and was going to drive home but her car was missing. No, she hadn't given anyone permission to drive it and no one else had a set of keys.

I was trying to get all the information on the stolen car when Bob, the "car thief" was spotted driving the stolen car into the area. Stopped, he seemed bewildered, not seeming to understand what was taking place, giving a flimsy excuse that someone had given him the keys. We have all heard that one before! Which, of course, the bartender denied.

Listening to Bob's story, I then checked with Dave Shaw who said he had given Bob a set of keys to his car to make some deliveries.

Taking a set of keys, they were found to work in both cars, I was later to learn that one key in 17 will fit another car. Dick said, Bob, perhaps making the light of the incident had said, "I would hope that even after this late date of 57 years and any statutes of limitations would have run out that the Herald-Review would print a retraction and restore my good name."

Now Ken Hickman was not above having a little fun and had printed an article of a local florist who may be hiring "shady drivers" to make his deliveries and that one of them had been in possession of a "stolen car."

Bob, as the officer in charge, this was written up as a misunderstanding. Please consider this publication in the Herald-Review as a retraction even though it may be a little late at 57 years. A full retraction of clearing your honorable name. Signed, Harvey Dahline.

162
A BIRD GOES TO CHURCH & HER FAMILY IS SAVED

June 7, a Sunday, nothing new was going to happen today.

I awoke this morning at about 6 a.m. Looking out the window, you could see it was going to be one of those mornings. We had all been waiting for - bright with the sun shining.

This had been a hard month for me as the passing of my wife had been just over a month.

All my friends were telling me this was going to take some time: "Don't try to forget, you have too many good memories over these last 60 years, savor them, learn to live with them; life goes on; time is your friend."

We all know the Lord giveth and taketh away for all living things. When our time comes, there is nothing we can do about it.

But is this really true?

Some things happen that can really make you wonder.

I was leaving my house, taking Third Avenue down to Fifth Street then east with some good music on the radio while heading for my church, the Assemblies of God, on the east end of town.

I was going up the hill close to Seventh Avenue when out of the corner of my eye I see a shadow. Then something struck my car on the right side. I thought, a bird. The sound had been very loud; so loud nothing could live through that.

I kept on driving for another block and thought that this was not right. You do not leave a living thing to die on the street.

I looked back, then made a U-turn. I could see quite a large bird sitting almost on the center line with its head hanging low, not knowing if it was still alive.

Just as I was passing the bird, I could see a very large black cat coming out of the tall grass some 30 feet away.

How the cat could know the bird was in trouble so fast was beyond me.

You could see the way he was moving, he had a meal in hand.

I started to make a fast U-turn to make it back before the cat was onto the bird. Stepping on it, the cat saw me coming and with the beep of the horn was in the grass crouching, his tail thrashing back and forth.

Looking down, I could see it was a large woodpecker with a large reddish spot behind his head and appeared to be dazed with some blood on its beak. It also had some worms in its beak. This must have been a mother feeding its young.

What to do? I had a large square bag in the car. The bird was in a daze. If I left it, the cat would have eaten it; in the grass, he still sat there waiting. Picking the woodpecker up, I set her gently in the paper sack. The worms still in her beak. I decided to take her to church with me and check her out later.

I sat for part of the sermon then went to check her out. Back at the car, looking into the sack, I saw she was moving her head and seemed to be alert, still holding onto the worms.

All at once, she flew out of the sack onto the dash of my car next to the windshield. I might say she left a deposit on my dash that would have to be cleaned up.

I had marked the spot on the road next to the trees to bring her back to, so I drove her back to her home area. She was just sitting there looking at me.

Pulling to the side of the road and opening three of the doors, I stepped back at this. She looked at me and took flight high in a half circle then into the trees. By the noise, you could tell she was welcomed there.

Her time had not come - hitting the car that hard with the cat seconds away and going to church.

Perhaps there are second chances and the little ones in the nest, one little incident. How many could have died?

Looking to the heavens, my reward for the day.

~

163
BETH

My girl, from the moment she was born.
She was dark and looked like Nat King Cole,
one of my favorite singers who sang
"They Say We're Too Young To Be in Love."
And like the song they were wrong.
This little girl stole my heart
from the moment I saw her.
And no it can't be true
I didn't drive them home
in a daze with my windshield
wipers on all the way.
Like my wife said,
from that time on I didn't
need a pup as she was
always under my feet,
such adoration for her father.
And as she grew, always there
to protect me as I having been
a soldier and a police officer
for many years, I sorely needed it.
As her four brothers all were
into wrestling, she was constantly
with the cheerleaders with
their long, beautiful Indian headdresses.
Soon they had made an
Indian costume for her with
a large feather in her hair.
She was now a little 6-year-old
mascot for the team.
And like the wind, the years
Were passing, she was growing
into a young lady always
with respect and a deep love
for her mother.
However, she never told me this,
but I think I had the edge.

She's still my little girl with
a husband I respect and four
beautiful children of her own.
The years have been good to me.
Could I ever ask for more?
Her mother is now gone and
is waiting for me.
In the meantime, we still have
each other.
And when I leave this earth,
I know I'll be leaving it
a much better place as
this girl of mine, now a nurse,
will be there carrying out her dream
of healing others.

~

164
THE LETTER OF FOREVER

Grandma has been gone a short time now and while going through her keepsakes, I found this special letter tucked away. A treasure of her's, she had never shared with me. One of many surprises, our grandson was a little mite when he came to us and many of his childhood days were spent with us.

As he grew into a beautiful, young man it was with great pride we watched him go through all of his training to become a Green Beret in the Army.

I can see the pride in her eyes as she read The Letter of Forever. I'm sure she took a copy with her. Sharing our hearts can sometimes help others.

Grandma,

This Christmas I thought about what I should give you and thought that maybe writing a letter that you can keep forever would be a nice gift to get. I'm writing you this to let you know how much I appreciate you, and how thankful I am to have you in my life. Words can't express how much you mean to me. You have taught me how to be kind and loving to others which is one of the greatest lessons to learn in life. You have taught me to be a forgiving person and always show how much you love someone. Even though you have many grandchildren you have always found a way to make me feel special to you. You have the biggest heart out of anyone I've ever met and I'll be very lucky if I'm even half the person that you are. I want to thank you for always being there for me no matter what I'm going through and showing me tough love when I needed it. No one else can make me feel as loved as you do. Your cooking will always be the best no matter who tries to top it and the quilt you made me will keep me warmer than any other blanket I've ever owned because I know there is love in every single stitch. You are the best grandma I could've asked for and I love you so much. Thank you for everything.

Love, Jared

~

165
CUTTING A ROCK

When someone we love dies, our whole life changes.

All the things we thought were so important to us - money, house, cars - have no meaning.

I have often times said, "We don't know what we ain't got till we ain't got it no more." So now we learn to cope trying to fill the emptiness in our hearts.

This morning, I received a call from the Northland Monument Company, located 12 miles past Remer, almost to Walker. I had ordered a garden bench for my wife's grave site. Premium black with a shear white granite foundation with two oval pictures and either art work.

Each step along the way has be approved. Once it is set in granite it cannot be changed.

It was a beautiful morning and I did enjoy the drive. After looking and approving the sketches for the garden bench, I was taken on a tour of the plant and was truly amazed at how a 10-foot rock once set and anchored in place could be cut through the middle by a 20-foot quarter-inch wire into two inch slabs in a few hours, possibly for someone's kitchen counter top, and how the printing was being done by taping and then sand-blasting the exposed granite. I left thinking of the artistic talent it must take to run Northland Monument.

On the way home, I came through the town of Remer, having been born there a short distance out of town in a log cabin. Driving by the old homestead, it was now indistinguishable from the surrounding growth.

Deciding to take Highway 200 to Hill City, I came into Grand Rapids from the south. As it was about 12:30 p.m., I thought I would drop into the Sawmill Inn and have lunch with some friends.

Checking the dining room, I found they had already left. As I was walking back to the entrance, I bumped into Pat Richards and his elderly parents.

Pat, some time ago, had worked for the sheriff department, so our relationship goes back a long way. Pat then introduced me to his parents, saying I had served in Korea at the same time as his father in 1952 and 1953. His father brightened at this, saying he now lived in Effie but had been a Marine Sergeant working with shot-up airplanes.

376

I then told him I had been a sergeant in a machine gun platoon and probably seen some of his planes dropping napalm bombs in the North Korean sector. We did reminisce for some time.

All this time, I was fully aware of her attention to her husband. So now I sit and see what once was for me.

This beautiful older couple. The adoration in her eyes as she prompts him to tell her favorite story of the plane without wings.

As he tells it, the Navy and the Marines at the air base flew the same type of planes. The Navy with the blue and white and "Navy" on the wings; the Marines, with their camouflage colors and "Marines" lettering on the wings.

It so happened one of Richards', a green camouflage plane, came back one day from a mission with the fuselage shot up. The only thing that could be saved were the wings.

A few days later, he was approached by a Navy pilot saying he had a good airplane but the wings had been shot up beyond repair and could Richards help him out. They got together that night and by morning the Navy pilot had new wings on his airplane.

The planes were all lined up the next morning on the air strip. The Navy with their blue and white colors. But one plane stood out from all the rest - a blue and white airplane with green camouflage wings and "Marines" printed on them.

I could see the glow and adoration in her eyes as he told her favorite story.

As I left them I again thought of where I had been that morning. Thinking if a 20-ton rock, 12 feet high can be cut into a beautiful shining slab with a thin wire in two hours, can a heavy heart be mended?

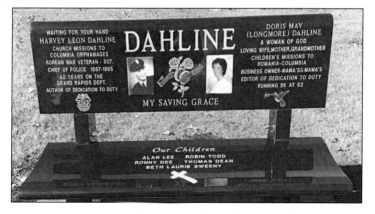

~

166

THE HOSTESS:
Given so other creatures of the forest might live

A short time ago, I was invited out to the country to see a friend's new house as the older one had caught fire and had to be replaced.

It was a place to admire, sitting on perhaps 10 to 20 acres with a large green pasture out back sloping down on all sides like a bowl into the large pond with a forest of maple trees surrounding it.

As I was shown about the new house, you could see Kevin was a master woodworker as the banister to the stairs and some of the walls were very well done. Soon we were out back onto a very large deck some eight feet off the ground looking at the pasture and a pony grazing there.

This young lady, Sue, began to tell me about some of the animals she had raised as pets over the years: a goat and wild turkeys. But the memories that stood out the most was of her 31-year-old horse Sunny.

When Sue was about 15-years-old, her mother was starting to worry about her like all mothers do. She thought her daughter needed something more constructive to do to keep her mind busy. She thought perhaps a horse would do the trick.

Soon they were at the Arne Schmidt Farm on the LaPlant Road a few miles south of Grand Rapids and taken to the pasture. There stood two beautiful twin copper-colored yearling colts with black manes, a white star on their foreheads, and a white line down their faces.

A choice to be made. They were both mares and registered quarter horses - one with the name Polly Pac Sunshine. This was Sue's choice. Her name from now on was to be Sunny. And it would be another year before she would be halter broken.

Sunny would grow to be 16 hands high and 800 pounds. A very gentle horse, especially with children. Something different, Sunny loved Mt. Dew and Sue made sure she had her can everyday.

There were many trail rides over the coming years around swamps, through the forest and hills. One day, Sue's four-year-old son couldn't be found. Finally looking in the barn, there he was sitting on Sunny's back without a bridal or anything.

Then some how she came up lame and was never ridden again by adults over the last 10 years. However, she was ridden by the children. The last couple of years she was blanketed in the winter with a heat lamp in the barn.

Now she was starting to shiver all the time. Sue knew her time was coming and was very sad. Then, one day she went out - it was 25 degrees and Sunny was shivering and in pain.

"What could I do now? It was winter and the ground was frozen," thought Sue. "I was recently visiting a friend of mine and she had told me what she had done in almost the same circumstances, that she had made her animal a hostess for others.

"I then thought Sunny was not to be put in the frozen ground to rot and decay but left in her favorite spot under her tree as a host to all the birds and animals of the forest so they might live.

"Soon I led her back into the woods to her favorite place under the maple tree.

"We cried our good-byes and she was put down."

"In just a few short weeks her Earthly remains were all gone.

Like her picture on the wall, she will remain in our hearts forever."

Wouldn't it be something when we all leave this Earth, we could somehow be a host to others?

~

167
LAST CHRISTMAS WITH GRANDMA

Some years ago, I don't remember exactly when it started, Grandma Dorrie and I would have a little tree with a few bulbs and some silver strands hanging from it. This was our little Christmas tree.

We didn't have much but each of the children always had their special gift to open in the morning.

Many was the time if it was quiet in town on Christmas Eve, I would slip into the house with a few bags of candy and help Dorrie wrap gifts for the morning.

One thing about Grandma, she was a stickler. Each of the children had to get equal gifts. Now you had boys and a girl she always worked it out.

Through the years, things started to change. We moved to a bigger house that we built together, the boys, mother and I. It had four bedrooms and a larger living room. The Lord had blessed us through the years,

We now had a much larger tree with an angel on top and many glittering bulbs with silver strands.

Along with the years came children and grandchildren. Our flock grew and a tradition was born.

Over 60 years, even though our flock had spread over the states, most of them always managed to make it home to Mother and I for that special evening of Christmas Eve.

They would all be at our house and soon after eating we would all gather around the tree and gifts would be opened. Always the younger ones first opening their gifts, we would work up through the ages.

For some reason, I would always be last then we would go to the youngest and so on until the gifts were all opened.

Soon the youngsters would all be helping each other open their gifts. There would be laughter and mounds of paper on the floor. I could see Mother with her camera, the delight in her eyes - priceless.

I couldn't help thinking back those many years to when we were very young and my sister Marjorie, perhaps 9 or 10 years old, would take us out of that old log cabin on a crisp cold Christmas night and looking to the sky at the blinking stars would tell us that was Santa going by.

Memories are made from this.

This night, however, was not over.

Mother, some 30 years ago, when she had her little shop in the mall had come up on some very unique Christmas stockings. Each of them were made of cartoon characters - the Tasmanian Devil, Daffy Duck, Tweety Bird, Snoopy and Bugs Bunny.

Each Christmas, they would be filled with candy and small gifts and as the evening came to an end each would be given their special stocking, some of the children now grown.

I look back now and wonder how could she have known?

I went to a basement bedroom today. There, in the closet in a box, were all of those big Christmas stockings which made me think how she seemed to sense on our 60 years married this would be our last Christmas together and told each of the children that each of their treasured stockings were now theirs and they were to take them home this night - none of them did.

Mother left us a short time later.

Memories of Christmas gatherings will always be in our hearts with a special thought for my wife Dorrie who made it all happen.

How do you say good-bye to 60 years? With a tight chest and a tear in your smile.

~

168
A FISH STORY (that can now be told)

They say that telling the truth can sometimes set you free.

I know this has some how seared my conscience and I started thinking, did I really do some thing wrong when the story gets out will I be chastised and shunned?

Many years ago, before most of you were born, a group of law men got together to plan a trip to Greenbay, Wis., to fish for salmon in the Fox River. As they were now running, the trip was hastly planned.

As this may be hard to talk about, some names may be changed to protect anyone who may be innocent of any alleged crime.

A friend, I'll call Mike at this time, came to see me asking did I like to fish and had I ever fished for salmon in the Fox River in Wisconsin and would I be interested in such a trip.

I said it did sound interesting. Mike then said I understand you have driven school bus many years and you don't drink.

I then thought one of this group owned a large yellow school bus and realized it was not my fishing abilities they were after but my driving.

After getting a few things together a few days later I was driving a yellow bus to Greenbay, Wis., carrying five law enforcement officers all who I had worked with for many years and had the utmost respect for.

This was to be a long trip of at least nine hours and I, the only driver, the group was telling many stories along with a few bottles of beer. At this time, it was legal to drink and drive as well as having open containers in the car.

I might say there were stops along the way for the bushes.

A rule was made and money put in to a pot for whoever got the first fish.

We arrived at our campsite after dark and some time was taken to eat and unpack our sleeping bags.

This was a beautiful area with quite a large river, the Fox flowing by. We would get a much better view the next day.

After settling in, it was quite late, some of us thought we would walk a short distance to a nearby bridge spanning a small stream to see if any fish were running.

We were now walking a small path along the side of some large trees coming around the point heading back to our left. At this time we could see at least three persons coming our way, perhaps 150 feet away.

All at once they were running into the trees and bushes, possibly thinking we were some game wardens. One of the men went into and under a bush a short distance from me.

At this, your instincts kick in. My dilemma, what to do?

I calmly walked over to the bush, stopped some 20 feet away and stood there for a few moments. Then, I said, "Come out," adding, "bring the fish with you."

At this, a young man of about 18 slowly rose up and came to me bringing a large salmon. Coming forward, you could see he was scared.

I was just standing there not saying a word when he started to plead, saying, "I'm so sorry, I have never done anything like this before. I'll never do it again. Please give me a break."

Standing a moment looking at him, I said, "You had better not. Leave the fish and take off."

He left at quite a fast pace, never looking back.

Did I do wrong many years later? I like to look back and think I helped a young man mend the errors of his way, perhaps saving him from a life of crime.

For some reason I never did get the money I so richly deserved for getting the first fish!?

The fish was quite good!

~

169
THE LADY

Recently, I came home one afternoon only to hear my phone beeping. I had a recorded call.

Pressing the play button, a young lady's voice could be heard saying, "please do not hang up this is not a crank call."

She then started to tell me that she had returned home after sitting in a business office in Grand Rapids for some time. While sitting there, she had talked to a pleasant man. They had a conversation that was very interesting.

She thought the man sounded very kind and had more to say but she then had to leave.

Upon arriving home, she was talking to her granddaughter telling her about the man who had lost his wife and they had something in common wishing they could have finished their talk.

Her granddaughter then told her she would see if she could find out who the man was by calling the business, which she did. She then told her grandmother to make the call.

After much soul searching, as in all her years, she had never done anything like this before. Finally picking up the phone only to find there was no one home she then left a message.

Upon hearing her call, and remembering talking to a lady, I thought she deserved a call as she sounded lonely. During the day I made two calls to her number telling her she may call if she wished, never hearing anything for over a week. Then last evening I received a call from the lady.

She told me she had been out of state, hoping I would not hang up on her as she had lost a loved one.

Thinking at this time she had found someone who would listen and understand what she was going through as she was 91 years old and very lonely needing someone to talk to in her loneliness.

At this time, I thought she must have a wonderful, understanding granddaughter to help her make a call like this.

Haven't we all had a moment in our lives when we needed someone to talk to?

I knew I wouldn't be hanging up the phone. I could feel the need, the want in her voice as we talked. As the minutes rolled by, a connection was being made. It was as though we had known each other for all our lives.

Soon we were sharing our recent losses and she was telling me of the love of her life and her 64 years of marriage.

We talked for over an hour. I was now thinking she was going to be alright and telling her before we hung up we would be talking again and she had my number.

The lady was now thanking me for not hanging up on a crank caller and she was feeling so much better, saying, "this is the happiest realization that has come into my heart."

A week or so later I called to see how she was doing. Her answer was so much better. Just knowing there was a friend out there who could fully understand and who could be called.

It hadn't been long into our first conversation that I realized I was not the person she had talked to at the business. She had some how gotten my number by mistake.

At a later time, she told me she realized there had been a mistake in getting my number. I then told her she could certainly call the other number. No, she told me, "God must have been guiding me to you."

Some time has gone by. I thought it was time to see how this lady friend of mine is doing.

She answered the phone cheerfully, saying things were going well and she had been thinking of me and now wanted to meet this man that helped turn her life around. We did set a time of 3:00 p.m. and she met me at the door, all five feet of her. I had also taken some of my stories along as she had told me she likes to read.

We were soon talking like we had met long ago. She was telling me how she had met her husband, the love of forever long ago, telling me how proud she was of this man of few words. How, after much prompting, he had told her some of his small part in World War II but of all his stories, one stood out.

Her husband, who I will call Ken, was a machine gunner and fought in the Battle of the Bulge which was one of Hitler's last major counter attacks of the war. Hitler, threw thousands of men and tanks into a surprise attack in the dead of winter and temperatures below zero. The Germans over ran many positions in this surprise attack.

Ken, in this battle, was soon the only one left in his squad. As he was walking out of the area alone, he came upon a very young German soldier. They stood eye-to-eye. Ken could not shoot him and walked on. This was her man.

As we talked, time was flying. I had a prior commitment at 6 p.m. and had to leave.

As I left, I knew I was leaving a stout little soldier behind - the lady. Will you be the next one to step forward and say: "Can I help?"

~

170
THE PLEA

I find myself sitting writing a letter to the Office of Adult Release regarding one Audie Fox who will be coming up for a parole hearing Jan. 12, 2016.

Audie Fox, 27, was convicted in May of 1982 of First-Degree Murder in the slaying of Deputy Robert "Beefy" Lawson.

Fox has since then been in the Minnesota Correctional Facilities.

Fox remains there to this day on a life sentence which expires in 2081.

On Oct. 29, 1981, Beefy Lawson went to the Fox residence in Pengilly on business relating to the custody of children.

Unaware Audie Fox was also in the house Beefy arrived at 10:30 a.m. and entered. Fox was hiding in the entry way holding a .357 magnum pistol aimed at Beefy's head and demanding to know where his wife was, according to a witness in the house at the time.

When Lawson refused to give him the information, Fox directed him to the floor and again demanded to know where his wife was, telling Beefy he would give him to the count of three. Beefy again refused. Fox then shot Beefy in the head.

Information was received by the sheriff office stating an officer was down.

This started an 18-hour stand off with many towns and counties offering their assistance of officers and equipment.

It was only after much negotiating, did Fox allow Don Irish, a Nashwauk police officer, to enter the home at 4:30 p.m. to retrieve and bring out Robert "Beefy" Lawson's body.

While inside the house, Fox kept his two small children, 2 and 5, on his lap using them as human shields so the authorities would not shoot. During the long cold hours, none of us had any idea how this would play out.

Early in the morning, negotiations seemed to be breaking down but an opportunity seemed to be opening. This was discussed with those in charge. Fox was getting about everything he asked for and seemed less alert. Also, the children on his lap would hinder his movement.

The three of us approached the front door. Fox's mother was there. I had talked to her much earlier and she held the door open as we approached. Turning to show we had no guns, without hesitation we were past her and onto Fox still holding the children.

After a short struggle, the 18-hour siege was over and the children were safe.

This short story was written to give you a few of the facts on a coward who had a long criminal history and was using his own children as human shields and the tactics of ISIS to kill an unarmed man, a police officer.

The following is my letter to the office of Adult Release:

Nov. 19, 2015
From: Harvey Dahline
Chief of Police (40 years police work)
To: Office of Adult Release

In 1981, I was one of the officers involved in the Audie Fox stand off and arrest.

Beefy Lawson's life was taken in a deliberate execution. He was on the floor face down, a gun put to his head by Audie Fox. Threats were made and a trigger was pulled.

Left dead was a police officer and a personal friend of mine.

Beefy was known throughout the area as a friend of everyone and an honest, hard-working deputy who went beyond duty to help not only citizens but law-breakers to get back on the right path. Beefy would work hard to send someone up for breaking the law and the first person they would look up when they got out would be Beefy and thank him.

I have been a police officer over 40 years and it seems inconceivable to me that the state could ever consider parole for Audie Fox.

This execution was planned and deliberate. Fox got a life sentence but he deserved more. I think this is a good illustration of what is wrong with our judicial system.

Don't you think it is about time we start meaning what we say? Forty years is 40 years and life is life. What kind of message are we sending?

Fox should never see the light of day outside of prison. I know Beefy Lawson never will.

~

171
LITTLE OFFICERS

Editor's note: Sometimes while writing stories, you come up on writer's block having ideas in your head that just won't come out. Where to go next?

I like to write about the Grand Rapids Police Department as I joined it in 1955. Once in a while you get a little unexpected help. Yesterday, I received a letter from some old friends of yester years, Tom Benton and his wife, Tammy. Both so well thought of in our community before making their home in Anchorage, Alaska many years ago.

I would like to share this letter with you as it is so well-written and is about our most respected Chief of Police at that time, Walter Craig. I think it shows the heart of the man and what we all would like to see in our police officers - humanity:

For part of one summer, my friend and I were employed as secret government agents; very much like the C.I.A., only we were Junior G-Men. Because of our age, it would have been more correct to call us Junior G-Boys, but that lacked the ring of authority that Men had. In truth, we weren't even called Junior G-Men. We just called ourselves that. Our correct name, according to Police Chief Walter Craig, was "little officers." We like our name better.

Walter Craig was the Chief of Police of the Village of Grand Rapids. He lived in our part of town so all of the neighborhood kids knew him and he knew all of us by our first names. I don't think that he was always Chief, but he was for all the time that I knew him. He was a man of the law, a man to be respected. He knew all about crooks, robbers, kidnappers, and all around bad guys. Not that he talked about these things, he didn't have to. We knew from the movies the type of work that he was involved in daily, and the really good police officers never bragged about their work. They just did it. Shoot outs, physical encounters, car chases, they were just part of an ordinary workday for a man of his position in a town of our size. He was good at what he did, be cause we were never afraid to walk the streets of the village - unless it was a really dark night with no moon, and that wasn't the Chief's fault. It had more to do with spooks and ghosts which were out of his jurisdiction.

Chief Craig was an unassuming man in appearance, with one exception. It looked as though one of his ears was glued to his shoulder. His head had a definite tilt to it - the kind that made you want to tilt your own head to the same degree as his so that you could maintain eye contact with him. There were several explanations for this condition. They ranged from a birth defect to a war injury to an automobile accident. The most repeated rumor was that God cast him that way.

One summer day, my friend and I stopped at the police station in the Village Hall to visit with the Chief. We din't have anything particular in mind, we just wanted to chat. Actually, we wanted to look at his display case. For in his office, he had the neatest collection of forbidden items that you could ever want. Starting with brass knuckles of all description. They ranged from the plain old brass knuckles to the really mean ones with the sharp little points on the ends. The kind that really could do damage to somebody's face. Then there were Billy Clubs. Not the big bulky ones that you see now but the little leather ones that you could carry concealed in your pocket. The ones made out of dark leather, neatly stitched and filled with sand. The kind you "bop" someone in the back of the head with and down they went, "lights out." A gangster's array of knives was prominently displayed. Not the little pocket knives, but the type of knives that you couldn't buy at the local sporting goods stores. There were switchblade knives with fancy pearl handles, stilettos and knives with special cut-outs on them designed to pull out your guts once they have been inserted into you. Knives as long as our little legs, complete with a leather sheath with fringes on it. Finally, there were the guns. Sawed off shotguns, little derringers, and homemade guns.

We were always welcome to look at the items but we were not permitted to touch. Nor were we to get our drool all over them. Man, did we ever lust for just one of these special weapons. It made us wish we had the opportunity to have purchased them from the criminal before he had been apprehended and his personal effects were confiscated. They were far better than the brass knuckles and knives of our own that were made out of rubber. And they appeared to be far more effective. We could only imagine the encounters that the Chief must have been involved in to have such a wonderful collection. The stories that he could tell, if only he wanted to.

This was a special day for the two of us. Not only did we have another chance to view all of the above items but the Chief asked us if we wanted to become Junior Police, "little officers." Would we! Who wouldn't jump at the opportunity to enter the field of law enforcement at such an early age? We wondered how much we would have to pay to join the force. It turned out that it was not going to cost us anything but that we wouldn't get paid either. The Chief said that it was a voluntary job, one of public service. We weren't issued any full uniforms but we were provided with two old badges that the Chief had laying in a desk drawer and two old police hats that he scrounged up from a back closet. He told us that we could put the badges in our wallets. We told him that we didn't have any wallets. We never had any folding money and as we weren't into girlfriends yet, we had no pictures of loved ones to carry around. We asked him if he had any old wallets in the drawer or closet. He said that he didn't, so we just pinned them on our cotton striped shirts. This worked, but there was a slight droop to the badges as their weight made them sag on our shirts. I think they were made to be pinned on still uniforms, not little kids' cotton summer shirts. We ended up putting them in our pockets so that we could be incognito.

The hats were of two different sizes, one was extra large and the other was even larger. The inside adjustable band could be pulled in only so far. Still, they were way too big and came to the top of our eyeballs. This was later solved by taking two white sweat socks and lining the inside of the hats. An attempt was made to make a chin strap, much like the motorcycle police had in the movies. As there was no provision for a strap on the hats, we had to improvise.

We took one inch slice out an old car tire inner tube and placed it on the outside and top of the hat and then under our chin. The hat stayed on better, but we looked like we were idiots. We abandoned that idea and went on wearing the hats with the sweat socks inside, taking care not to move too fast nor to turn our head to the side too quickly, as our head would freely turn but the hat would remain stationary.

Our instructions from the Chief were simple. We were to be his eyes and ears in the community. We were to carry no weapons and we were not to attempt to arrest anyone. If we spotted suspicious activity, our job was to report it to him and let him and his men take over. Even though we were to receive no pay, we were entitled to any rewards that may be posted and that would lead to the capture, arrest and conviction of the criminals. Having told us this, and having us agree to the terms and conditions of our employment, the Chief took out a big old dusty book, made us place our hands on it, and swear our allegiance. After our swearing in ceremony, the two youngest and shortest members of the local police force left the Village Hall, proudly wearing our new hats but walking carefully so that they wouldn't fall off. We immediately headed for the post office. They had wanted posters. And many of the wanted posters had big rewards on them. We were soon to become rich. In our minds we were already spending our new fortune.

We studied closely the pictures posted on the wall at the post office. Mostly, we were swayed by the size of the reward. The higher the reward, the higher was our interest in the fugitive. We soon noticed a pattern. The greater majority of the criminals were from minorities, black, Mexican, etc. This would be our area of specialization. As there were no minorities living in Grand Rapids, or even in the county that we were aware of, we would need only to look at new people. New people passing through town. Minority people that looked as though they were up to no legitimate purpose. Especially, minorities that were hanging around the First National Bank Building. They obviously had to be crooks and potential bank robbers. The type of people with a big reward on their heads. It was to the bank we went, hats off and badges in our pocket so that we would be unnoticed.

After three or four days, this no longer seemed like such a good idea. We hadn't seen a single minority person. We discussed this and then recalled that the only person of color who had been in Grand Rapids recently was Aunt Jamima. And she was only there at the invitation of the local Lions Club for a pancake feed upstairs at the Village Hall. Her picture wasn't on any of the posters we saw. She was just a big black lady with a polka dot headband and white apron who flipped flapjacks. We had to come up with a different strategy.

Local white men. We would focus on suspicious looking local white men. That was our next approach to crime solving. We would go to the hangout of the suspicious looking white men and just observe. Sooner or later, they were going to do something evil. First, we had to find the local hangout of these people. Once again, our movie going paid off. We would have to go to the bar. That's always where the bad guys are. At the bar. Which bar, was the next hurdle that we faced. Grand Rapids had many, many bars and taverns and we certainly couldn't watch them all. Ozzie's had to be the one, we reasoned. IN the other bars, we would sometimes see women go in. In the movies, the really criminal bars rarely had a woman in them. There were only men. We never saw a woman go into Ozzie's, only men. Tough-looking men. Chronically unemployed men, card sharks, sharpies, and, we reasoned, criminals. Off to Ozzie's we went. Again without hat or visible badge.

We knew that we never would be able to get into Ozzie's so we just stood outside and looked natural. As natural as two young boys can look standing outside of a bar with the door open. We decided against wearing our fake mustaches and plastic buck teeth. We thought that the best disguise was to have none; just appear to be two small boys. Little would they know that we were watching their every move and listing to every word they uttered. Men would go in and men would come out. To an untrained eye they may have looked like suspicious men. But we were professionals and knew better. We also knew, or were familiar with, almost all of the men going in and out of Ozzie's. None of them had their picture hanging in the post office with a price over their head. They were just local people that had been around forever.

Men like One-eyed Ernie. He had his right eye slit almost down to his nose. It never seemed to be working as it was always full of a white puss and never stayed synchronized with his left eye. It never even blinked. He looked like and probably was an old injured lumberjack from days gone by. If we turned him over to the Chief, we would just let him go back to the bar.

The Chief would probably do the same with Peg Leg McDougal. He was the only man that either one of us had ever seen with a real wooden leg that ended in a stump. We were told that he even carved it himself. From the looks of it, this was a real possibility. I am sure that Peg Leg had a proper Christian first name but it must have gotten lost forever at the same time he lost his leg. Like One-eyed Ernie, Peg Leg was also harmless. He lived in a shack by the old thoroughfare bridge and rarely came to town. He was no criminal.

After one week of near constant surveillance, the job of Junior G-Man had lost its interest for us. We weren't any richer than when we started, there were no major or even minor crimes committed in town during that period and the whole thing was stealing time from our precious summer vacation. We resigned. We got to keep the hats and badges and the Chief gave us a verbal thank you for our efforts. It was the end of our careers as those little officers who fought crimes.

~

172
THE LONE WOLF

This is how Brady thinks of himself. It has to be this way, no friends, don't confide in anyone. Ninety percent of the time someone gets caught because someone talked. Being a Lone Wolf has worked well the past few years.

Now he waits back in the darkness. He's always been good at this. Finally, here they come, slowly the spotlights probe the darkness. He can see the white doors, then they are gone, they won't be back for some time.

Plenty of time to do his mission. He's like a doctor, always planning, working out the details.

When he was in prison, it was like being in school. You get a chance to learn from the best. Always sitting, talking and exchanging information. He will never get arrested again. He has learned his lessons well.

Brady thought, move into a community, work your way into their lives, and gain their trust. Always picking up information, he plays baseball with them, goes to community events, drives a school bus—what better way to work your way into the system? Along the way he has picked up a master key to the school buildings and the bus garage.

He uses his locker at the school bus garage as his home base. Who would think to look there for his shoes, gloves, clothes or his black pull-over mask that helps hide him in the dark on his missions?

He has lived in Grand Rapids for some years. How many places he has burglarized, he can hardly remember. No, that's not true. He can remember every one, every detail. Several times robbing three places in one night, coming in late after driving to a sporting event or taking the band on trips.

Go to my locker, get my masks, gloves, dark clothing and shoes, and hide my car at some distance from the target. First, Itasca Flour and Feed, it doesn't take long. The high school next, three or four hundred dollars. Then the Northside Lumber.

This has been going on for some years, will they ever catch on? Yes, it seems they are because as soon as they discover one break-in, they go check for more and find the other two.

Time to change the routine. Tonight it's Dick Distributing. A little snow on the ground, he comes across a field. Sure, they will see my tracks, measure them and take pictures. They have checked me before but the shoes will go back in my locker when I'm through tonight.

The safe does take a little time, but once you have peeled a safe or knocked the dial off it gets to be routine. Having the right tools with you, a five pound maul with the handles cut off to about 18 inches and good quality metal chisels and pry bars, shielded flashlights to keep the glare down. After a few jobs get rid of all the tools in the river so tool markings can never be compared to the tools you have in your possession. Sometimes you take the tools from the bus garage and return them after the job.

Vary your break-ins six weeks or more, sometimes even a year apart. If you need a little cash then you wait until the kids leave their billfolds or purses on the bus for safe keeping while they are out competing. Go through the purses careful to put them back the way they were, only taking a few dollars from each one. They think they have miscounted. Maybe only getting $25 to $75 in a night, but you know the old saying, "A hundred here or hundred there, pretty soon you are talking big money." I never hear any kids complain so they may not notice.

Getting close to people, he gains their trust. One I'll always remember. A good friend. Will Sarkela, Athletic Director for the school, watching him put the receipts from the football game into the trunk of his car, several thousand dollars, locking the trunk, driving home.

Will never knew he was followed home that night and watched to see if he took the proceeds from the trunk. Just locking the car and garage doors, then into the house.

The next morning I was called to Sarkela's house; there had been a forced entry to Will's garage. The trunk of his car had been forced open. The proceeds of several thousand dollars were missing. Look as we might, no real evidence was left behind. There was no doubt in my mind that it was an inside job, as I had investigated break-ins at the schools and surrounding businesses over the last couple years, including thefts of small amounts of money from purses and billfolds left on buses. Although nothing could be proved, the same name always came up. When I asked Will if he had seen Brady at the game or close by last night, he said, "Yes, several times."

The men in our department had been discussing Brady, having checked his shoe prints more than once. He had always taken it cheerfully as he had spent some time in prison, so he didn't hold that against them for doing their job. Brady was very friendly and probably thought he was a good friend of everyone in the department including myself.

We had tried to put a case together the last couple of years, checking to see what time the school bus got in, what time he had arrived home; his wife was never of much help to us. We just couldn't put it together. I had talked to Brady and my gut feeling was there. He was good and he knew it. The break-in at Will Sarkela's garage was one of many that were laid at Brady's feet.

It might take a while, but his time will come. I don't forget. One was 17 years before it was solved, the Royal Bar robbery which Thomas Franklin committed.

This brought back memories of different burglaries we had in the past.

We suspected Brady, one of them being Gordy's SuperValu and this a long time go. At that time the SuperValu had a system where they would load your grocery bags, place them in plastic bins and send them to an opening in the wall to the outside to be loaded in your car. The bins were pushed on rollers. On this night someone had worked his way through the opening and spent a good part of the night peeling a large safe, making off with a considerable amount of money. The method used was similar to other peeled safes that were to come.

We knew the person getting away with these burglaries must be thinking a lot of himself and rightly so, but even smart people make mistakes. Patience pays off. On a night to come, Lady Luck smiled on us.

Brady, thinking it was time to change his tactics, had been sitting in his car some distance from the east end Minit Mart watching customers come and go. The manager was working. Thinking it had been some time since he had some extra cash, this was to be his mission for tonight. It looked to be very easy and he had new ideas on how to go about it.

Not wanting to force the door since it was in a brightly lit area, he had gone on a reconnaissance mission a couple times into the store. Walking around the store, working into the back when he could not be seen, he knew what he would do. Shortly before closing time while there were others there to distract the cashier, he walked into the store. When he thought it would be safe, he walked into the back of the building.

In the back was a large walk-in refrigerator with some clearance between the top and the ceiling of the building. With some difficulty he managed to climb up on top of the refrigerator. Getting as far back as he could, then out of sight, he settled in to wait the short time until closing. From the traffic in and out of the store and the gas sales, he knew he was going to be a much richer and happier man in the morning. And the police were going to be wondering, as with so many other thefts, how someone had gotten in. Did they have a key?

He had just gotten comfortable when the manager began locking up and coming to the back of the store. Perhaps he could see where the money was hidden. As Brady watched the manager, he did not realize that he himself had been seen.

Then the manager was moving fast, securing all the doors which needed a key to open once they had been locked. He then called the police and stood outside the building waiting.

Brady sensed there was something wrong, thinking, "I had better get out of here." But the entrances were all locked. He was going to have to pretend he had been locked in. He was standing pounding on the glass door yelling that he was locked in when officers Gene Bennett and Bill Litchke pulled up in the patrol car.

They took Brady into custody as soon as the manager told them how he had been seen hiding in the back room on top of the refrigerator. He was caught red-handed, he knew that. What could he do to help himself? He didn't resist. These officers knew their jobs well. He was given his rights and taken to jail.

Still he was pretty proud of what he had done and gotten away with in the past. The next day he was talking to me after being given his rights. I asked about some of the crimes he was suspected of doing. The statutes of limitations had run out on many of them. He admitted knocking over the Gordy's Supervalu safe and explained how he had made his way through the wall entrance where the plastic bins went through. He spent part of the night getting into the safe. He also admitted going into the grocery store in Cohasset and cracking the safe by spreading the metal siding on the back of the building which was about 3 feet wide, 14 feet high.

This then brought us back to Grand Rapids, the back of the Moose Club and the prize of all the stores, the L&M. He had split the seams of the metal siding behind the tire racks at the L & M Supply, going in there several times. This was located on the 4th St N.E., since then they have moved to a more modem building south of town.

Brady then went through the court system, and it seemed like it was no time at all before he was back on the streets. We knew what would be happening and sure enough, after a few months, Dick Distributing was burglarized, the high school, and the Northside Lumber.

In the summer of 1990, Brent Bradley, a Grand Rapids police officer, set up a burglary alarm system in a room at the high school. The office had a large safe in it. The alarm would sound off at the sheriff's office if someone entered the room after hours.

On the night of September 29, 1990, the alarm went off. Law enforcement from the Grand Rapids area swiftly converged on the site.

Some going to strategic points watching for anyone leaving the building, other officers entered the building, searching it for anyone that might be in there. No one was found.

A hat with some gray hairs in it was found close to the safe along with a bag of burglary tools. The tools were later to be identified as coming from the bus garage.

While the search inside of the high school was going on, Officer Serfling in a patrol car reported finding a car parked out of the way in St. Andrew's church yard a few blocks away from the high school.

As soon as we were finished with our investigation in the school, we left in our cars. Where he would not be seen, Officer Leigh Serfling was dropped off, working his way back through the brush and trees. He was soon able to observe the parked car which had been identified as belonging to Brady. Soon a dark figure was seen approaching the car and trying to get in.

Serfling stepped out with his flashlight on and recognized Brady. A search was made and a master-key to the high school was found in his pocket. He also had in his possession a flashlight belonging to the school. As Serfling first approached him the only thing he said was, "Oh, shit!" Later his explanation for being there was that he was just out walking to unwind. He then was taken to the sheriff's office and given his rights again, read from the Miranda card, and agreed to talk to us at the jail if he could have his lawyer present at the time, to which Pat Medure, Itasca County Sheriff and I both agreed.

Looking back, I don't think it was such a good idea for him as he locked himself into a story that later would be hard to change. A warrant was issued for his locker at the bus garage where some items were found later that would help our prosecution.

The prosecuting attorney, Bernard Bodien, gave a compelling case, saying among other things, that Brady had a master-key for the high school in his pocket, that his hair matched the hair found in the hat at the high school, and that burglar tools were found in his possession.

The defense addressed the jury, "You will hear only circumstantial evidence on Brady as he was only walking late at night near the high school as he often did to unwind. He was stopped and arrested. My client was raised in the Minnesota woods. Also, there were at least two or three other master-keys out there someone could have used. Once Brady was arrested, the police stopped looking for anyone else. A suspect still could have been hiding in the building. Also, the police didn't follow standard procedures by removing the burglary tools from the school."

The defense rested.

Brady went to trial for two felonies in April 1991:
1. Burglary in the 3rd Degree.
2. Possession of burglary tools.
3. He was found guilty on both charges before District Court Judge William Spooner.
4. He was found guilty for the unauthorized use of a school bus.
5. A pre-sentence investigation was ordered.
6. He was given five years but spent only a short time in jail.
7. Brady was also charged with burglary and theft of the L&M. However, the L&M charge was dismissed under a plea agreement.

It may be attributed to old age or that he had just gotten careless having beaten us so many times. Just a few short years later he was arrested for arson, having set fire to his own house for the insurance money. It seems one night his house had caught fire, but everything of value was found upstairs in his garage. The source of the fire was a stack of newspapers on a support beam underneath the kitchen floor which burned through the floor, but due to the density of the newspapers it only burned part of them and had gone out.

Pat Medure of the sheriff's office led the investigation. Brady was arrested for felony arson, found guilty and imprisoned.

It seems like the Lone Wolf ensnared himself more than once in his career. For a criminal who had to work alone through all these years so no one could give him up, once the wolf was caged, he may have been the most talkative of all.

It does make me wonder after all these years, where is Brady? Who is he befriending? Where is the Lone Wolf?

(Herald Review April 7 1991/Itasca County Records)

On advice of counsel, some names have been changed to protect family members.

~

REFLECTIONS

Some times we who write stories or columns for newspapers think we know all the answers. This is history; people have the right to know. Where do you stop? There are always two sides to a story. There is the victim's side - it does not stop there - and his or her family is affected. Parents and relatives, we think after a time they have forgotten. It never will be.

You have a young boy, 14, who makes the biggest mistake of his life. He is going to live with it. Where will this all end, time served? What about his mother, grandmother, the rest of his family? They, like the victim's family, is as close to him and suffer over the years at the loss of a loved one.

Then, we start to write thinking so many years ago no one is left. Get all the information you can, make it correct, names, places. There is always someone left. Some of them feel guilty. "If I was there could I have prevented this?"

So, I keep writing my stories. Can I do a better job? I have to - there is so much to tell.

Am I going to make mistakes? I'm sure I will as I have in the past.

My conscience must be my guide.

- Harvey Dahline

~